THE
MYSTERY
OF INIQUITY

South Atlantic Modern Language
Association Award Study

THE
MYSTERY
OF INIQUITY

Melville as Poet, 1857-1891

W ILLIAM H. S HURR

The University Press of Kentucky

ISBN: 0–8131–1276–1

Library of Congress Catalog Card Number: 70–190535

Copyright © 1972 by The University Press of Kentucky

A statewide cooperative scholarly publishing agency
serving Berea College, Centre College of Kentucky,
Eastern Kentucky University, Kentucky Historical Society,
Kentucky State University, Morehead State University, Murray
State University, University of Kentucky, University of
Louisville, and Western Kentucky University.

Editorial and Sales Offices: Lexington, Kentucky 40506

for Georgia Grey

CONTENTS

ACKNOWLEDGMENTS

I would like to express my gratitude to the directors and staffs of the Houghton and Widener Libraries of Harvard University for the use of the Melville manuscripts and related materials and for their courteous assistance. I must also thank the director and staff of the Louis Round Wilson Library of the University of North Carolina for their cooperation with my research.

Professors Richard H. Fogle and C. Carroll Hollis of the University of North Carolina and Professor George C. Connor of the University of Tennessee (Chattanooga) have read parts of the manuscript, and I have benefited from their comments. Professor Robert C. Ryan of Boston University interrupted his own editorial work on the Melville poetry manuscripts to share his immense knowledge of them with me. His generous offer to read my book in typescript has added to the accuracy and, I hope, to the clarity of the final result.

Mrs. McKay, mother of the present owner of Arrowhead, was at home when I was in the Berkshires in pursuit of Melville's spirit. The request would have been extraordinary—to see the inside of a private home—but her offer preceded it. Her enthusiasm for the famous chimney, the room where Melville wrote, the view of Saddle-Back Mountain, made the afternoon glow with an almost mystical brightness.

I would also like to record my gratitude to the University of Chattanooga Foundation for two generous grants enabling me to carry on my study of Melville. For careful secretarial work I would like to thank Miss Donna Weaver, Miss Sandra Poe, and Mrs. Peter McGraw.

In writing this book I have been constantly aware of the work of Melville scholars who have gone before me, specifically those who are listed in the Bibliography with which this work concludes. I hope that I have been scrupulous enough in acknowledging their work in my text and notes. I should particularly like to thank Howard P. Vincent and Walter E. Bezanson for permission to use their editions of the collected poems and *Clarel* respectively as my basic texts. The portrait of Herman Melville by Joseph Oriel Eaton is reproduced on the jacket by kind permission of the Fogg Art Museum of Harvard University.

Finally, the book could not have been written without the shared enthusiasm of my wife, to whom it is dedicated.

Missionary Ridge
Spring, 1972

INTRODUCTION

His works trace a spiritual experience of
unequaled intensity.

Albert Camus, "Herman Melville"

The fight of all fights is to write.

Mardi

OUR UNDERSTANDING of Herman Melville rests at the moment at a peculiar stage of incompleteness. Nearly all the critical attention given to him has been concentrated on one decade of his literary life. The fierce energy that produced ten such works of fiction in eleven years is among the most impressive accomplishments in American letters, but even the casual student of American literature must be puzzled to learn that there were three and a half decades left, that Melville continued to write and publish during these years, and that—as one scholar has pointed out—there was more poetry published than even a professional poet like T. S. Eliot produced in a lifetime.[1] Encouraged then by the knowledge that here is quantity at least, one may find his pursuit aided by the various editions prepared by Walter E. Bezanson, Hennig Cohen, Howard P. Vincent, and Robert Penn Warren. But otherwise, the few existing treatments of Melville's poetry mostly tend to disappoint. A typical commentary will be subsidiary to a study of Melville's fiction; it will begin with a few items brought forward for praise and end quickly with the admission that, finally, Melville was no poet, that he never mastered the craft, and that the poetry is mostly embarrassing or unreadable.

The present book is based on the conviction that such judgments have been made too hastily and that not enough study, even of a descriptive kind, has yet been devoted to Melville's poetry.

From a purely theoretical point of view one would expect the later work of a writer's career to be more mature, considered, developed. Such a view in the case of Melville has been hindered by the widely held theory of "the long decline." At the same time those who hold this theory will often admit that the later writings are complex and difficult. It is possible that there may be a contradiction here. As Melville grows older and becomes more and more isolated it can be considered a logical development for his evaluation of the world to become more complex and, therefore, more difficult. But this may be anything but a long decline or sign of debilitated genius. The fault, in other words, may be not so much with the writer as with his readers. This is hypothesis, of course, and the following chapters are an extended test of that hypothesis.

The external events of Melville's life during the years he was writing poetry may be told quickly. In 1856–1857, at the age of thirty-seven, Melville was traveling alone through Europe, the Mediterranean, and the Holy Land. Money for the trip had been spared only with difficulty, since the family was in financial straits. There were four children between the ages of two and eight; income from his books was down; and farming in the Berkshires was a marginal enterprise at best. While he was traveling, the last work of fiction he was to publish, *The Confidence-Man*, was with the printer. Nathaniel Hawthorne, American consul at Liverpool, was overseeing the British publication of the book, after recording his last depressing remarks on Melville after their conversation on the dunes nearby.

When Melville returned from this trip, with an important notebook filled with jottings, he was to spend the next three winters traveling the difficult lecture circuit, hardly regaling lyceum enthusiasts with his one-nighters on Roman statuary, the South Seas, and his journeys. At the same time he was writing poetry. When the opportunity arose in 1860 for him to cruise around the world with his ship captain brother Tom, he left a collection, to be called simply *Poems*. His wife, his brother Allan, and Evert Duyckinck were left with detailed instructions on how it was to appear. As it was, no publisher could be found for a volume of poems that probably included, in some version, "The Berg," "The Maldive Shark," and some of the travel poems that would later go into *Timoleon*. The next year another disappointment occurred when he failed to get a consular appointment to Florence, although in the course of the attempt he managed to shake hands with the new president, Lincoln.

In October of 1863 the family home, Arrowhead, had to be sold and the Melvilles moved to New York in order to economize. These were the Civil War years, and Melville's thought and emotions were intensely involved in the conflict. *Battle-Pieces*, his first book of poetry, was published in 1866 as its author was just turning forty-seven. That same winter he began his job as a New York customs inspector, at four badly needed dollars a day. He was to work at this for nineteen years, until he was sixty-six. His first few years as customs inspector were full of dark shadows. His health was better, but there were deaths of close family members. The worst of these was the self-inflicted death of his eighteen-year-old son Malcolm, in 1867. Two years later his other son left home to wander aimlessly for seventeen years, financially always hopeful yet never successful, dying in 1886 in a San Francisco hospital. It was probably around 1870 that Melville began shaping his trip to the Holy Land into the long *Clarel*.

Life had presented him with materials enough for a tragic view, and one should not underestimate the influence of his portrait painted by Joseph Oriel Eaton in this year. Eaton gave him the picture of a man whose stature was heroic and whose eyes were full of dreams and pain.

And then too a new book had just come out by a wild young humorist whose views on the Holy Land may have helped focus Melville's own. At any rate the more than eighteen-thousand-line poem occupied him and wore down his strength and his family's morale until it was finally published in 1876. The next nine years are almost totally devoid of recorded incident, though Melville continued to write during these years. There was the experiment with sandwiched prose and poetry (the *Burgundy Club* sketches) and poems on the shape of a man's life and the relation of a writer to fame. Finally there was some money from family bequests, and he was able to retire from the customs office after nineteen years of service.

These were the lonely years; one can only imagine with whom he was trying to communicate in *Clarel* and in these sketches, in the incessant study he did (partly in library reading rooms, which left no visible record), in the short poems he wrote when leisure and thought coincided. Even the family correspondence of these years reveals little that is dramatic, except for the insight which two famous letters from Mrs. Melville to relatives give into the state of Melville and of his whole household when a book was nearing readiness for the printer. The year before *Clarel* was printed she wrote: "Herman is pretty well and very busy—pray do not mention to anyone that he is writing poetry—you know how such things spread and he would be very angry if he knew I had spoken of it—and of course I have not, except in confidence to you and the family. We have been in much fear lest his pay should be reduced, as so many others have, but it has not been, so far—it is hard enough to get along at all." Eleven months later, when they were all reading proof for *Clarel*, Elizabeth wrote: "If ever this dreadful *incubus* of a *book* (I call it so because it has undermined all our happiness) gets off Herman's shoulders I do hope he may be in better mental health."[2]

One wonders what would have happened if the legacies had come twenty years earlier. He had already written the greatest American novel, but no one knew that at the time, and possibly he did not know it himself. Much of the "mental" distress came from financial worries. Had these been alleviated, the question still remains whether Melville yet felt within himself and in his accomplishments a secure enough base to build on confidently. As it was, these were the years of his Babylonian exile, while the universe kept piling up concrete proof of its malevolence.

After retirement there were to be almost six years left of unobstructed leisure, carefully guarded and efficiently used. All his poetry manuscripts were reworked, and new poems were written. The first result of this new surge of energy is *John Marr and Other Sailors*, published at his own expense in a limited edition of twenty-five copies. As soon as this was finished, he was at work on more poetry and on *Billy Budd*. Three years later, in 1891, he published *Timoleon*, again in a private and limited edition, and he had *Billy Budd* very nearly ready to be recopied for the printer. Melville died in September of that year, with another collection, *Weeds and Wildings*, almost complete. Several dozen other finished poems were carefully preserved by his widow.

A preliminary problem had to be dealt with concerning the texts of Melville's poems. Howard P. Vincent's *Collected Poems* and Walter E. Bezanson's *Clarel* have become standard editions, but the former needs to be studied with close attention to the errata sheet as well as to the pages of manuscript variants which were offered only with copies of the subscriber's edition of the book. Hennig Cohen has edited a good annotated and illustrated edition of *Battle-Pieces* as well as a small book of *Selected Poems* with illuminating commentary. But almost every book of Melville's poetry has its own set of special problems. After *Battle-Pieces* was published, he continued to revise some of the poems in his own copy. I have chosen to quote the poems from this first book of poetry as they appeared in Melville's original edition, noting the effect of his later revisions where they seem especially interesting or significant. For *Clarel* I have used Bezanson's fine edition. For the remaining poems I have used Vincent's edition for my basic text. Where I have chosen to vary the text it has been on the basis of Melville's original editions, his manuscripts, and the surviving corrected galley sheets for *John Marr*. All such variants are noted. Very helpful are two unpublished dissertations: Norman Jarrard, "Poems by Herman Melville: A Critical Edition of the Published Verse" (University of Texas, 1960) and Robert C. Ryan, "*Weeds and Wildings Chiefly: With a Rose or Two*, by Herman Melville: Reading Text and Genetic Text, Edited from the Manuscripts, With Introduction and Notes" (Northwestern University, 1967). The study of Melville's poetry will become considerably easier with the publication of Ryan's edition of it for the Northwestern-Newberry edition of the writings of Herman Melville.

There were special benefits to be had in working with the actual manuscripts of Melville. One is, of course, more certain about the printed versions. One also has more information that helps to interpret individual poems, as he sees the final result emerging from a mass of shiftings and changes represented by the struckover lines and words. In addition unexpected benefit accrues to the scholar here: Melville has left notations or jottings here and there among his manuscript sheets which help to date a poem or give a further insight into the thought developed in it. The accurate dating of all Melville's poems will probably never be possible. He seems to have kept many of his poems in process over a period of several years, recopying and throwing away all old material when a page became too full of corrections. Nevertheless there are many bits of evidence about dating, some of which is from these manuscript jottings and some from the poems themselves. In some cases the evidence allows a poem to be dated exactly; in other cases one or other *terminus* for the poem can be established, or the dating for a particular stratum of a poem is indicated.

Among the points of interest that have emerged in studying the poetry of Melville is the concern he gave to shaping his individual collections. In every case a Melville poem can stand by itself, but all the books of poetry which he published, as well as *Weeds and Wildings*, are characterized by a careful arrangement of the poems in relation to one another and of smaller groups in relation to the whole. Everyone knows that Melville's thought in his novels needs a large amount of room to maneuver and develop. The case is similar with his poetry. Each of his books has a unity of its own, yielding further meaning which is not accessible to a reader who knows only anthologized selections. This phenomenon has never been studied, nor even noted, except for a few attempts to deal with Melville's statement that there is a natural order to *Battle-Pieces*.

Another point of interest resides in the intellectual content of the poems and the insight they give into the poet's mind during the later decades of his life. The poems are a record of his thoughts as well as a creative entry into the currents of thought in the late nineteenth century. Melville continues his polemic against Emerson, and it shades into a polemic against the new optimism that is produced by one strain of thought deriving from the new data concerning evolution. Thus Darwin and Lyell are present in his mental universe. So also, in a more concrete way than has yet been noticed, is Arthur Schopenhauer. Another surprise is Melville's early perception of the dark thought of Mark Twain. The long-dead Hawthorne continued to exert control over Melville's mind. Melville was also aware of Browning, Swinburne, and James Thomson, among his contemporaries, and he creatively used such nineteenth-century favorites as Horace, Plutarch, Cervantes, Camoens, and Montaigne. Several passages clearly show that Melville was reading Buddhist literature during these years. Source study becomes interesting here, since it shows one method by which Melville continued to develop and enrich his personal symbolic systems. The poems are the attempt of a painfully isolated man, isolated from the intellectual camaraderie he enjoyed and even from a readership, to engage his world and probe its meaning.

The continuing development of Melville as an imaginative writer of considerable theological sophistication and depth has also been considered. The development is predictable, given *Mardi* and *Moby-Dick* and given the quality of thought in the second half of the nineteenth century. Still the content is uniquely Melville's own, as he expands his metaphysics of an evil universe and explores the problems of discriminating various levels of reality. The speculations are fullest in *Clarel*, but refinement of the system goes on until the last year of his life. Unfortunately Melville's large collection of theological books was dispersed unrecorded shortly after his death,[3] but in some instances internal evidence provides clues to the writers who shaped his thought here. Much of Melville's poetry lies in that area of theology where it comes close to psychology and to metaphysics in the broadest sense of that term. Its greatest affinity is with those writers who create a symbolism for ultimate realities, as those realities impinge most disturbingly upon the author's own consciousness. The primary writer in this class is Dante. Melville does not have his scope or his organization, but there is a symbolic system latent in Melville's poetry which shows detailed organization. Finally, we must say that for all the similarity in imagination and technique, his vision is the obverse of Dante's. All poets have an implied universe, built with their words, to correspond to their inner feelings of what the significant realities are. Perhaps this is to say that Melville can more profitably be studied with Blake and with his own nineteenth-century contemporaries, with those imaginative philosophers who wrote as they felt, like Dostoyevski, Schopenhauer, and Nietzsche; like Baudelaire and James Thomson; like Arnold and Tennyson when they verged close upon despair. Yet an individuality must be claimed for Melville, and it is one of my purposes to establish this individuality.

The light that the poetry sheds on *Billy Budd* is of great importance. Melville published *John Marr* the year that he probably began *Billy Budd*. The year of his death he finished that manuscript and also published *Timoleon*. During the three intervening years he worked through his remaining unpublished poetry. The poetry and the last work of prose, in other words, were developing at the same time, and in the final chapter I will propose several patterns from the poetry which must be considered in evaluating *Billy Budd*.

Finally our attention must be on the poetry itself. I must record an experience, visible about halfway through this book, of beginning to refer to Melville as "the poet." The realization was present to Melville much sooner than it has been to his readers. The poems in *Mardi* are not profound or magnificent, but they are skillful genre-pieces: work songs and chanties, drinking songs and love songs. They read with a vigor and precision that must force some acknowledgment of Melville's skill at the craft as early as 1849. When he left elaborate directions for the publication of his 1860 volume of *Poems*, there is no indication that he feared or even suspected that they would never find a publisher. Melville was quite at home with the idea of himself as a poet. This could be beginner's arrogance in someone else, but Melville by this time was thoroughly knowledgeable in the traditions of literature both written in and translated into English. His supple pen could mimic other writers at will. His poetic taste was highly formed. It is possible that he was wrong, and that has been the judgment of many critics who grant him a minor role, if any at all, in the history of American poetry. On the other hand one may choose to trust Melville's well-formed instincts a bit further. Some have faulted him for his use of the four-stress line in *Clarel*. But the traditional English five-stress line was showing signs of debility. Lowell's deadening hand rests on it, as a vehicle for philosophical narrative, throughout *The Cathedral* (1870), for example. It may be that we are just getting used to Melville's favorite four-stress line and are beginning to appreciate the flexibility with which he used it. As his poetry becomes better known, more familiar to the ear, I believe this difficulty will disappear. So too the problem with his peculiar rhymes (*law-o'er*, for example) will disappear even more easily when one grants it to be an experiment by a died-in-the-wool New Yorker to establish his regional pronunciation as normative.

To write a poem is one way of trying to define a perception. Traditionally the qualities of grace and harmony have been expected of poetry, and we shall have to watch these qualities in operation in Melville's poems. Economy and verbal felicity are also regarded as assets, and they characterize many of Melville's poetic passages. More important is significant structure, that pattern of image and meaning which seems to make the poem an entity by itself or a self-sufficient mechanism for insight. All these methods are derived from our experience with actual poems, and each poet of any significance redefines their operations and their limits of possibility for himself. Each new poet makes a new set of demands upon the reader, and Melville is for all practical purposes a new American poet.

I

BATTLE-PIECES

Great geniuses are parts of their times, and
possess a corresponding coloring.

Melville on Hawthorne

A structure of a thing is the way it is put
together. Anything that has structure, then,
must have parts, properties, or aspects which
are somehow related to each other. In every
structure we may distinguish the *relation* or
relations, and the items related.

*Suzanne Langer, An Introduction
to Symbolic Logic*

FOR MANY YEARS individual poems have been excerpted from *Battle-Pieces* for anthologies, but evidence in the book itself makes it clear that Melville saw the series as an organic whole. In the Preface he says, "They were composed without reference to collective arrangement" (and some were published separately in Harper's *New Monthly Magazine*[1]) "but, being brought together in review, naturally fall into the order assumed." The problem for the reader is to find this natural order. One critic has said that the organization of *Battle-Pieces* is chronological, and that this is the only principle of organization to be found in the book.[2] This is true, but only roughly so, for the first part of the book. There still remain the epigrammatic "Verses Inscriptive and Memorial" and the three poems which conclude the book. One is tempted to insert these poems back into the chronological arrangement, which could easily be done, but is prevented by the fact that they already exist—to Melville's expressed satisfaction—in their natural order.

Another reader has suggested that there is a larger unity given to the collection by the subject of the war itself.[3] This seems vague, but it may have stimulated a later insight that has helped to bring the poems into better focus. Melville was not the kind of writer who was stimulated primarily by introspection into the workings of his own mind or by the possibilities latent in various literary forms. He needed an event outside of himself, an action grand enough to furnish correlatives for his own feelings and emotional patterns. Life on a merchant ship, a navy gunboat, or a whaler had served in the past. In this instance it was the Civil War. William Bysshe Stein has argued this, as have F. O. Matthiessen and Robert Penn Warren. Warren's point is made in the more recent of two articles he has written on Melville's poetry: "the deep divisions of Melville's inner life, from the struggle between his natural skepticisms and his yearning for religious certitude, to his sexual tensions, which had found expression in previous work, now found, we may hazard, in the fact of a *civil* war an appropriate image which might, in some degree, absorb and purge their pains."[4]

Two decades ago Henry F. Pommer demonstrated how pervasive was the influence of Milton on Melville's imagination and literary style. When Pommer turned to *Battle-Pieces*, he too was inspired to speculate about the Preface and its insistence upon the unity of the collection. Pommer's particular approach to Melville yielded the insight that the "use of symbolism drawn from Milton does give *Battle-Pieces* some degree of structure,"[5] and he believed that such an outside source could retain its full power only over the relatively short time in which the poems were composed. Pommer cited lines from some of the more prominent poems in the collection to show how Melville amplifies the issues of the war between the states by allusions to Milton's treatment of the war between Heaven and Hell.

Helpful though these attempts to find the unity of *Battle-Pieces* have been, they have not yet fully described the complexity with which a mind as ambiguous and ironic as Melville's would have viewed the personal and national history through which he lived, nor do they quite justify Melville's own strong assertion of order here. For this one must dive, not so much with the sources or the subjects, as with the mind itself that forged such a collection.

Thematically the poems in *Battle-Pieces* are unified by two cycles of thought. Each cycle represents a single dominant idea by which the poet seeks to understand the forces controlling events during the Civil War period. The cycles are superimposed one upon the other, in the sense that signs of both can be found throughout the book. But it must be noted that one of the cycles fails to give sufficient understanding of the events, and that the other cycle emerges as dominant. The intellectual tension generated by the logical impossibility of both cycles coexisting as the final explanation is responsible for one of the more fascinating conflicts in the book. Within the cycles one can also notice several other groupings of related poems—poems on youth or on sea-battles, for example. Let us plunder the title of that warmly enlightening book by Melville's granddaughter and call them "epicycles."

THE CYCLE OF LAW

In his first attempt to find a pattern of meaning in the political and social chaos of the Civil War, Melville experiments with the tenets of the conservative tradition. States and individuals ought not to rebel against duly constituted civil authority. The destruction and pain of the war result directly from breach of the law. In this cycle harmony and peace will return to the cosmos when law is reasserted.

Fragments of this cycle can be found throughout the collection; the most concentrated statement of it appears in the fine poem entitled "Dupont's Round Fight." The poem describes a naval maneuver which involved several Union ships engaging two Confederate fortifications guarding Port Royal Sound in the mouth of the Broad River above Savannah. *The Rebellion Record*, a documentary history of the Civil War which Melville used constantly for factual and even verbal materials, provides a map of the battle plan and describes it thus: "The plan of attack was simple and effective, being for the ships to steam in a circle, or ellipse, running close to one shore as they came *down* the river, drifting or steaming as slowly as possible past the batteries there, and paying their fiery respects, then making the turn to go back, and as they went *up* the river, favoring the other batteries with a similar compliment."[6] The tactic allowed the Union ships leisure for reloading and maneuvering, since each ship was within range of the shore batteries for only a short time, while the forts themselves were under constant bombardment and were soon reduced. As Melville conceived it, the textbook simplicity of the strategy created a kind of beauty, the beauty of "Law" prevailing.

> In time and measure perfect moves
> All Art whose aim is sure;
> Evolving rhyme and stars divine
> Have rules, and they endure.

The poem itself is an example of "measure perfect": iambic fourteeners perfectly rhymed and varied only by an extra unstressed syllable in the word "Unity"—a word to which attention is quite rightly called since it is Melville's point that something more than the "Union" was responsible for the Confederate defeat here. The poem elaborates a neoclassical or ideal concept of Law, confirmed in the word "type." Law is an Idea which can be embodied at all levels and in all items of the great chain of being. The poem envisions Law as responsible for beauty and harmony and order to the exact extent that it pervades such diverse things as art, rhyme, stars, or a warring fleet. The "geometric beauty" recalls the confidence which the classical Greeks had in numbers and in mathematics as the most fundamental science; one may recall the line from a later poet: "Euclid alone has looked on beauty bare." The choice of the name "Port Royal" reinforces this line of thought. "Broad River" or "Fort Walker" were equally available metrically, and geographically as precise. But only "Port Royal" starts the series of associations linked with Blaise Pascal, whose genius encompassed both mathematics and the science of ethics, who mastered the elements of Euclid's geometry by himself as a child and whose life was so closely connected with the moral precisions of the Jansenists at Port-Royal. The allusion not only demonstrates Melville's learning, but opens up still further areas in which the thought patterns of the poem can be seen operating. Melville's platonic conception of Law in this poem puts it at the key position of this first thematic cycle to be found in *Battle-Pieces*.

We have launched our inquiry with a discussion of the central state-
ment in this first cycle, but the cycle is begun with the book's first poem,
"The Portent." Melville, from the vantage point now of retrospect, here
contemplates the multiple significances in the pre-Civil War image of
John Brown, who was hanged in accordance with the law against
insurrection.

> *Hanging from the beam,*
>   *Slowly swaying (such the law),*
> *Gaunt the shadow on your green,*
>   *Shenandoah!*
> *The cut is on the crown*
> *(Lo, John Brown),*
> *And the stabs shall heal no more.*
>
> *Hidden in the cap*
>   *Is the anguish none can draw;*
> *So your future veils its face,*
>   *Shenandoah!*
> *But the streaming beard is shown*
> *(Weird John Brown),*
> *The meteor of the war.*

Those who fault Melville on the score of metrics must ignore this open-
ing to *Battle-Pieces*. The stanza form is Melville's own, as indeed are
most of his. (I have been unable to find that he has used a single poetic
form twice in the collection.[7]) Here the individual stanza shows no
particular pattern in meter or rhyme. One then finds that the second
stanza sets up a mirror image, metrically; corresponding lines have the
same number of stressed syllables and several lines of the second stanza
rhyme with corresponding lines in the first stanza. It is likely that *law,
draw, Shenandoah, war*, and *more* all are meant to rhyme, in accordance
with Melville's regional pronunciation. The eye rhyme, *crown-shown*,
increases the number of correspondences between the two stanzas. The
parallels are worth examining more closely. The participle followed by
a prepositional phrase in the first line, "Hanging from the beam," is
paralleled by the same sequence in the first line of the second stanza,
"Hidden in the cap." But there is an advance to a closer view of the
subject in the second instance. So also "Shenandoah!" is repeated in
line 4 of each stanza, but the exclamation gains intensity in the second
stanza from the words "anguish" and veiled "future." So too the paren-
thetical "Lo, John Brown" is intensified to "Weird John Brown" in the
corresponding line of the second stanza.

Melville's investigation of the Law issue in this poem seems minor on first consideration, a mere parenthetical mention of the word in the second line. One quickly discerns that the word is ambivalent, working on two levels. The shadow of the hanged body sways back and forth like a pendulum—such are the laws of physics. But the civil law is intended here too, which imposes such a penalty on insurrectionists. The notion of Law operating at several levels, which characterizes "Dupont's Round Fight," provides one of the basic thematic patterns in this poem also.

Once this ambivalence is established, one can go on, for example, to "crown" in line 5. Brown was wounded on the head when he was captured; but the incident in which he was involved, as portent of worse violence, is a cut upon the crown in another sense. In the American political structure "crown" must mean civil authority. Civil law and order are also "cut" by his insurrection.[8] And so one level of meaning in the ambivalent word "crown" carries forward the analysis of Law and its function in this poem.

The second stanza takes a closer look at one feature of the scene described in the first stanza. The head of the hanged man is hidden by an executioner's black hood, but the image can still yield two items: the specific details of the Shenandoah Valley's future are likewise veiled, yet "the streaming beard" becomes a meteor (conventionally described as bearded), a "portent" of the anguish it will experience. Thus John Brown can be described quite rightly as "weird." Melville, who knew Shakespeare well, could recall the three weird sisters in *Macbeth*, agents of the Fate (*Wyrd*) that works for man's destruction.[9] That he was aware of the connection between *weird* and *fate* is obvious from a passage in *Pierre* (IV, ii) where he speaks of the Fates as "those three weird ones." The hanged Brown, then, can be seen as an item in the larger fate that will work itself out in history. The cut is on the crown: the law is already broken and signs of the evil to come are there to be discerned, at least in retrospect.

Several terms associated with the Cycle of Law are usually capitalized by Melville. In "Dupont's Round Fight" appear the words *Right* and *Unity* as well as *Law*. Several other poems in this thematic cycle add other capitalized words, to indicate something like a constellation of values associated with Law in Melville's mind. Two short but related poems in the "Verses Inscriptive and Memorial" section concentrate on *Right* and *Cause*. The poems follow one another and are entitled "Inscription for the Graves at Pea Ridge, Arkansas" and "The Fortitude of the North Under the Disaster of the Second Manassas."

Both poems attempt to show how those soldiers are happy who have not only died, but died in a battle which was a defeat for their side. Paradoxically they are "victorious" because they did not surrender "the Cause / Hallowed by hearts and by the laws." They are fortunate because they "warred for Man and Right." There may be reason for considering the poems in this section of *Battle-Pieces* as superseded when the work assumed its final order. Generally the poems of the "Inscriptions" section are neither as distinguished nor as convincing as those of the main body. But the two poems were worth saving: for the paradox which ends the first one (they "fell—victorious!"), and the extended metaphor for the Right Cause which ends the second:

> The Cape-of-Storms is proof to every throe;
>   Vainly against that foreland beat
> Wild winds aloft and wilder waves below:
>   The black cliffs gleam through rents in sleet
> When the livid Antarctic storm-clouds glow.

A few pages later one finds a poem which adds still more concepts to the Cycle of Law—"Presentation to the Authorities by Privates, of Colors Captured in Battles Ending in the Surrender of Lee." The words *right* and *laws* appear in this poem, but only *Country* and *Duty* are capitalized. The verse is low-keyed and seems to straggle because of the many instances of enjambment. However, this seems appropriate to the situation: ordinary Union soldiers at the end of the war present the enemy flags they have captured, before returning to their farms and trades. The resolution of the conflict, as they see it, is the "foredoomed" victory of Right, of "the just cause." With sober dignity, mindful of the deaths of comrades "whom duty as strongly nerved," they make this final formal gesture and return "to waiting homes with vindicated laws." One senses in the poem that this kind of sentiment had once been planned as resolution to the whole collection, but this poem too was superseded and placed in the "Inscriptions" section.

Another poem which furthers the Cycle of Law investigation is called "The Victor of Antietam." It could also be included in another category of poems, those that focus on personalities involved in the Civil War, but it connects the deeper thematic cycles at several points and is best considered here. The poem includes most of the essential information about General George B. McClellan, the controversial Union officer who was relieved of his command after the Seven Days' Battle (l. 12), then reinstated to win the battle near Antietam Creek, and finally relieved of his command again. Melville finds a euphony in the man's name; the single word "McClellan" rings out at intervals in the course of the poem. The regularity of the intervals rewards study. The last four stanzas regularly have the refrain standing just after the first line and just before the last line. These four stanzas alternate from nine to ten to nine to ten lines. There is also the attempt to end all the lines of a stanza with a single rhyme. The earlier part has no such regularity. The easiest conclusion to be drawn is that Melville was not master enough of his craft to duplicate a chosen stanza form the required number of times. But another conclusion must be given consideration. The poem may be read as a poem in search of itself; that is, as a poem in which the process of creation has been left visible. The first half of the poem experiments with the placement of the one-word refrain; the stanzas of the second half proceed with the stanza finally achieved.

Three items in "The Victor of Antietam" relate it to the Cycle of Law. The first is the function of "authority." The word calls attention to itself by setting up a chiming effect between lines 16 and 27: "Authority called you"; then "Authority called you" again; then "she recalled— / Recalled you"; and finally "Recalled you." Authority is clearly connected with Law, though the system here stands on uncertain feet because of the vacillation of those in control. Melville must have intended the irony two lines after the last "recalled you," when he wrote of McClellan that "you propped the Dome." The Dome, always capitalized, appears in five poems. It is primarily the newly constructed dome of the Capitol in Washington, and as such it is symbolic of the order which struggles to reassert itself in this cycle. In propping the Dome, McClellan has sacrificially supported an authority which topples him, time and again.[10]

Associated with the concept of authority and the image of the Dome is an echo of "Dupont's Round Fight" in lines 7–8: "Through storm-cloud and eclipse must move / Each Cause and Man, dear to the stars and Jove." Melville thus considers the reversals in McClellan's career to be closely associated with the powers that are struggling toward resolution and equilibrium in the Cycle of Law. The universal order (stars and Jove) will eventually reassert itself. Storm and eclipse are natural phenomena of this Order, but they are considered to be merely temporary.

A final note may be added to this poem. Line 22 applauds McClellan's military accomplishments in the skillful chiasmus, "Arrayed Pope's rout and routed Lee's array." For the Union cause McClellan ordered ("arrayed") the disorder left by General John Pope, whose army was routed during the Peninsular Campaign. So also he broke up ("routed") the orderly army ("Lee's array") of the masterful enemy tactician. The line thus shows McClellan to be an agent working within the Cycle of Law; it also accomplishes a subtle editorializing in favor of the Union's position on the side of the angels here. "The Victor of Antietam" is by no means among Melville's best poetry, but it nevertheless shows a complicated creative mind at work.

More in the tradition of popular nineteenth-century poetry is "Gettysburg: The Check." This was one of the five poems from *Battle-Pieces* chosen by Melville or by his publisher, Harper and Brothers, to appear in *Harper's New Monthly Magazine*, perhaps as part of a promotional technique to interest readers in the collection which was to appear a month after this poem was printed. The first half of the poem consists of two stanzas, one of eight lines and then one of ten. The second half repeats the sequence. One finds that corresponding lines in each half, with few exceptions, carry the same number of stresses. The rhyme scheme of the first two stanzas, irregular but unmistakably there, is also repeated almost exactly in the second half of the poem. Melville frequently employs this mirror technique in rhyming. Finally the introduction of a strong system of allusive imagery characterizes the first shorter stanza of each half. The poem is filled with conventional techniques: assonance and alliteration, near-rhyme linking the two halves ("renown" and "strown"), and internal rhyme used for heightened intensity in four separate places. Melville was capable of traditional metrics where a particular poem demanded it.

Connecting this poem with the Cycle of Law is the only capitalized abstraction, the word "Right" which brings the first half of the poem to a climax. Melville prepares for this crisis by viewing the Union cause as identical with that of the Israelites in their fight against the Philistines. The First Book of Samuel, Chapter 5, tells of the power of the right cause even when suffering defeat. The Ark of the Covenant, carried by the Israelite armies as a standard around which to rally, had been captured by the Philistines, who deposited it in their temple beside the statue of the god Dagon. The next morning Dagon was found toppled face down. The statue was set up again and the next morning was found in the same position with head and hands cracked off. Melville assumes an identity, not merely a similarity, between the Israelites and the Union—"our holy cause" in line 3. In this poem the Cycle of Law gains another dimension. Melville here experiments with the rhetoric of the holy war, which must be as old as religion itself. The conflicting parties become the Right and the Wrong, or the agents of Good and Evil. God will always, or at least eventually, cause Good to emerge victorious, and there is never any hesitation about which side the speaker's party is on, even if spokesmen for both sides are praying simultaneously. The concept of "our" side fighting for good against the agents of evil continues in line 7—"God walled his power"—and culminates at the end of the first half of the poem: "Right is a stronghold yet." This same concept of right side and wrong side, of Union as good and Confederacy as evil, can be found in several other poems of the Cycle of Law. It will still be in evidence, though with greater subtlety and with theatrics borrowed from Milton, when this cycle is superseded by another and more profound analysis of the Civil War.

The second half of "Gettysburg" opens with the vivid image of a beach desolated by September gales, standing as a simile for the battlefield after warring armies have retired. What is the thoughtful man to make of such destruction? It is to be sanctified "with hymn and prayer" (l. 34); memory is to retain the fact that the ground "our centre held" is still held by the remains of those who died "in honor there." Melville's note to this final stanza records the fact that part of the battlefield at Gettysburg was Cemetery Hill. One of the monuments toppled in the battle marked the grave of a Union officer killed the year previous. Without directly mentioning Lincoln's address at Gettysburg, Melville "foresees" the rededication of the ground two years later, July 4, 1865: "The warrior monument, crashed in fight, / Shall soar transfigured in loftier light." The historical progression rises to an apotheosis. In its final view the Civil War will be understood best by the visionary who is sensitive to its reverberations through all the levels of meaning: "transfigured" and bearing "a loftier meaning."

The transfiguration of Civil War issues and events climaxes in the final poem of the main section of *Battle-Pieces*, "America." This poem also contains some of the concepts of the Law Cycle, now appearing as allegorical figures. And finally it shows the major problem Melville experienced with the Cycle of Law, and why it was superseded. If Melville had been a lesser poet, or if he had allowed the idea to prevail that war is merely a temporary breach of law and order, one can easily conceive of this richly dramatized poem as standing as climax and conclusion to the whole volume.

The poem is a dream vision which proceeds through four stanzas, four stages, to present allegorically the meaning of the Civil War and the victory which concluded it. America is pictured as a young woman, "Maternity," lovingly protecting the Land and its children, standing under the banner of the United States. A protective Dome, which may be the firmament or the dome of the Capitol building again, looms over all. The picture is typical of allegorical newspaper cartoons and popular art throughout the century. The banner and the woman appear in each of the stanzas, as in a series of four pictorial panels. In the second panel the banner becomes a battle flag, while "the lorn Mother" stands "Pale at the fury of her brood." The battle at this stage is full of ambiguities: valor, despair, and pride characterize each side equally; in this stanza one cannot tell who is rightfully carrying the banner. The third stanza contains a dream within a dream. One must probe to a deeper level to resolve these ambiguities. The Land-Mother sinks into a deathlike trance while the banner wraps around her like a shroud. An anonymous "watcher" sees her face contorted and guesses at the terror she is experiencing. In her trance she has a vision "revealing earth's foundation bare, / And Gorgon in her hidden place." The Gorgon is a powerful and precise image for Melville, a model he has taken from classical mythology to express the central reality of the universe. This is the figure which when gazed upon has the power to become active and suddenly destroy the gazer. In her vision of "earth's foundation" the Land-Mother is undergoing the same experience which drove Pip mad in *Moby-Dick*.

> The sea had jeeringly kept his finite body up, but drowned the infinite of his soul. Not drowned entirely, though. Rather carried down alive to wondrous depths, where strange shapes of the unwarped primal world glided to and fro before his passive eyes; and the miser-merman, Wisdom, revealed his hoarded heaps; and among the joyous, heartless, ever-juvenile eternities, Pip saw the multitudinous, God-omnipresent, coral insects, that out of the firmament of waters heaved the colossal orbs. He saw God's foot upon the treadle of the loom, and spoke it; and therefore his shipmates called him mad.
>
> *(Chap. 93)*

The doctrine of this passage, key to Melville's thought throughout his writing career, is that the final divinity is to be found below rather than above; that this reality is evil, not good; and that knowledge of this god causes not the peace that surpasses all understanding, but madness. Thus the heterodoxy, or obverse Christianity, of Melville. We shall later have occasion to speak of another powerful symbol of Melville's, the shark who inhabits this world beneath the sea and who is connected with the present stanza in "America" by the link word "Gorgon."

In the final stanza the sleeping Mother has awakened, has shaken off the effects of the trance, and has found strength again in the renewal of Law (l. 45). The flag reappears, again performing its natural function. The final panel seems more staged than the rest, more contrived.

There is too great a leap from the convincing vision of stanza three, and no signs of how this deep terror is to be banished. If the vision had been such a terrifying one, then how does it function in reasserting peace and fertility and how can they endure? "Light" is brought in to vanquish the shadow (l. 47), but it is a light which does not have its source within the universe of the poem. The Cycle again breaks down at what was clearly intended to have been one of the pivotal moments of the collection.

One other poem shows the breakdown quite conclusively. "Lee in the Capitol" is one of the longer poems printed at the end of *Battle-Pieces*. In many ways it is a moving portrait of a noble character. Like the prose supplement which shortly follows it, the poem is concerned with the problems of justice and retribution in the Reconstruction period. In a note Melville explained that Lee appeared briefly before the Reconstruction Committee of Congress, but that Melville has taken considerable liberty in preparing a lengthy speech where Lee offered only a few short and dignified answers to the questions he was asked. Lee is the ideal loser in the tidy universe of this Cycle: "His doom accepts, perforce content, / And acquiesces in asserted laws" (ll. 14–15). Melville gives Lee the words to bring into focus a climactic moment in history, the moment at which the North must decide the future of the Union and the terms of coexistence.

> Shall the great North go Sylla's way?
> Proscribe? prolong the evil day?
> Confirm the curse? infix the hate?
> In Union's name forever alienate?
> *(ll. 187–90)*

The other alternative is the reestablishment of the Union in a more organic sense: "What sounder fruit than reestablished law?" (l. 145) The last line of Lee's speech to the congressmen is a plea against vengeance: "Avoid the tyranny you reprobate" (l. 200). In his personal copy of *Battle-Pieces* Melville later changed the line to read "Forbear to wreak the ill you reprobate." There are several instances of this kind of mollification in his copy. Surely he had little hope that his book would see a second edition. By 1868 only 486 copies of the book had been sold. But in the years following the Civil War he must have felt that emotions were still running too high, and that even the private citizen must do what he could to check the lust for vengeance, even if it were only by making a gesture towards controlling his own innermost thoughts. Melville concludes the poem, after the presentation of Lee's speech, with a commentary on how little the plea for justice and order influenced the congressmen: Lee's earnestness "moved, but not swayed their former mien" (l. 202).

In this poem a new word is introduced into the constellation of concepts associated with the Cycle of Law. Lee feels that events of such magnitude as those with which he was associated can only be accounted for by "Fate." He had surrendered when he felt "that the hour is come of Fate" (l. 3); early in the speech he says, "All's over now, and I follow Fate" (l. 112). He asserts that whatever the crimes, on both sides, that seemed to cause the war, still "this I feel, that North and South were driven / By Fate to arms" (ll. 156–57). After a few lines Sulla is recalled and his method of exacting vengeance upon his conquered enemies by putting them on his proscription lists. The allusion is integral to the themes of the poem since the concept of Fate oppressively dominated the Greek and Roman classics. In the same context Melville describes Lee leaving the Capitol building after finishing his speech "through vaulted walks in lengthened line / Like porches erst upon the Palatine" (ll. 204–5). The passage continues: "Historic reveries their lesson lent, / The Past her shadow through the Future sent." Up until the last six lines, then, Fate is the controlling concept, rendered more powerful by allusions to the era in which it was most powerful. It still threatens the present and the immediate future with violence and irrationality.

After this the conclusion presents a jarring contradiction. The penultimate image of a future filled with vengeance is rejected:

> But no. Brave though the Soldier, grave his plea—
> Catching the light in the future's skies,
> Instinct disowns each darkening prophecy:
> Faith in America never dies;
> Heaven shall the end ordained fulfill.
> We march with Providence cheery still.
>
> (ll. 208–13)

The lines are full of problems and evasions. "Light" again appears from nowhere within the poem, as it had in "America." Optimism is encouraged on the weak basis of "instinct." The next-to-last line is merely asserted. Providence is high-handedly substituted for Fate. And the word "cheery" so harshly conflicts with the formal vocabulary of the poem that one would gladly read this conclusion as irony, if the lines would support such a reading.

The contradictions of the poem are now apparent. On the one hand it clearly belongs to the Cycle of Law. As such it must foresee a future in which the discords of the war finally resolve "in time and measure perfect." But the platitudes which end the poem are undermined by the earlier statement of real issues and probabilities. Melville's attempt to create a pattern of concepts constituting a Cycle of Law breaks down here.

THE CYCLE OF EVIL

The phrase Cycle of Evil may be used to characterize the poems linked by the second major theme in *Battle-Pieces*. The poems in this cycle are noticeably better—more dramatic, more convincing, more ironic. The poems are mostly to be found in the main section of the book, a clue to Melville's own final evaluation. This cycle too is culminated by a short striking statement, a poem as fine as "Dupont's Round Fight," in which the most concise formulation of the cycle is to be found. Finally we may note that the issues in these poems are frequently given dramatic power by allusion to Milton's war in heaven and to other mythological events of cosmic significance.

"Misgivings" immediately follows the prefatory poem on John Brown.[11] The date (1860) which stands as a subtitle shows that the situation described is still before the actual outbreak of war.[12]

> When ocean-clouds over inland hills
>   Sweep storming in late autumn brown,
> And horror the sodden valley fills,
>   And the spire falls crashing in the town,
> I muse upon my country's ills—
> The tempest bursting from the waste of Time
> On the world's fairest hope linked with man's foulest crime.
>
> Nature's dark side is heeded now—
>   (Ah! optimist-cheer disheartened flown)—
> A child may read the moody brow
>   Of yon black mountain lone.
> With shouts the torrents down the gorges go,
> And storms are formed behind the storm we feel:
> The hemlock shakes in the rafter, the oak in the driving keel.

From the first line the strong cadences indicate a firmer hand in control here. At the very beginning of the collection the poet assumes a larger view of the conflict by immersing himself in the processes of Time and Nature, the only two hypostatized abstractions in the poem. They contrast nicely with the abstractions in the Cycle of Law. Here they are two very basic concepts, and each is central to a stanza.

The first stanza introduces a powerful but vague image of a storm. Its effect is devastating, but hills, valley, spire, and town are so general, so unspecified, as to be typical items. The storm itself immediately becomes useful only as an analogue for "my country's ills." A poetic mind working at a lower level would have chosen specific parallels between storm and war. But Melville immediately reaches the metaphysical level, in a line that sharply concentrates his view of history: "The tempest bursting from the waste of Time." He will elaborate this theory of history more in detail in *Clarel*, but the essence is here. Time is a desert or wilderness. But "waste" also suggests that time is a process of attrition and decay. The destructive storm of war has been generated by and within Time, the process which encompasses man and all his institutions. At the present moment it "bursts" forth to destroy the best that man has been able to create. The profound intellectual content of Melville's symbolism is again visible. The stanza concludes with a reference to America as "the world's fairest hope," an Eden image like those which R.W.B. Lewis has shown to be established in the American imagination of the mid-nineteenth century.[13] The line also carries a strong condemnatory reference to slavery—"man's foulest crime." The poems in the Cycle of Law allude to slavery only very indirectly; the issue moves to the center only in this cycle. Finally the first stanza shows a continuity with the powerful imagination that had produced *Moby-Dick:* the storms of evil which overwhelm man are associated with, generated by, "ocean." The poem is neatly bracketed by its only references to the ocean, in the first and last phrases.

The second stanza opens with an unequivocal statement of Melville's viewpoint, his antitranscendentalist polemic: "Nature's dark side is heeded now— / (Ah! optimist-cheer disheartened flown)—." Even "a child" can hardly misread the kind of evil now beginning to show itself. The last poem of *Battle-Pieces* will confirm this view by repeating "a darker side there is."[14] The fundamental institutions of civilization are threatened by this bursting forth of evil: church, home and ship of state—the spire, the rafter, and the driving keel. Finally the word "hemlock" chimes curiously in the reader's ear. Surely as a tree it provides useful and durable building materials. But it is also an herb, and no civilized reader can now see the word without being reminded of Plato's description of the death of the good man—a motif which is congenial to the Cycle of Evil, and which Melville will fully exploit during the second half of his writing career, in *Clarel* and in *Billy Budd*.

A poem like "Misgivings," then, immediately dives to the heart of the evil universe. Its controlling concepts, Nature and Time, two profoundly metaphysical concepts in nineteenth-century thought, are presented as sources and contexts for the storm of chaos that is shortly to come.

The poem "The Conflict of Convictions" is the most complex in *Battle-Pieces*. A problem arises in identifying the "voice" which speaks in several short italicized stanzas. These stanzas are also set off from the rest of the text by parentheses. This is the most difficult of the voices to identify, but there are also two others: the lines in ordinary roman type and the final stanza which is printed in capital letters. It would simplify matters greatly if the "roman" voice were the voice of naive optimism and the italics were the voice of pessimism and despair.[15] Such a clear division seems indicated by the title, and such a conflict seems resolved by the final stanza: "YEA AND NAY—EACH HATH HIS SAY." But the poem itself will not allow such simplicity. For experimental purposes one may read just the "roman" voice in the poem. Clearly this voice is carrying on a debate with itself, alternating between hope and despair. It is the speech of the ordinary but highly intelligent man faced with the chaos of issues and alternatives presented by the war. Significantly he seems to be an ex-mariner, who takes incidents from his experience at sea as models for his understanding of historic forces, as in lines 63–68. His categories are classical and biblical and Miltonic, derived from the inherited wisdom of the culture. One can identify the voice even more precisely: the figure in line 32, "and heaps Time's strand with wrecks," shows that this is the same voice that had misgivings in the previous poem about the "ocean-clouds" generated by "the waste of Time." In contrast the "italic" voice seems to have a larger view, is more remote and detached from actual events, is in fact cynical about finding a workable explanation, and opposes the sincere inquiry of the "roman" voice with a sneering humor. The final voice of the poem speaks from a standpoint still more removed, and alludes both to the voice from the whirlwind in the Book of Job ("NONE WAS BY WHEN HE SPREAD THE SKY") and to the vanity of vanities section in Ecclesiastes ("WISDOM IS VAIN AND PROPHESY"). Thus the conflict of convictions announced by the title is a multiple conflict: it is found in the roman voice's desire to see all sides and to understand; it is found also in the conflict between this honest inquiry and the ironic skepticism of the italic voice; finally it is found in the last voice, which declares both approaches inadequate.

The struggle toward understanding is opened by the roman voice in the first twelve lines with an immediate leap to the cosmic level of interpretation. The setting includes both "starry heights" and the "deep abyss." The combatants are seen as Raphael and Christ's martyrs against Satan and Mammon's slaves. The issue is nothing less than "man's latter Fall." In the latter half of his writing career Melville was deeply immersed in the myth of the American Eden and the likelihood that the Civil War was the new Adam's sin and the end of his innocence, as well as the betrayal of the fresh start which the American experience offered to the human race. The outcome of the mythical battle seems predetermined in this stanza by the characterization of the two leaders: "a white enthusiast" against the skillful old captain.[16] Presiding over this cosmic scene is a sinister presence: "*Derision* stirs the deep abyss." Melville does not say whose this disembodied sourceless voice is. Lines 11 and 12 end the opening statement with an insight into the possible significance of this historical moment. Melville must have in mind Saint Paul's easy tolerance of slavery[17] and the fact that the church had been unable to abolish the institution during its long history. The voice wonders whether Mammon will now step forward to accomplish this moral end. The stanza thus focuses on a moment of historical change. Melville will return to the point later, in this poem and in other poems of the cycle, to worry about the implications for society once the secular forces of Mammon have achieved a moral superiority in this issue.

The italic voice, with its more detached view of history, responds in the next five lines. All this self-torture to achieve understanding is useless. Cynical comfort is taken from the fact that, in the perspective of eons, so much worry about human particulars is meaningless: the primal sea will once again cover the scene of man's struggles.

The roman voice is apparently unaware of this cynicism. In its second stanza (ll. 18–23) it goes on to consider the more optimistic possibilities. The religious view of affairs involves patience. God's ways, though slow, are inexorable. Faith must stand patient, content that the reign of evil is temporary. But the last five words of the stanza shift to a mood of panic: while faith waits, she also grows old.

The italic voice picks up the word "wait" and in four short lines dismisses the idea. The image Melville uses is sharp—"a stony gate, / A statue of stone, / Weed overgrown"—but tantalizingly indefinite. The lines seem to evoke the people of a bypassed civilization who thought their final destruction was only a momentary eclipse. Like faith they thought a short wait stood between them and restoration.

The roman voice returns to its argument, this time considering darker aspects. The "but" which opens the stanza begins a contrast to the previous statements of the roman voice, not to the italicized passage. Melville has framed his debate on different levels in this poem: the roman voice ponders real historical events and issues, oblivious to the detached cynical considerations which engage the italic voice; the italic voice responds to the points made by the roman voice, but is itself unaware of the still larger view of the final voice in caps. In this stanza the roman voice considers "necessity" as a counterpossibility to faith. The verses mount in choppy intensity to a state very near hysteria. Necessity, the *anankē* of classical Greek tragedy, drives men and events, heaping "Time's strand with wrecks." Time and Ocean are brought together here from the previous poem. America, as a third Adam "who wouldst rebuild the world in bloom," is crucified again. Kings, the old monarchs still surviving into the nineteenth century, stand around the dying young democracy and "wag their heads—now save thyself" as the jeering crowd had insulted the second Adam. Melville's language here is close to the evangelist Mark's: "And they that passed by railed on him, wagging their heads, and saying, Ah, thou that destroyest the temple, and buildest it in three days, save thyself" (15:29–30).

The italic voice then takes up the jeering "ha ha" and emphasizes the sense of vanished possibility glimpsed by the roman voice. Four metaphors are enlisted to describe democracy's offer of a new political and social Eden; one line then points out that the newly constructed symbol of that hope is already showing signs of decay (l. 44).

In the next stanza the roman voice rejects its previous moment of panic and returns to faith. Milton's mythology is again invoked, where cosmic wars are always won by the powers of right. The short stanza ends on a note of hope: "The light is on the youthful brow."

The cynical voice pounces on the metaphor of light. It may be on the youthful brow, but it sits there like a flickering candle on the cap of a miner, who gropes his way in near blindness through the enfolding darkness.

The roman voice continues his meditation on youth and age, shifting from confidence to despair to confidence again and finally to despair in the short space of two rhymed lines (55–56). The italic voice then jeers to see this "cloistered doubt" break out again at still another point in man's history.

The roman voice finally works out a theological foundation upon which to base his hope: God may be old, but he is also forever young; evil must be part of his continuing process toward good. This methodology of paradox is summed up in a vivid statement: "I know a wind in purpose strong— / It spins *against* the way it drives." The paradox is then enlisted as technique for understanding the present destruction: it is really the first stage in the construction of "the final empire and the happier world."

The detached italic voice, whose forte is history in its larger cycles, turns a patronizing sarcasm on this view of suffering as a foundation for some "blissful Prime" in the future. His last word in the poem is a cynical pun.

In its final statement the roman voice is unable to hold firm in the convictions of the previous stanza. The voice is not that of the congenital optimist. The thought of usurpation or tyranny ("power unanointed" in line 72), as the result of a military conclusion to the conflict, appalls him. Though it may begin an era of wider American domination, it would be at the expense of "the Founders' dream" of individual freedom. The result of the roman voice's conflict of convictions is that there can be no real change: institutions spring ultimately from man's heart, which never changes (l. 82). All optimism concerning change is negated, by the silent negation of death.

There is no response given this time by the italic voice, nor is there need for one. They are in accord—in their final view of the present, if not in their temperaments or in their range of philosophical abilities. But unknown to either of them still another voice speaks, and with more authority, of the obscurity which was the final wisdom for both Job and Solomon. At this point one is forced to read back through the poem for a firmer identification of the two voices. The roman voice is very much like that of Job, searching honestly for answers while very close to the edge of despair; and in the italic voice one finds a cynicism close to that of Solomon in the Book of Ecclesiastes. For Job the acceptance of obscurity was demanded by the voice from the whirlwind; as Melville has the final voice summarize it: "NONE WAS BY / WHEN HE SPREAD THE SKY." And for Solomon the stance was to consider all action and thought as vanity; the final voice puts it: "WISDOM IS VAIN, AND PROPHESY."

The poem is immensely demanding and rewarding. What Melville has done is to approach the current manifestation of the age-old problem of evil, basing his inquiry on two classical approaches to the problem, both of which end not so much with an answer to the problem as an attitude toward it. The final voice of the poem summarizes the two biblical positions and hints at a higher truth which will remain unknown.

In "The Conflict of Convictions" Melville had touched briefly on the theme of youth and age as it relates to the problem of evil. The role of youthful thought and conduct is explored further in several poems belonging to the Cycle of Evil. The topic may be a conventional one for a collection of war poetry, but Melville's treatment of it goes beyond the usual lament for young lives cut off before their potential could be fulfilled. "The March into Virginia" creates the experience of green but enthusiastic troops who marched into their first battle and their first defeat at Bull Run. The poem is brilliantly written, deriving some of its formality from legal and medical diction, some of its meaning from classical and biblical allusion, and possibly the sharpness of its distinction between innocence and experience from William Blake.[18]

The poem opens formally. "Lets and bars" is probably a substitution for the metrically impossible "lets and hindrances," an example of the legal terminology which appears again in lines 13 and 15. The key to the opening lines is the word "ignorant" in line 4. The ignorance of youth is a necessary condition for the "trust and cheer" they experience in the present conflict. It is only by the exploitation of this innocence that the horrors of war can flourish. Melville's compressed syntax makes lines 8–11 difficult, though the point is important. "Ardors" and "joys" are both qualified negatively: they are both attractive qualities of youth, though the ardors may be cloudy ("turbid") with regard to their final object, and the joys may be ill founded ("vain"). Still (and here one must supply some missing words) such qualities do not "abate" with age without leaving some good results. Melville uses medical terminology to describe these results. "Stimulants to the power mature" is clear; the joyful energies of youth can lead one on to further exploration of reality, to greater knowledge and control as an adult. But Melville suddenly adds another dimension in the next line: these youthful qualities are also "preparatives of fate." Maturity, then, is characterized by greater freedom ("power") and also by a greater subjection to the irrationalities of fate. A paradox lies beneath these two compressed lines: what looks to the adolescent like the freedom of maturity is actually experienced as a greater domination by the uncontrollable forces to which the mature man is subject.

More verbal difficulties appear in the next four lines (12–15).[19] The contrasting views of youth and age on war continue to develop. The question is "*Who* here forecasteth the event?" Youth ("heart") spurns precedent, believes that the past need not repeat itself, that this war can be victorious, quick, magnificent. Youth also condemns the adult world's "foreclosures of surprise." Foreclosure has the general meaning of "exclusion, prevention." The legal sense, which is within the same circle of meaning, has an interesting nuance for the poem. Legally the word signifies the extinguishing of a right that one previously had. (It is interesting to note that "foreclose" appears in the epilogue to *Clarel* also, and this progression of meanings is also operative there.) Here it adds a precise item to the characterization of youth: they will not easily give up their right to buoyant optimism for the future. The word "precedent" two lines above is a further indication that the legal meaning of "foreclosure" is operative here.

The poem then proceeds through a finely realized description of youthful soldiers on the way to their first battle. The first break in the poem occurs then, and a short conclusion of six lines dramatizes how this gap in generations is bridged. Ignorance becomes experience in three days. Enlightenment comes, with pitiless irony, by "the vollied glare" of actual battle. Those who survive the shame of defeat at First Manassas become hardened for the shock of Second Manassas.

Behind this poem is a series of distinctions that would develop more fully and clearly in a paragraph that was at one time a part of *Billy Budd*. In a paragraph headed "Lawyers, Experts, Clergy: An Episode," Melville says that doctors are sometimes called as expert witnesses. He suggests that perhaps in extreme cases clergy might be called in also to testify concerning "those intricacies involved in the question of moral responsibility." [20] The gradations of "the mystery of iniquity" indicated here, and the various professions competent to deal with it, can be seen to be already taking shape in this poem.

A similar enlightenment is the subject of the frequently anthologized "Shiloh." The poem commemorates one of the disastrous early battles which Melville sees as dampening the initial childish enthusiasm for war. It is a poem of brilliant visual quality. The church stands at its center while the swallows, wheeling and skimming in patternless curves, constantly draw the reader's attention away from its fixed solidity. Chaos and cosmos are in rhythmic conflict here.

The poem is another carefully wrought one, though its techniques seem constructed just for this occasion. The rhyming creates a four-line framing stanza at the beginning and at the end, which accords with the sounds and images repeated in the two groupings. The rhyme scheme also serves to divide the body of the poem, between lines 9 and 10. The structure of the poem allows three possible climaxes: the shortest line (12); lines 14–15 immediately before the framing stanza begins to repeat itself at the end; or the line dramatized by parentheses and an exclamation point. The complex theme of the poem is also deceptive. Swallows seem to indicate joy, as they do for example in Keats's "To Autumn," or possibly even the Incarnation or the Resurrection.[21] Spring rejuvenation is continued through the "April rain" in line 5. This train of association leads quite naturally to the church in line 9, where one now becomes aware of the deception: Sunday and church are desecrated by "pain" and "fight." The third section then focuses on the drama the men have undergone who lie here awaiting death in surroundings so suggestive of resurrection and religious consolation. As a result of the battle they at least are undeceived, both about the glorious myth of war and about who the enemy is. The fourth section begins, or, according to the logic of the poem, this section ends, with the magnificent "what like a bullet can undeceive!" The whole poem is laid out to dramatize this ironic epigram. "Shiloh" ends with repetitions from the opening lines, except that the vitality of the swallows who there "fly low" now becomes the absolutely different reality—and the feminine rhyme emphasizes it— "lie low." Deception, then, is a part of the nature of Evil as Melville analyzes it in this cycle. War is unmasked, finally, as a concrete histori- cal eruption of Evil. Man can be deceived about this reality, but those who found themselves most directly involved came away, or perished, "enlightened."

In several poems Melville explores this process of transition from youthful innocence and enthusiasm to an adult sense of crass casualty ruling the world. "The College Colonel," "Commemorative of a Naval Victory," and "In the Turret" are three such studies. The college colonel had led his regiment out two years before, much as the soldiers who had trooped in Bacchic glee into Virginia for First Manassas. They are now a remnant, and he himself is a remnant. Several of the thematic motifs that unify *Battle-Pieces* are here. The "Indian aloofness" in this poem contrasts with the "young Indians" feared for their exuberance in "Apa- thy and Enthusiasm." The sea once again is used for its metaphoric power. In "Misgivings" and in "The Conflict of Convictions" it has been defined as the wasteland of time, source of the irrational violence that bursts out upon man at irregular intervals. The colonel and his men had momentarily wandered into this waste; the survivors barely escaped out through the surf (ll. 8–12). Here too the word "Boy" is used (l. 19), but now only in the sense that a lifetime of experience has been com- pressed into a short space, and that he is only chronologically a boy now. The experiences that matured and enlightened him are enumerated in the last six lines: battles, surgical operations, and the barren listless experience of a prison camp. (Melville had described this at length in the previous poem, "In the Prison Pen.") The italics in the final line manipulate the reader, at least momentarily, to accept Melville's dark version of reality. What the boy has learned from these horrors, and what has changed him, is *"truth."*

Similarly "Commemorative of a Naval Victory" focuses on a man who had also plunged into the depths of that Sea-Time, and is con- demned to finish life in the isolation imposed on one who carries the secret of what was really there. The poem is well made. There are three stanzas of nine lines each. The rhyme scheme is an odd one, but it is the same in each stanza. The prevailing meter is a calm four-stress line. Each stanza dips and then swells to three stresses and then to five in its sixth and seventh lines. The third stanza ends with a sharply discordant image presented in two rough lines of trimeter.

The first stanza characterizes a particular kind of sailor, one that stands on a line which can be drawn from the early idealizations of Jack Chase all the way through Melville's works to *Billy Budd*. The discipline of the sea has refined the qualities of strength, grace, and gentility. Melville mentions Titian's portrait, where three props are unobtrusively used to suggest the qualities of his subject. Hennig Cohen, in his edition of *Battle-Pieces* (p. 285), has reproduced the portrait Melville seems to have in mind here. There may also be an allusion to *Walden*, which had recently appeared. "I long ago lost a hound, a bay horse, and a turtle-dove, and am still on their trail" (Chapter 1). Thoreau throws an air of mystery around himself and the exact identification of these symbols of lost ideals. He was asked for the meaning of the symbols, and his replies were mystifying.[22] The three items seem made to stand for one's private version of the vanishing, the unattainable. Melville may have had the passage in mind as he noted how "the hawk, the hound, the sword" in Titian's painting were also necessary symbols in the characterization. There is a similar air of mystery about the sailor who is the subject of the poem.

The second stanza sketches such a personality "in years that follow victory won." He seems to embody the prestige and authority that Melville had recently hoped for his cousin Guert Gansevoort. Melville wrote to his brother Tom (May 25, 1862), in a letter alluding to recent events in the war, that "Guert has recently been appointed to be commander of a fine new sloop of war. I am rejoiced to hear it. It will do him good in more ways than one. He is brave as a lion, a good seaman, a natural-born officer, & I hope he will yet turn out the hero of a brilliant victory."[23] Gansevoort was at this time already living under a tragic cloud. The *Somers* mutiny affair had occurred in 1842. Gansevoort had been the presiding judge in a trial that ended in a hanging similar to Billy Budd's. Thus the other side of such a character is equally interesting, and Melville proceeds to consider it in the final stanza.

As the stanza develops Melville focuses on the division that exists within a man who has had a revelation of evil, the kind of self-division that sets him apart even in the midst of those who would praise him. That part of one's spirit which would ordinarily respond to adulation is now oblivious to it. The situation recalls the fine psychological insight of Hemingway's early stories where Nick Adams fears sleep because Death might catch him off guard and looks forward to Melville's late characterization of persons whose one "transcendent act" sets them apart from the rest of humanity. One part of the ex-officer's spirit is constantly alert for the reappearance of the shark. The stanza ends with one of the finest dramatic moments in Melville's poetry. The period and the dash bring the reader to a long stop, as if building energy for the leap across to an image which is grammatically and logically detached from the rest of the poem: "The shark / Glides white through the phosphorus sea."

The shark powerfully affected Melville's imagination throughout his life, especially so at this moment. A few pages later in *Battle-Pieces* he will use the image again in "A Scout Toward Aldie." The guerrillas of the Confederate Colonel Mosby are dangerous and seem to appear from nowhere: "As glides in seas the shark, / Rides Mosby through the dark." Most striking of all the shark poems, of course, and the locus where all the power of evil is concentrated, is the poem Melville was to publish twenty-two years later in *John Marr*, "The Maldive Shark."[24] The symbol is closely associated with what Pip glimpsed at the bottom of the sea and with the vision of the mother-figure in "America."

The third case of an individual who passes from innocence to wisdom in the experience of war concerns the commander of the Union ironclad *Monitor* who sustained severe eye injuries while canned up in his novel armored ship. The poem is framed as a setting for the speeches of Worden and the surrounding presence of which he is unaware, the "spirit forewarning." The honest sailor finds himself in the midst of forces which the poet can describe only in mythological terms; he threads his way through them only by devotion to a single concept and thereby finds glory. The dominant note of characterization, "duty," is struck in the first line and surges in crescendo to be repeated five times in the last stanza. The devotion is maintained in a confined and terror-ridden atmosphere. Melville compares Worden's iron-clad turret to a diving bell (l. 4), an image used elsewhere. In a poem published many years later, "In a Church of Padua," Melville describes the Roman Catholic confessional booth:

> Dread diving-bell! In thee inurned
> What hollows the priest must sound,
> Descending into consciences
> Where more is hid than found.[25]

One is alerted, then, to the possibility that in "In the Turret" the diving bell may also be a vehicle for descent into moral and spiritual depths.

The image fits well with Melville's frequent contrast between those who skim and those who dive. He had written to Evert Duyckinck in 1849: "I love all men who *dive*. Any fish can swim near the surface, but it takes a great whale to go down stairs five miles or more."[26] The notion is not one tending towards heart's ease; one need only recall the report of Pip who had also been there.

Melville uses the unusual word "cribbed" (l. 13) to describe Worden's confinement in his turret. One must look to the major landmark in the history of this word in *Macbeth*. Macbeth has just experienced his first reversal: "Most royal sir, Fleance is 'scaped." Stunned by the implications, Macbeth replies:

> Then comes my fit again: I had else been perfect,
> Whole as the marble, founded as the rock,
> As broad and general as the casing air:
> But now I am cabin'd, cribb'd, confined, bound in
> To saucy doubts and fears.
>
> *(III, iv)*

It is nearly impossible for Melville (or his reader) to have known the word without knowing this context. Shakespeare's play about the perversion of duty suggests a rich contrast to the example of Worden here.

The most interesting feature of the poem is the anonymous "spirit" which dominates the third stanza. The honest man is walled up in his "turret"—an image that suggests the besieged towers of romance as well as Civil War battle technology. A morning calm before the battle prevails. Og, the mythical giant of the Book of Deuteronomy, awaits him. The tutoring spirit, a monitor in another sense, must inspire ambiguous courage: it not only forewarns but *derides*. The spirit, then, is the same that distressed the naive voice in the earlier poem "The Conflict of Convictions." There it had been a disembodied quality: "*Derision* stirs the deep abyss." Here the same word is used to describe the voice of the spirit who threatens the simple generous man in pursuit of his duty. Derision, the cosmic laugh, is a spirit and therefore real and pervasive. It will soon, in intellectual history, be called absurdity.

The thematic universe of *Battle-Pieces* begins to take shape. The derisive spirit warns the man against reliance on his clumsy gadget. The armor can protect, but it also can imprison. Cunning can be error, "monstrous error." But more can be deduced about the nature of this spirit from an important word at the end of the spirit's speech. The sailor is being trapped in a "*goblin*-snare." The spirit here drops its disguise for those who can notice the clue. The only other use of the word "goblin" in *Battle-Pieces* is in the culminating poem of the Cycle of Evil, "The Apparition." What Worden finds himself alone with is nothing less than the cosmic spirit of evil pervading and controlling the universe.

One of the tasks Melville sets himself in the Cycle of Evil is the identification of the agents of good and evil. Here too one can see Melville's thought progressing from one level to a deeper one. Several poems rest content in the conviction entertained by all people at war that "our" side is the good side, while the enemy are minions of pure evil. The poems in which Melville momentarily identifies Evil with the South are among his most emotional poems in *Battle-Pieces*. For example "Look-out Mountain" is written in a stirring meter that recalls "The Battle Hymn of the Republic," and it draws upon the mythical structures of *Vathek* and of *Paradise Lost* for added power.

The poem described what was called by contemporary historians "The Battle above the Clouds." Confederate forces occupied the plateau atop Lookout Mountain just outside Chattanooga. When Union forces began their assault, low clouds obscured the top of the mountain, and the first Union soldiers to reach the top found that the Confederates had withdrawn. The Union banner was raised, as Melville describes it in the last stanza. "Mountain" is capitalized in each stanza, as if it were the abode of the Holy. One is tempted to think of Moses and Sinai until the allusion is made clear in the fifth and sixth lines. This is the mountain of Kaf, which in Islamic mythology rings the world and is the abode of Eblis, the Evil One. Melville would have read the two names in William Beckford's *Vathek* (Sealts #54). Beckford's immature mock-heroic, at the beginning of the book, must have been less than pleasing to Melville, though there are passages of allegory and moral intensity that make the book considerably more interesting as it progresses. Beckford's description of the hall of Eblis, which climaxes the book, is impressive. His note on "Eblis" would have interested Melville: "D'Herbelot supposes this title to have been a corruption of the Greek . . . *diabolos*. It was the appellation conferred by the Arabians upon the prince of the apostate angels, whom they represented as exiled to the infernal regions."

There can be no doubt then which side the Confederacy represents. The description of the hall of Eblis naturally suggests Satan's Pandemonium in *Paradise Lost;* Beckford quotes frequently from Milton in his notes, and a further link is furnished here. The Miltonic echo occurs precisely with the word "anarch" in the second and third stanzas of Melville's poem. The word is from *Paradise Lost* (II, 988), but the entire context is relevant, lines 890–1055 at the end of the second book.

Satan has just left the gate of hell and finds the whole area between him and the created world to be "a dark Illimitable Ocean"—the element essential to Melville's cosmology. Presiding over it are Night and Chaos. Milton calls them "Ancestors of Nature [who] hold Eternal Anarchy." The ocean is "the Womb of nature and perhaps her Grave." Chaos is then given his other name, "the Anarch" (l. 985), and he allies himself with Satan for the destruction of the world. The Anarch is not Satan, but the pervasive Chaos, the "womb" of the created universe. We can now understand the mythology of "Look-out Mountain" quite clearly. The peak of the mountain, occupied by the Confederate forces, is "the fastness of the Anarch," chaos. The withdrawal of these forces is "the Anarch's plunging flight." The Civil War is identified as "the war of Wrong and Right." And if there can still be any doubt about the allegiance of each side, we are told that the Union armies in the valley "are fortified in right."

Melville's temporary flirtation with this view of the war continues through three more poems. One of them is "The Battle for the Bay," a descriptive poem about the encounter in Mobile Bay in August 1864 between Admiral Farragut's small fleet and the Confederate ironclad *Tennessee*, with its three attendant gunboats. Once again the action is mythologized into the eternal struggle between Good and Evil. Farragut himself is one of the "noble hearts" (l. 1), and his men enjoy divine protection: "Behind each man a holy angel stood" (l. 35). The Confederate ship *Tennessee*, on the other hand, is "strong as Evil, and bold as Wrong" (l. 75). The Confederate ship is called "the bad one," "this Man-of-Sin" (ll. 95, 97–98). The latter reference puns on man-of-war and also alludes to the apocalyptic section in St. Paul's second letter to the Thessalonians, Chapter 2: "Let no man deceive you by any means: for that day shall not come, except there come a falling away first, and that man of sin be revealed, the son of perdition." Four verses later in the same chapter occurs Paul's famous expression, "the mystery of iniquity," which was to continue to fascinate Melville through the writing of *Billy Budd*. Finally, in the next stanza of Melville's poem, the Confederate ironclad is made to stand as hate personified. The concepts associated with the Confederate cause in this poem, then, are the Satanic ones of hatred, evil, perdition, and sin.

The same identification can be seen in "Rebel Color-Bearers at Shiloh," where the Confederate armies are compared to martyrs—"and martyrs for the Wrong have been." But the strongest poem on the theme of the South as Evil is one called "The Frenzy in the Wake." It is conceived as a diatribe delivered by the southern voice after Sherman's devastations.

The poem is similar to the biblical genre of taunt speeches delivered by the defeated. Satan has several of them early in *Paradise Lost*. The voice created by Melville for this poem, a voice of hatred and despair and defiance toward the conquerer, sounds very much like that of Milton's Satan; there are correspondences between the poem and Book I, lines 84–124, of *Paradise Lost*. Melville's South rails against the victorious "Oppressor"; Satan derides whatever "the Potent Victor in his rage can else inflict." Neither speaker is willing to "repent or change." Each sees the war continuing beyond defeat and surrender. Satan vows "immortal hate" and the final promise of the South is that "even despair / Shall never our hate rescind."

The preceding poems show that there was a momentary temptation for Melville, while probing the ethical and metaphysical issues of the Civil War, to fall into typical patterns of war rhetoric by identifying the enemy with evil and the Union cause with good. But reality could be not quite so simple nor so partisan. The intellectual strength of *Battle-Pieces* is to be found in Melville's diving to deeper levels for his truth. Men are still the evil-doers at this deeper level, but in a poem called "The House-Top" they are northerners, those who participated in the draft riots in New York, late in the summer of 1863.

The poem is one of Melville's rare examples of blank verse. Pentameters have generally become languid and slack by this time in the nineteenth century, but the vigor of Melville's lines is remarkable. Melville's poem contains two movements. The first begins with a magnificent linking of words and phrases to suggest the atavistic lust for violence which is still active in the jungle of man's soul. Even the sea is here (in lines 6–7) to terrorize with its mixed and muffled threat of destruction. Atheism is once again personified, and together with Arson it presides over the rats (used three times in two lines) which now infest the town. Neither law ("civil charms") nor religion (now reduced to "priestly spells") can control the outbreak. Primitive forces burst out in the civilized city, "and man rebounds whole aeons back in nature." The focus is now on man, not on one or other faction, as evil.

In the second part the poem becomes a profound commentary on history and a categorical denial of the optimism on which the Constitution of the United States is based. Melville himself "rebounds"—to a theory of man held by the Puritan oligarchy which was superseded by the theories of the founding fathers. The lines become heavy with a plodding and jarring alliteration. In his own copy the author intensified this effect by changing "shakes" to "jars" in line 18. Much of the meaning in this second part is carried by the sensitive irony of the adjectives; they seem to be employed perversely, though the reader soon realizes that Melville is in earnest about them. Thus Draco, whose laws carried brutal punishments, is called wise. So also, cynical tyrants are "honest": they are the only realists in the science of mob control. The older theory, Calvin's creed of man's innate depravity, is proved true in the events. Of many possible citations from Calvin the following description of humanity, from the *Institutes*, is typical: "Those whose feet are swift to shed blood, whose hands are polluted with rapine and murder, whose throats are like open sepulchres, whose tongues are deceitful, whose lips are envenomed, whose works are useless, iniquitous, corrupt and deadly, whose souls are estranged from God, the inmost recesses of whose hearts are full of pravity." With the restoration of law and order through military force, the Town is relieved and grateful, but does not understand that its gratitude implies a "grimy slur on the Republic's faith." Man is simply not naturally good; one of the principles upon which the American Constitution is based is false.

The same pessimism is suggested by the last stanza of "The Fall of Richmond." In his preface to *Battle-Pieces* Melville had said that most of the poems "originated from an impulse imparted by the fall of Richmond." The impulse is perhaps hinted at in the poem commemorating the event, and my reading of the whole collection is corroborated by Melville himself. The third stanza is:

> Well that the faith we firmly kept,
>   And never our aim forswore
> For the Terrors that trooped from each recess
> When fainting we fought in the Wilderness,
>   And Hell made loud hurrah;
> But God is in Heaven, and Grant in the Town,
>   And Right through might is Law—
>   *God's way adore.*

The poem must be read against the background of ideas more fully developed in "The House-Top." One must also note the parody of Browning's optimism in the third-to-last line. On first reading the poem appears to belong to the Cycle of Law; but law is here redefined as the reestablishment of right through military force, necessary because of the evil now manifested in man. Grant in the town seems to be vicar of God in his heaven. Only repressive might can bring man's corrupt nature under control. This is "God's way," *pace* Browning and the founding fathers.

We are now in the midst of those poems in *Battle-Pieces* which contain Melville's profoundest thought on the nature of evil as he apprehended it in the events of the war. It would be difficult to praise these poems too highly. Only two more remain to be discussed: one of them looks into the heart of a man closely associated with a major catastrophe in the war; the other, I believe, contains the whole of Melville's philosophy of evil in its most concentrated form.

"THE COMING STORM"

A Picture by S. R. Gifford, and owned by E. B.
Included in the N. A. Exhibition, April, 1865

All feeling hearts must feel for him
    Who felt this picture. Presage dim—
Dim inklings from the shadowy sphere
    Fixed him and fascinated here.

A demon-cloud like the mountain one
    Burst on a spirit as mild
As this urned lake, the home of shades.
    But Shakespeare's pensive child

Never the lines had lightly scanned,
    Steeped in fable, steeped in fate;
The Hamlet in his heart was 'ware,
    Such hearts can antedate.

No utter surprise can come to him
    Who reaches Shakespeare's core;
That which we seek and shun is there—
    Man's final lore.

The title and subtitle contain in abbreviated form two pieces of information that are essential to an understanding of the poem. The painting is a landscape with a placid mirrorlike lake in the foreground. To the left are a rocky coast and a forest, bathed in sunshine. To the viewer's right a mountain rises whose reflection darkens much of the lake. Black storm clouds seem to be rolling in from the right, obscuring the peak of the mountain and menacing the sunny part of the landscape.[27] Second, the E. B. of the subtitle is Edwin Booth, the famous Shakespearan actor whose brother assassinated Lincoln. (The poem previous to this one, "The Martyr," is a meditation on the assassinated president.) The sense of the poem is seriously impaired unless one realizes that Edwin Booth is "Shakespeare's pensive child" and also the man who bought this painting.

Several different items are linked here. The title recalls the picture:

clouds that threaten a storm. The assassination in the previous poem presages the turmoil of an unjust Reconstruction to come once the storm of war itself has passed. But the particular buyer of the picture, and the knowing "Hamlet in his heart," also feared a more personal tragedy might follow the assassination if an enraged public were to seek vengeance on him for the deed of his brother. The evil that bared itself at that moment will be long in working itself out both on the national level and the individual. Edwin Booth thus becomes a tragic figure in the most classical sense: the individual whose story involves the civil order as well as his own personal destiny. This man is highly conscious of tragic action: "Never the lines had lightly scanned, / Steeped in fable, steeped in fate." He has become the materials he was acting. Melville's final thoughts on this profoundly significant coincidence reflect his own understanding of Shakespeare: Booth, from the vantage point where he can view the workings out of national and personal tragedy, cannot be surprised when evil erupts; he has already penetrated "Shakespeare's core" and "man's final lore." The rhyme of course makes the identification of the two even stronger.

The word "core" links this poem with "The Apparition: A Retrospect," and brings us to the final statement of Melville's synthesis. I believe that the poem is the most concise statement of Melville's philosophy to be found anywhere in his writings. In the present collection, as has already been stated, it stands at the climax of the Cycle of Evil, just as "Dupont's Round Fight" stands at the climax of the superseded Cycle of Law. It may well be Melville's most characteristic work.

THE APPARITION

(A Retrospect)

Convulsions came; and, where the field
    Long slept in pastoral green,
A goblin-mountain was upheaved
(Sure the scared sense was all deceived),
    Marl-glen and slag-ravine.

The unreserve of Ill was there,
    The clinkers in her last retreat;
But, ere the eye could take it in,
Or mind could comprehension win,
    It sunk!—and at our feet.

So, then, Solidity's a crust—
    The core of fire below;

All may go well for many a year,
But who can think without a fear
Of horrors that happen so?

There are fine phrases here: "Convulsions came," "The unreserve of Ill was there," "Solidity's a crust— / The core of fire below." The poem is carefully made: stanzas match one another in rhythm and rhyme scheme, both created especially for the present poem. Melville has added an extra rhyming line at the middle of the conventional quatrain, causing each stanza to swell with a natural crescendo. The poem is dominated by the single image of a volcano whose destructive force can suddenly and inexplicably burst forth in a serene landscape. "The Apparition" reaches back into the collection for a restatement of several themes and images: "goblin" recalls "In the Turret," for example, and the volcano here has the same force as the imagery of "Misgivings." The poem also points to other works of Melville, to the intent of the "pasteboard masks" section of *Moby-Dick* (Chapter 36) as well as to the volcano image there and in *Clarel*.[28] Curiously, and quite significantly, the Civil War is not even mentioned in this poem. Placed as it is toward the end of the main section of *Battle-Pieces*, the poem may be presumed to be a generalized retrospective view of the war. But the fact that the war is not mentioned leaves the reader with the impression that this is not only the explanation of the war, but also a revelation of "Solidity"—that the war offers an insight into the nature of reality generally. An America dominated by transcendentalist optimism had been sleeping, "was all deceived." The truth is that solidity's a crust; the unreserve of Ill was present all along, the core of fire below, the horrors that happen so. Such destructive evil cannot be adequately described as a temporary breach of permanent and all-pervasive law. Instead evil is the permanent and controlling reality.

II

CLAREL:
THE STATIC
ELEMENTS

The problem of philosophy, according to Plato,
is, for all that exists conditionally, to find
a ground unconditioned and absolute.

Emerson, Nature

For evil is the chronic malady of the universe;
and checked in one place,
breaks forth in another.

Mardi

MELVILLE published his *Clarel: A Poem and Pilgrimage in the Holy Land* in 1876. It is a long poem of some 18,000 lines, nearly twice as long as Virgil's *Aeneid*. Behind the poem lies Melville's own experience as a pilgrim in the Holy Land during the winter of 1856–1857. He kept a journal of the trip[1] and some of the seeds of *Clarel* are clearly discernible in it. Twenty years of reading and reflection added a great deal more, until the finished poem can very nearly be called a case study of the nineteenth-century representative man.

The poem, however, was badly received by contemporary reviewers, some of whom could have given it only the slightest glance;[2] even into the late 1950s there was little attempt to probe the complexities of *Clarel* with any sympathy, at a time when the major fiction was receiving the utmost respect.[3] More recent analyses of the poem tend to take a subordinate position in larger studies of Melville's work as a whole. Merlin Bowen, for example, read it as a significant stage in the author's mental biography. By the time Melville came to write *Clarel*, he concluded, "the search for a life-sustaining balance—a vision adequate to the needs of both heart and head—has become the central concern."[4]

Tyrus Hillway returns all the way to Weaver's interpretation of Melville's life, dealing with *Clarel* in a chapter entitled "Long Decline." (He also dislikes the poetry generally: "the loss of all his verses would probably detract nothing from the stature of Melville as an American writer."[5]) Hillway concludes: "To escape despair, Melville was impelled in *Clarel* to turn from science to the faith he found in his own heart. The belief in God in some guise, whether just or unjust, he found necessary to the peace of his soul."

Robert Penn Warren has written two articles on Melville's poetry. In 1946 he was quite critical of "this poet of shreds and patches," though willing to admit some fine lines and images. He considered Melville's theory of history to be "a guarded meliorism" and spoke of *Clarel* as ending on a note of affirmation.[6] In 1967 Warren came back to Melville's poetry considerably more appreciative, finding it the tough-minded personal searchings of a man not easily satisfied with conventional answers to the mysteries and tragedies of life. The Civil War made Melville a poet because it gave him the right subject for exploring public as well as private tensions and conflicts. Of *Clarel* Warren says: "The poem is an important document of our modernity, as it is a document of Melville's own mind." He adds: "Clarel is left alone, as man always is in the end, to make what terms he can with the polarities and antinomies of life, and to try to make terms with himself by achieving the selfhood of the sort exemplified by the Druse guide and by Rolfe." Warren still holds that the poem is flawed. Its main weakness is that it originates from ideas and not from the significant kind of action that inspired Melville's best writing, but he judges it a major step beyond the typical nineteenth-century debate: "We see that ideas are not merely to be judged abstractly as true or false; in one sense the personal tone, the quality of commitment a person has to an idea and the depth and richness of his experience of an idea, are related to the 'truth' of an idea." Warren cites Bezanson approvingly, saying that Melville "goes increasingly from asking whose beliefs are right to asking who is the right kind of man." This focus on "selfhood" provides the key to Warren's interpretation of the poem. It functions, surely, in the reader's evaluation of the characters, but one finishes the poem realizing that Clarel himself disappears at the end with his problem unsolved and his own selfhood unachieved.[7]

The earliest reviewers' dislike for Melville's poem is matched by one of its most recent critics. Hyatt Waggoner, in his *American Poets: From the Puritans to the Present*, exercises little restraint in his scorn for Melville's poetry generally. He says that "Melville never really found a voice for his poetry. Or rather, the voice that speaks is not the voice of anyone alive, and it is not speaking to anyone in particular, not even to itself. It is a voice neither colloquial nor literary, a voice such as we have never heard, even with the mind's ear." He feels that "if the author of *Moby Dick* had not written [these poems], they would now be unknown—except to specialists in minor American nineteenth-century poets and to antiquarians. . . . For the most part they are painful to read." He speaks of *Clarel* as "this immensely long and almost completely unreadable poem." "This is amateur poetry," he says, "written by a man with no ear for speech and only the most abstract sense of the reality of his own characters. . . . They are all merely pasteboard figures." Waggoner judges it to be a narrative poem, but seems irritated by "the brief narrative interruptions of the interminable debate." He concludes: "Even on the thematic level of its most general meanings, the poem is deeply incoherent."[8]

One can concur with Waggoner's last statement, concerning the incoherence (or, I would prefer, the inconclusiveness) of theme in the poem. But Richard H. Fogle finds this very quality one of the poem's virtues. The conflict between faith and doubt, so characteristic of nineteenth-century literature, is the theme of the poem. Characteristic also is the rarity of generally acceptable solutions for those who explored the problem seriously. Fogle therefore insists that, at the thematic level, *Clarel* "does not push to definite conclusions."[9]

The inconclusiveness of the poem provides the key to the present study. If we can set up the model of a literary work as a structure having many levels, the problem becomes clear. At the level of simple geography, for example, the poem is inconclusive. The journey is circular: from Jerusalem, through various Holy Land sites, back to Jerusalem.[10] At the chronological level the story is also inconclusive. Prominent at the beginning of the poem is the Epiphany season. Toward the end the time is Ash Wednesday and then Lent. The concluding cantos of the poem go through Holy Week and Easter to Pentecost. But the pattern of the church year functions less and less consciously as the poem goes on, except perhaps as a counterpattern against which the action takes place. In other words there is no resolution for the poem to be derived from chronological patterns. At the narrative or plot level, there is no resolution, no final clarification. The main character merely fades into the background with his problems heightened and developed, but with no sign of how a solution could possibly occur. And thematically, as we have seen, the poem "does not push to definite conclusions."

One must read then, if possible, to a deeper level of the poem for its final judgment. Melville himself gives the clue to what he was doing and how his work should be read. In Part II we find the lines "Thy wings, Imagination, span / Ideal truth in fable's seat" (II, xxxv, 18–19).[11] The work of a literary artist, conceived in terms of the romantic esthetic to which Melville was heir, is the creation of symbols, models for truth, by the highest of the faculties—the imagination. Critics of *Clarel* have not yet analyzed the symbolic level of the poem in detail, a level which must finally be considered for the kind of resolution not achieved at the other levels in the poem. And there is a definite choice made here from among the conflicting options which arise in the poem.

At first reading there appear to be several symbolic systems operating simultaneously: the main system of city-landscape-desert, with a separate category of sea images performing a subsidiary function; a secondary set of symbols for the shaping of history and time; and finally another extensive system of Pastoral-Edenic-Christ materials. A more thorough acquaintance with the poem shows these systems to be working together to form one massive and complex symbolic system, carrying the burden of meaning in the poem. This massive symbol is composed of what might be called the static elements: those images out of which the major picture (of the universe, as it turns out) is constructed. The major static elements are the city, the landscape of the Holy Land, and the Dead Sea. Vitalizing these are what may be called the dynamics of the symbol, the elements which add a temporal or sequential quality to it.

Clarel opens in the city to which its eponymous hero has come quest-
ing for the grail of clarity. Immediately we are in a place of something
more than bricks and mortar. Mounting the rooftop of the hostel where
he is staying, Clarel[12] looks over Jerusalem at sunset:

> The mountain-town,
> A walled and battlemented one,
> With houseless suburbs front and rear,
> And flanks built up from steeps severe,
> Saddles and turrets the ascent—
> Tower which rides the elephant.
>
> *(I, i, 128–33)*

Nearby he sees the houses of the city, "All stone—a moor of roofs. No
play / Of life; no smoke went up, no sound / Except low hum, and that
half drowned" (ll. 143–45). A more precise description follows shortly:
"Blind arches showed in walls of wane, / Sealed windows, portals
masoned fast, / And terraces where nothing passed / By parapets all
dumb" (ll. 163–66).

In this opening canto, taken up entirely with introducing the musing
hero on his first night in the Holy City, clearly the city itself carries its
own kind of message to Clarel. Three phrases seem strongest: "no play
of life," "blind arches," and "parapets all dumb." The city is dead; it
has no eye for his problems, no voice to speak to him. There are indica-
tions that the city will not only be neutrally dumb and unenlightening
for him; there appears to be, in addition, some positive lumbering men-
ace in a city compared to the chess rook (l. 133). The qualities of blind-
ness and lumbering strength suggested in this opening canto will come
to function more strongly as the poem goes on.

Within the next few days Clarel explores Jerusalem in more detail.
The buildings of this blind city particularly attract his attention:

> In street at hand a silence reigns
> Which Nature's hush of loneness feigns,
> Few casements, few, and latticed deep,
> High raised above the head below,
> That none might listen, pry, or peep,
> Or any hint or inkling know
> Of that strange innocence or sin
> Which locked itself so close within.
> The doors, recessed in massy walls,
> And far apart, as dingy were
> As Bastile gates. No shape astir

Except at whiles a shadow falls
Athwart the way, and key in hand
Noiseless applies it, enters so
And vanishes.

(I, vii, 1–15)

The same symbolic contours are apparent here as in the first passage:
the silence and sense of isolation; the blind windows which seem to shut
him off from any communication, contrary to their ordinary function;
the vague menace suggested in "Bastile gates." An element added here
is the mysterious "shadow" who possesses the "key" to the city; but in
his noiselessness and quick vanishing he seems almost to belong to
another dimension, another universe, which Clarel is not allowed to
enter. A second added element is the similarity between Nature and
the City, in the silence and loneliness of both; this similarity is later
pushed to a continuity and identity between the two.

   Clarel goes with Nehemiah to the latter's house in an especially poor
section of the town:

A little square they win—a waste
Shut in by towers so hushed, so blind,
So tenantless and left forlorn
As seemed—an ill surmise was born
Of something prowling there behind.
   An arch, with key-stone slipped half down
Like a dropped jaw—they enter that;
Repulse nor welcome in the gate:
Climbed, and an upper chamber won.
It looked out through low window small
On other courts of bale shut in,
Whose languishment of crumbling wall
Breathed that despair alleged of sin.

(I, xxii, 6–18)

Once again the town is "blind," and the indefinite menace is perceived
lurking there; vacancy is repeated ("tenantless"), but a vacancy now
filled up: "something prowling there behind." The city now is personi-
fied for Clarel: the arch becomes a jaw into which he is expected to
step. The place exudes an atmosphere of despair for some "alleged" sin.
All this is very strange, for this is the place where Clarel is shortly to
meet Ruth, the one real possibility for salvation held out to him in
the course of the poem; and the site is the home of Nehemiah, one of the
most purely good characters of the poem. Melville returns here to the

phenomenon of ambiguities which fascinated him in *Pierre*. Finally one should note the word "waste" in the first line. Melville's symbols tend to touch upon one another throughout the poem; here we find a hint of similarity to the desert which figures so largely in the second, third, and fourth parts of the poem.

The passages discussed so far include the impressions both of Clarel and of the narrator independently of his main character. A new character, Rolfe, now reports similar impressions of the city. Melville, in other words, is saturating the reader with one impression from several narrative sources.

> "O City," Rolfe cried; "house on moor,
> With shutters burst and blackened door—
> Like that thou showest; and the gales
> Still round thee blow the Banshee-wails;
> Well might the priest in temple start,
> Hearing the voice—'Woe, we depart!' "
>
> (*I, xxxiii, 64–69*)

Rolfe notes the city's similarity to a "moor," the aspect which had struck Clarel on the rooftop of his hostel. He sees also the empty lifeless house— not merely lifeless, but sterile, unable to support life. Rolfe perceives too something menacing about the city ("Banshee-wails"). It is a city which even the gods have forsaken.[13] Rolfe's impressions continue to be important in the poem. The exploring party has now grown to include Clarel and Rolfe, Nehemiah and Vine. They visit the chapel of the Ascension and then climb to its tower for a panoramic view:

> "Is yon the city Dis aloof?"
> Said Rolfe; "nay, liker 'tis some print,
> Old blurred, bewrinkled mezzotint."
>
> (*I, xxxvi, 29–31*)

Melville has already developed his City as symbol to a considerable degree. Here he stresses the most significant aspects of the symbol by having Rolfe see it as one of the cities in Hell. In the translation of Dante's *Inferno* owned by Melville (Sealts, #174), he would have read of "the City, that of Dis is named." It is a city of fire "that inward burns"; "the walls appeared as they were framed of iron." [14]

Immediately Rolfe goes on to include the whole setting of Jerusalem in one vast impression. Both Holy City and surrounding countryside are seen to be "lifeless," "dead," and "baleful." It is suggested that something sacral, "the *hymn* of rills," has also departed from this country:

"And distant, look, what lifeless hills!
Dead long for them the hymn of rills
And birds."
                        (I, xxxvi, 32–34)

The impression of lifelessness and malevolence has already been well
established; what is new is the impression that the Holy Land generally
is seen to possess these symbolic qualities.

The setting for Part I is Jerusalem and its immediate environs.
Clarel's last strong experience of the city in this part comes just after
finding that he will not be able to see Ruth for several days, during the
period of formal mourning after the death of her father. He is turned
away from her door and wanders about:

                 . . . in a street,
        Half vault, where few or none do greet,
        He paced. Anon, encaved in wall
        A fount arrests him, sculpture wrought
        After a Saracen design—
        Ruinous now and arid all
        Save dusty weeds which trail or twine.
        While lingering in way that brought
        The memory of the Golden Bowl
        And Pitcher broken, music rose. . . .
                        (I, xliii, 9–18)

The ruined fountain may be only one detail of the city as a whole,
but it assumes importance from its position in the action, coming as it
does at Clarel's major disappointment, the climax of Part I. It is impor-
tant also as furnishing a symbol for the city in miniature: "ruinous,"
"arid," "dusty"—though presumably once the fountain of living waters.
The city too was once a source of living waters, but now shows only the
face of arid decay. The music Clarel hears at the end of this passage
turns out to be the music of a funeral procession. For Clarel the whole
event brings to mind the preacher's words in Ecclesiastes, Chapter 12.
Here only verse 6 is alluded to, concerning the golden bowl and the
pitcher, but the context is important: "desire shall fail, because man
goeth to his long home, and the mourners go about the streets: Or ever
the silver cord be loosed, or the golden bowl be broken, or the pitcher
be broken at the fountain, or the wheel broken at the cistern. Then shall
the dust return to the earth as it was; and the spirit return into God who
gave it. Vanity of vanities, saith the Preacher; all is vanity." [15] It seems
to be the ruinous state of the fountain that brings the passage to

Clarel's mind, though the funeral procession is there too. It seems likely that Melville intends to use the reader's general recollection of Ecclesiastes to underline the mood he is bringing to a climax here. Ecclesiastes is jarring for its pessimism and skepticism in the midst of the Old Testament, asserting the inscrutability of God and the uncertainty of man's fate.

Part II begins with the assembled pilgrims leaving Jerusalem for their ten-day excursion to Jericho, the Dead Sea, the monastery of Mar Saba, Bethlehem, and then back to Jerusalem. Melville has the pilgrimage begin "adown the dolorosa lane." They ride before daybreak, their horses' feet "striking sparks in vaulted street . . . as in a cave" (II, i, 5–6). The images suggest more a dark journey to the underworld than a pilgrimage in the Holy Land, and the suggestion will grow. As they reach the outskirts of the city, they are able to see it in its setting:

> Sheep-tracks they'd look, at distance seen,
> Did any herbage border them,
> Those slender foot-paths slanting lean
> Down or along waste slopes which hem
> The high-lodged, walled Jerusalem.
>
> *(II, iii, 1–5)*

Melville uses this departure from Jerusalem to accomplish two things. First there is an explicit denial of any pastoral element in his observations of the Holy Land. The significance of this will emerge later. Second, he takes this opportunity to stress the continuity of impression between the city and its surrounding countryside. They blend into one, into one massive symbol we shall see, because of the "waste slopes" stitching them together.

Understandably there is little reference to Jerusalem once they have left the city and are traveling in the countryside. The exceptions must be noted. One of the most remarkable among the later references to the city Jerusalem occurs while the pilgrims are staying at the Monastery of Mar Saba during the fourth through sixth days of their ten-day pilgrimage. They are invited to witness a "masque," consisting of the monologue of the Wandering Jew, framed by a short prologue and epilogue. The reference to Jerusalem in this masque may tell why Melville felt the city to be empty, blind, lifeless, even vaguely malevolent. The prologue introduces the Wandering Jew sitting on a rock in the valley of Jehoshaphat, "underneath the hem / And towers of gray Jerusalem: / This must ye feign" (III, xix, 11–13). Part of the Wandering Jew's apostrophe to the city follows:

"O city yonder,
Exposed in penalty and wonder,
Again thou seest me! Hither I
Still drawn am by the guilty tie
Between us; all the load I bear
Only thou know'st, for thou dost share.
As round my heart the phantoms throng
Of tribe and era perished long,
So *thou* art haunted, sister in wrong!"
(III, xix, 19–27)

Three times in these opening lines the Wandering Jew refers to the similarity between the city and himself: "the guilty tie / Between us," "thou dost share," and "sister in wrong." The parallel is established. Melville had earlier given his own version of the sin of the Wandering Jew, among the many that have developed during the centuries the legend has been current. In Part I of *Clarel* Melville's short-lived Celio overhears a monk pointing out one of the sights to a coreligionist:

"Thou mark'st the spot where that bad Jew
His churlish taunt at Jesus threw
Bowed under cross with stifled moan:
Caitiff, which for that cruel wrong
Thenceforth till Doomsday drives along."
(I, xiii, 112–16)

The two passages can obviously be considered together, because they deal with the legend. In addition they are linked verbally. "Caitiff I am," exclaims the Wandering Jew of the Mar Saba masque (III, xix, 97), repeating the unusual epithet the monk had used in the earlier passage. The implication is that the city, like the Jew, offered churlish taunts as response to Jesus; both then are abandoned, damned.

Melville, nearly prostrate with nervous exhaustion,[16] was sent by his family on a vacation trip to the Holy Land. The normal expectations would be spiritual renewal and refreshment. Years of Sunday hymn singing would have educated one to such a response to Jerusalem and the pastoral Eden of the psalms. Melville obviously found himself responding in the opposite way. The development of his massive Jerusalem symbol shows him attempting to express the contours of this negative reaction. Finally, in an attempt to find the basic cause for this unconventional response to the Holy City, Melville hit upon the parallel between the city and the Wandering Jew: both have tormented and rejected the truly divine among us; both then must remain through history, dead and yet not dead, estranged from the presence of God, unable to make any constructive use of their prominence and length of years.

The contours of Jerusalem, the city and the symbol, are repeated briefly twice more before the poem ends. Traveling through the highlands toward Bethlehem, an old sailor who had joined the party at Mar Saba "sent his gaze / As from the masthead o'er the pale / Expanse" (IV, i, 177–79). He cries out: "Wreck ho,—the wreck!" (181) The party questions his outburst:

> Forth did his leveled finger go
> And, fixing, pointed: "See ye, see?
> 'Way over where the grey hills be;
> Yonder—no, there—that upland dim:
> Wreck, ho! the wreck—Jerusalem!"
> *(IV, i, 187–91)*

His cry reinforces the general symbolic values of the city. The narrator goes on to describe what the party saw:

> Abandoned quarry mid the hills
> Remote, as well one's dream fulfills
> Of what Jerusalem should be,
> As that vague heap, whose neutral tones
> Blend in with Nature's, helplessly:
> Stony metropolis of stones.
> *(IV, ii, 7–12)*

The sight stimulates comparisons by the other members of the party with "the town / Erst glorious under Solomon" (ll. 13–14) and the same city "so bright / With sardonyx and ruby" (ll. 17–18) of Saint John's Revelation. Here they only see "lone crag where lone the ospreys wheel!" (l. 22) It seems a matter of heightened significance that Melville here gives this perception to a sailor and that he says it in the idiom of his trade. The old sailor sees Jerusalem as the final terror for sailors, a wreck at sea. Quite possibly Melville felt this to be a metaphor for his own attitude about Jerusalem, for he has put the old sailor into the pilgrimage only at this last stage and he says little else during his short appearance in the poem.

The travelers close the circle of their tour and approach Jerusalem by night. Coming from Bethlehem, they would ordinarily have to pass through the valley of Hinnom just under the city walls.

> And now those skirting slopes they tread
> Which devious bar the sunken bed

Of Hinnom. Thence uplifted shone
In hauntedness the deicide town
Faint silvered.

(IV, xxix, 127–31)

The "skirting slopes" again suggest the continuity between Jerusalem and the rest of the Holy Land. But to the riders down in the valley the city seems to loom above them with special menace ("hauntedness"), suggesting also that here is the heart or the point of greatest concentration for the symbol. Here Melville brings to a climax his perceptions about the city and its meaning for him. He has already made sure that his readers realize that the "Valley of Hinnom" (*Ge Hinnom*) has developed linguistically into our modern word *Gehenna*, and that in biblical times it furnished the imagery for realistic portrayals of Hell. From the pilgrims' perspective as they ride up, Jerusalem seems to preside over the demonic world. Melville here clinches the final meaning of Jerusalem in the phrase "the deicide town." It is a town not merely depressing in its physical and geographical aspects, but a town actually damned through the centuries for the evil that was perpetrated there. Melville would situate the heart of darkness in Jerusalem.

As the party travels through the wilderness from Jerusalem to Jericho, they pass a region called Adummim, generally associated with the place in Christ's parable where the Samaritan traveler came upon the man beaten and robbed. Melville describes the approach:

In order meet they take their way
Through Bahurim where David fled;
And Shimei like a beast of prey
Prowled on the side-cliff overhead,
And flung the stone, the stone and curse,
And called it just, the king's reverse:
Still grieving grief, as demons may.

In flanking parched ravine they won,
The student wondered at the bale
So arid, as of Acheron
Run dry.

(II, ix, 1–11)

Aside from reaffirming the desiccated quality of the Holy Land ("parched," "arid"), the poet has here described a place presumed to be of special holiness, and weighted it with references to a biblical story of menace to King David's reign and to Virgil's approach to Tartarus.

The first seven lines, set off by a space as prologue to the canto, refer to an episode late in the life of David—his tactical withdrawal from Jerusalem during the conspiracy against him by his son Absalom. Shimei was a member of Saul's family, the dynasty David had replaced. Melville may have had his King James Version open to II Samuel 16:5–14, where several details of these lines (here italicized) are to be found.

> Shimei came forth, and *cursed* still as he came. And he *cast stones* at David and at all the servants of King David. "The Lord hath returned upon thee all the blood of the house of Saul, in whose stead thou hast reigned; and the Lord hath delivered the Kingdom into the hand of Absalom thy son: and behold thou art taken in thy mischief, because thou art a bloody man." [Melville wrote in line 5 that he "called it just, the king's reverse."] And as David and his men went by the way, Shimei went along *on the hill's side* over against him, and *cursed as he went, and threw stones* at him, and cast dust.

To the biblical account Melville has added the prowling beast of prey and the comparison with demons; he has completely omitted David's reaction—that all this cursing and stone-throwing is allowed by a providential God. The menace of the place, then, and the suggestion that it is under demonic influence are the elements Melville wants noticed here.

The demonic reference may lead by association into "Acheron" in line 10. The place is like the entrance to the classical Hades, though worse: here even the horrid river has run dry.[17] Clarel wonders at the "bale" of the place, a curious word which can mean simply sadness or sorrow; but the "demonic" context may also hint at something more personified, some "dire evil" or "malign influence" as Webster would have it. (It will appear later, in some detail, that I consider Melville to have constructed a highly personified universe; to find traces of that in these lines will seem more reasonable as the study progresses.)

The main business of this canto is a retelling of the story of the Good Samaritan. The mad mystic Nehemiah, for whom all the pilgrims feel a protective reverence, is the one who tells the story, and he ends with the assertion that even now, if someone were to be waylaid and beaten by robbers, a modern Good Samaritan would soon come along. Nehemiah's assertion is met with well-bred respect, but with no sign of agreement; and meanwhile the guides of the party are chasing off a group of would-be robbers. Clarel's reflections end the canto:

> With thoughtful mien
> The student fared, nor might withstand

The something dubious in the Holy Land.
(II, ix, 103–5)

Melville seems almost to retard the development of his symbol with his understatements, or at least to employ for his symbol the kind of suspense technique usually associated with the narrative levels of a story. He seems not content with an easy identification of the "meaning" of his symbol.

Clarel's reflection immediately precedes a canto beginning with a long (some thirty lines) catalog of stones and their occurrence in the Bible: stones for altars and for idols, sling-stones and stones used for execution, stones piled as memorials or rolled back from tombs, stones even taken up against Jesus. It concludes:

> attesting here the Holy Writ—
> In brook, in glen, by tomb and town
> In natural way avouching it—
> Behold the stones! And never one
> A lichen greens; and, turn them o'er—
> No worm—no life; but, all the more,
> Good witnesses.
>
> *(II, x, 27–33)*

The pilgrim's observation of the stony landscape, in other words, fits in with and confirms the expectation raised by scripture, and a new and immediate perception of the actual stones shows their utter lifelessness, their inability to support even the parasitic life of lichen or the low life of a worm. Two things are insisted upon: the omnipresence of these objects throughout the geography and history of the Holy Land, and the strong impression of lifelessness and sterility they convey. Melville ends the sections cryptically: by their very lifelessness they are good witnesses. He leaves the question hanging: witnesses to what? The vagueness of his generalization increases its scope of application. The vagueness is not dispelled in the course of the canto, but another item is added. Rolfe speaks of the "bland indifference" (l. 140) of the stony desert, thus forging another link between the blank indifference of Jerusalem and the stony landscape which is its setting.

The next canto, "Of Deserts," is climactic, and Melville explains more fully the emblematic quality of the desert. There is no narrative content to the canto, no advancement of the plot, but only description of the desert and inquiry into its significance.

Melville begins by conceding the beauties of the desert, the brisk fragrance of its dawns and the "pomp of night" (II, xi, 5), but insists on the power of the desert to overwhelm one with its own "forsakenness" (l. 12). He continues:

> Darwin quotes
> From Shelley, that forever floats
> Over all desert places known,
> Mysterious doubt—an awful one.
> He quotes, adopts it. Is it true?
> Let instinct vouch; let poetry
> Science and instinct here agree
> For truth requires strong retinue.[18]
>
> *(II, xi, 13–20)*

Here are powerful aspects of human experience—poetry, science, and instinct—to confirm the impression of "mysterious doubt" given by "desert places." The addition of Shelley's "awful" in Melville's next breath again seems to suggest personification of whatever it is that floats over all desert places.

The desert as symbol reaches its fullest development toward the end of the canto. Melville returns to the desert of Judah; he gives first an overall impression of it, and then the significance of its geography: a river of "anguish" connecting a hill of torment with a sea of death:

> For Judah here—
> Let Erebus her rival own:
> 'Tis horror absolute—severe,
> Dead, livid, honeycombed, dumb, fell—
> A caked depopulated hell;
> Yet so created, judged by sense,
> And visaged in significance
> Of settled anger terrible.
>   Profoundly cloven through the scene
> Winds Kedron—word (he scholar saith)
> Importing anguish hard on death.
> And aptly may such named ravine
> Conduct unto Lot's mortal Sea
> In cleavage from Gethsemane
> Where it begins.
>
> *(II, xi, 68–82)*

The overall impression of the desert conveys hellishness: it is a deserted waste but still menacing. It is personified ("visaged"), but beyond humanity and beyond even the ordinary personifications of the Christian divinity. Geography here has become highly symbolic, and the landscape psychologic.

These are the central cantos, the focal points, as far as the desert symbol is concerned. The imagery appears in less concentrated form throughout the poem wherever there is occasion to refer to the landscape. The symbol does not remain static; it is established early in the poem and continues to grow throughout. Seven cantos later there is another extended reference to the desert, with many of the same images again brought together, with a clarity that has been straining to break through but which until now has not found such exact expression. The episode takes place just outside Jericho. The party comes upon a young Syrian monk, a mystic, another one of Melville's religious fanatics. After some persuasion he tells them why he has chosen this life of a desert hermit. " 'Twas sin, he said, that drove him out / Into the desert—sin of doubt" (II, xviii, 37–38). The lines are interesting for two reasons: they connect with the plot at the intellectual or dialectic level: the problem of doubt is at the heart of the intellectual movement of the poem; the lines also suture the intellectual and symbolic levels of the poem, connecting doubt and the desert, a nexus which Melville had earlier made following Darwin and Shelley. The monk describes his flight into the desert and his climbing of the same rocky hill where tradition held that Christ was tempted by the devil during his forty days in the desert. When he reached the top,

> Hence gazed I on the wilds beneath,
> Dengadda and the coasts of death.
> But not a tremor felt I here:
> It was upon the summit fear
> First fell; there first I saw this world;
> And scarce man's place it seemed to be;
> The mazed Gehennas so were curled
> As worm-tracks under bark of tree.
>
> (*II, xviii, 56–63*)

Here the desert becomes an emblem for the world. The monk stresses that the desert is hell and also that this desert-world-hell is not "man's place," not really under his control and dominion as he would perhaps like to think. "Worm-tracks" are clearer evidence of who controls this world. Through the monk Melville provides a dramatic advance in the symbolic development of the poem. Granted the advance is made through a fanatic; the seed however is planted, and we shall see it grow and develop to an overwhelming element in Melville's symbolic universe.

Part II of *Clarel* concludes with a series of events in quick succession:

the burial in the desert of the Jewish mystic Nehemiah, the one who had brought Ruth and Clarel together; a rushing landslide that occurs near-by as they finish the burial; and the "fog-bow" which appears and then disappears over the Dead Sea. The pilgrims are apparently unable to see the landslide, which seems to take place nearby but is hidden by one of the ranges of hills and the mist from the sea. But they hear it crashing down, then hear its echoes which "bowled / And bowled far down the long El Ghor" (II, xxxix, 147–48). (El Ghor is the long valley in which the Dead Sea is situated.) The echoes then die down to a silence which is even more striking. This ominous and dramatic aural experience shifts immediately to an exclusively visual one:

> They turn; and, in that silence sealed,
> What works there from behind the veil [of mist]?
> A counter-object is revealed—
> A thing of heaven, and yet how frail:
> Up in thin mist above the sea
> Humid is formed, and noiselessly,
> The fog-bow: segment of an oval
> Set in a colorless removal
> Against a verticle shaft, or slight
> Slim pencil of an aqueous light.
> Suspended there, the segment hung
> Like to the May-wreath that is swung
> Against the pole. It showed half spent—
> Hovered and trembled, paled away, and—went.
>
> *(II, xxxix, 149–62)*

We seem to have two opposed signs confronting one another—Melville calls the second, "a counter-object." Conventionally the bow in the clouds should be a sign of God's peace over the world, a sign of the covenant God made with Noah (Genesis 9:15). Melville had explained his version of this convention powerfully in "A Canticle" in *Battle-Pieces*. The poem celebrates the end of the Civil War and is based on an image with two elements: a great waterfall with a rainbow at its base. The waterfall represents the flow of social history: powerful, chaotic, inexorable. The rainbow above it, constant though on an ever-shifting base, represents transcendence and glory presiding over the successful outcome of cataclysmic events. The image conveys hope triumphant.

But in *Clarel* the bow has been put to a different use. It is much less hopeful, for it is now a *fog*-bow, generated by the miasma rising from the Dead Sea. The background, no longer the powerful foaming white falls, is a slim shaft of light. Its presence is not enduring: the "thing of heaven" is "yet how frail." The long final line calls attention to itself, and the dash before the last word emphasizes the fleeting quality of this ambiguous sign. Melville seems to intend a dramatic confrontation of two powers at the end of Part II: the invisible, terrifying, irrationally destructive landslide, and the religiously hopeful sign in the sky. His trust, however, is not with the second; chaos presents stronger evidence than cosmos in this symbolized landscape.

Chaos sounds one of the opening notes of Part III, as the party continues its pilgrimage, turning from the Dead Sea, to Saba and Bethlehem and back to Jerusalem, completing the circle. The rest of the poem is outlined, geographically, and the tone of the landscape is set down clearly:

> For now, to round the waste in large,
> Christ's Tomb re-win by Saba's marge
> Of grots and ossuary cells,
> And Bethlehem where remembrance dwells—
> From Sodom in her pit dismayed
> Westward they wheel, and there invade
> Judah's main ridge, which horrors deaden—
> Where Chaos holds the wilds in pawn,
> As here had happed an Armageddon,
> Betwixt the good and ill a fray,
> But ending in a battle drawn,
> Victory undetermined. Nay
> For how an indecisive day
> When one side camps upon the ground
> Contested.
>
> *(III, i, 34–48)*

Here we find concentrated much of the previous imagery and epithet from which Melville has built his landscape: the waste, the pit, dismay, the deadening horror. But an explicit step forward is taken by placing the personified figure of Chaos over the scene, and by indicating the extent of its control by the phrase "holds ... in pawn." A cosmic struggle is suggested: "Betwixt the good and ill a fray." It is remarkable that Melville appears to slip into a conventional piety concerning the indecisiveness of the battle between Good and Evil: "battle drawn, / Victory undetermined." But this attitude yields to a wave of honesty; Melville rejects the convention: Chaos is the only ruler apparent in the field.

Leaving the monastery early in Part IV, the pilgrims again submit themselves to the countryside. And again the nightmarish landscape envelops them.

But here, 'twixt tent-lapped hills, they see
Northward, a land immovably
Haggard and haggish, specked gray-green—
Pale tint of those frilled lichens lean,
Which on a prostrate pine ye view,
When fallen from the banks of grace
Down to the sand pit's sterile place,
Blisters supplant the beads of dew.
Canker and palmer-worm both must
Famished have left those fields of rust:
The rain is powder—land of dust:
There few do tarry, none may live—
Save mad, possessed, or fugitive.
Exalted in accursed estate,
Like Naaman in his leprous plight
Haughty before Elisha's gate,
Show the blanched hills.

          (IV, i, 146–62)

"Haggard and haggish" may be precious—one word too easily suggesting another—except for the fact that "haggish" repeats the idea of a personal evil emanating from this landscape. In this passage Melville mythologizes the landscape more explicitly than usual, though unemphatically, in a word that could easily be read over quickly: "the banks of *grace*" (l. 151). One concludes from this that lush growth represents goodness, wholeness, grace; the desert landscape represents evil, sterility, damnation. And there is a remarkable concentration of such opposing qualities in this passage. Melville would force his perceptions of the Holy Land upon the reader by having him consider a series of opposites and realize that all the negative elements are those of the Holy Land. Finally, lest there be any doubt about the diseased and decayed quality of the setting, it is compared with the leprous Naaman.

One of the final impressions of the Holy City had been given by the old Greek sailor: "Wreck, ho!—the wreck—Jerusalem!" Two cantos later he is called upon to give an extensive emblem for the landscape of Palestine as a whole. Vine is impressed by the sailor, who seems to him "authentic; man of nature true; / . . . naught . . . slid between / Him and the elemental scene" (IV, ii, 196–98). Vine feels his impressions would be valuable and asks if anything can compare "with Judah here" (l. 207). The old sailor mentions "one far isle forever banned" (l. 211). When pressed by the pilgrims, the sailor delivers a canto-long comparison between the Encantadas and the Holy Land. Melville's sketch of these islands had been published serially in the new *Putnam's Monthly Magazine*, in the spring of 1854, two full years before he began his tour of the Holy Land. Yet the first two pages of the *Encantadas* sketches are filled with comparisons between these deserted islands and the desert landscape of the Holy Land: Melville finds in the Encantadas a "special curse . . . which exalts them in isolation above *Idumea*." "Like split *Syrian* gourds left withering in the sun, they are cracked by an everlasting drought beneath a torrid sky. 'Have mercy upon me,' the wailing spirit of the Encantadas seems to cry, 'and send *Lazarus* that he may dip the tip of his finger in water and cool my tongue, for I am tormented in this flame.'" "It is deemed a fit type of all-forsaken overthrow, that the jackal should den in the wastes of weedy *Babylon*; but the Encantadas refuse to harbor even the outcasts of the beasts."[19] Melville had been prepared to see the Holy Land the way he did long before he actually visited it.

The old sailor in *Clarel* reverses the process and compares the Holy Land to the Encantadas. He situates them "in waters where no charts avail" (IV, iii, 1). The waters are dominated by sharks and whales ("only fin and spout ye see," l. 2). These sea creatures are powerfully menacing. The old sailor recalls his first sighting of the isle: "The smoke-wrapped peak; the inland one volcanic" (ll. 8–9). The volcano also suggests violence: "It burns by night—by day the cloud / Shows leaden all and dull and sealed" (ll. 11–12). Surely the old sailor is here referring to the pillar of cloud by day and the pillar of fire by night which led the Israelites through the desert (Exodus 13:21). The general connection between the Encantadas and the present landscape is thus made. But it must also be noted that the pillar of smoke and fire was also symbolic of the presence of the deity for the Israelites. The force of Melville's words here seems to be that the Encantadas (and the Holy Land) are not at all godforsaken, but the nature of that presiding god must be recognized for what it is in Melville's developing symbol.

The sailor continues his description of the islands. As his party penetrates the interior of one of the islands they encounter several paths "as it were traveled ceaselessly— / Century after century" (ll. 31–32). But there is no sign of anything living that could have made the paths. The paths wind among bushes, but "no berry do those thickets bear, / Nor many leaves" (ll. 38–39). There is, in other words, a mysterious sense of life, but no sign of life: "The surface rubbed to unctious gleam / By something which has life, you feel: / And yet, the shades but death reveal" (ll. 51–53). Finally a dull booming sound introduces the first living creature:

Lo, 'tis the monstrous tortoise drear!
Of huge humped arch, the ancient shell
Is trenched with seams where lichens dwell,
Or some adhesive growth and sere:
A lumpish languor marks the pace—
A hideous, harmless look, with trace
Of hopelessness; the eyes are dull
As in the bog the dead black pool:
Penal his aspect; all is dragged,
As he for more than years had lagged—
A convict doomed to bide the place;
A soul transformed—for earned disgrace
Degraded, and from higher race.

                              (IV, iii, 62–74)

One's first impulse is to identify this monster as the deity of the place. He moves slowly into view, mysteriously, agelessly; but he is a creature "doomed" here like a convict, subject to some larger power, constantly at the mercy of the place. Perhaps the tortoise is the image of man: "a soul transformed," "degraded . . . from higher race." A third possibility is forced. The word "lumpish" links the tortoise with another of Melville's powerful elemental objects, the iceberg: "Though lumpish thou, a lumbering one— / A lumbering lubbard loitering slow" ("The Berg," ll. 32–33). Lifted out of context, the two lines apply equally well to iceberg and tortoise. We seem confronted once again with Melville's indirection and suggestiveness, with an organic universe, one in which objects and background fit into one another to form a whole, and the whole animated by some vague sense of life. The universe is organic, but the romanticism is surely inverted.

Clarel, at least, takes the old sailor's story as a parable of the way the world is, and it tempts him to a complete skepticism:

Since *this* world, then, can baffle so—
Our natural harbor—it were strange
If *that* alleged, which is afar,
Should not confound us when we range
In revery where its problems are.—

                              (ll. 116–20)

He wonders if he may be too influenced by Rolfe's skepticism. Part IV is just beginning and Clarel still has a few more stages of development ahead of him. The importance of his statement here, for the dramatic development of the symbol, is that it affirms Melville's suggestion of its cosmic applicability.

The final major element in what we have been calling the static conception of Melville's symbol is the sea. His preoccupation with the subject is lifelong, and it pervades the body of his work. He has used it both as the realistic setting for purely narrative adventures and as psychologized seascape for the interior adventure. One would naturally expect the sea to function prominently in *Clarel*, but the use which Melville creates for it is highly complex, created specifically for the occasion.

Unusual as it may seem in a poem whose setting is a desert, there are a great many references to the sea in *Clarel* which are spread throughout. They divide neatly into two quite distinct categories. Examples of the first category are found in every part of the poem, usually cast in similes, and refer to the great seas or oceans generally. Examples of the second are concentrated in the middle section and refer directly to the Dead Sea.

The first category is not unimportant for its effect on the poem but the fact is that in the majority of instances the meaning remains constant. The ocean at large makes two significant contributions.

As the pilgrims wend their way up from the Dead Sea, they hear the tolling of a bell rolling across the desert hills. It is the bell of the Mar Saba monastery, which is not yet in sight but toward which they are heading for a three-day stay. The sound is described:

> Where the sexton of the vaulted seas
> Buries the drowned in weedy grave,
> While tolls the buoy-bell down the breeze;
> There, off the shoals of rainy wave
> Outside the channel which they crave,
> The sailors lost in shrouding mist,
> Unto that muffled knelling list,
> The more because for fogged remove
> The floating belfry none may prove;
> So, yet with a difference, do these
> Attend.
>
> *(III, vii, 58–68)*

"The sexton of the vaulted seas" seems to be a deity presiding over the gloomy fog. He has already buried some drowned sailors "in weedy grave." Others are afloat in the same area, out of the safe channel they had been seeking, and in the vicinity of the shoals which had wrecked previous ships. The fog has muffled the sound of the buoy-bell so that they cannot tell its direction. The situation has entirely slipped from their control; the outcome is completely up to chance, and chance seems under control of the menacing sexton.

Two meanings emerge: the sea is a threat to man. It is irrational: its ways cannot be understood nor can it be placated. As so many of Melville's symbols for the evil universe have been, it is vaguely personal or is controlled by a person. Second, it is characteristic of the sea imagery in this category that it is used in similes. In the present example the "so" in the next-to-last line makes this clear. Melville is holding the actual sea at a distance in this poem. The simile maintains the separate and distinct identities of the two things compared. There is no sense of identification in a simile, as there is in a metaphor and more especially in a symbol. The effect of this, I believe, is to strengthen subtly, throughout the poem, the fact that Melville is here turning his attention away from the sea as the area to explore for deeper meanings. His scene is now the landscape of the Holy Land. Comparison drawn from his earlier experience with the sea can momentarily illuminate patches of the meaning he finds in the Holy Land, but the two are entirely distinct and are kept so throughout the poem. His focus is the Holy Land, and the distancing he achieves by using similes for his allusions to the sea keeps the focus where he wants it.

The second example in this first category of sea imagery involves a monastery again: the pilgrims have left Mar Saba and are approaching their next stopover, the monastery at Bethlehem. The comparison is long and complex, but the elements are kept clearly distinct by the mechanics of the Homeric simile, a form which Melville uses sparingly but with interesting effects.

> As shipwrecked men adrift, whose boat
> In war-time on the houseless seas
> Draws nigh to some embattled hull
> With pinnacles and traceries—
> Grim abbey on the wave afloat;
> And mark her bulwarks sorrowful
> With briny stains, and answering mien
> And cenobite dumb discipline,
> And homely uniform of crew
> Peering from ports where cannon lean,
> Or pacing in deep galleries far,
> Black cloisters of the god of war;
> And hear a language which is new
> Or foreign: So now with this band
> Who, after desert rovings, win

The fort monastic, close at hand,
Survey it, meditate it—see,
Through vaultings, the girt Capuchin,
Or list his speech of Italy.

(*IV, vii, 1–19*)

The two major elements of the Homeric simile are the ship and the monastery. The complexity arises in the first part where metaphors of a monastery are used to enrich the image of the ship: "grim abbey," "cenobite," "black cloisters." The effect enhances the forbidding aspect of the ship at sea by reinforcing it with forbidding aspects of monasteries generally. Then the whole ship, thus reinforced, is turned to illustrate the menacing appearance of one particular monastery.

The two characteristics of this first category of sea imagery recur. Sea and Holy Land are kept rigidly apart. The former is used to evoke powerful effects of menace and uncertainty, but the focus is quite plainly on the latter. The passage also illustrates again the use of the sea as a threat to man. The contrast could hardly be drawn more sharply: the castaways adrift and helpless in a small boat, coming up against the powerful warship. And once again the vagueness of the personal element at the heart of this evil is stressed: there is a sense of life aboard the ship, but it is foreign and only glimpses of it are caught peering through the portholes or "pacing in deep galleries far." [20]

Moving on now to the second category of sea imagery, that describing the Dead Sea of Palestine, we encounter it as the pilgrims camp on its shores overnight on their third day out, before beginning to circle back toward Mar Saba and Bethlehem. The imagery here differs from that in the first category in two specific ways: it refers to a particular sea rather than the sea at large, and is used directly rather than figuratively. Melville seems quite consciously to be integrating the sea into a larger and more meaningful landscape. He had earlier used the sea for his quest for meaning, for example in *Mardi*. Now this sea appears as inadequate and is kept at a distance by the use of simile whenever it is alluded to. The sea is an important part of the landscape of *Clarel*, but only a part. In *Mardi* the sea was adequate model for Melville's world. Here it is confined and limited and particularized.

The travelers' first glimpse of the Dead Sea comes from a tower commemorating the Ascension of Christ from atop Mount Olivet. The travel book Melville was using mentions the tower as being famous for its view both of Jerusalem and the Dead Sea. Jerusalem elicits Rolfe's allusion to Dante: "Is yon the city Dis aloof?" In the other direction they gain a view of the Dead Sea:

Far peep they gain
Of waters which in caldron brood,
Sunk mid the mounts of leaden bane:
The Sodom Wave, or Putrid Sea,
Or Sea of Salt, or Cities Five,
Or Lot's, or Death's, Asphaltite,
Or Asafoetida; all these
Being names indeed with which they gyve
The site of foul iniquities
Abhorred.

(*I, xxxvi, 38–47*)

The two words "caldron" and "bane" seem to go together and suggest a setting for witchcraft. Not only is the preternatural at work in this landscape, but it is concentrated at this one particular spot, Death's Sea, glimpsed in the distance. Melville's catalog follows, presenting an unpleasant series of names by which the Dead Sea has been called. One of its names still in use, Asphaltites, which Melville shortens to "Asphaltite," seems to be taken from the black pitchlike mineral deposits there. "Asafoetida" is a foul-smelling resin from an Oriental plant. Together with "Putrid," "Salt," and "Death," they heavily load this description of the Dead Sea with sensory images of corruption. "Foul iniquities" and "Sodom" imply moral corruption as well. These are the names that have been shackled ("gyved") to the Dead Sea. It is a sea toward which the pilgrims move as a goal they have set for themselves, yet it is "abhorred." The sea seems a magnetic evil center for this symbolic universe, drawing the pilgrims toward itself much as the evil whale had drawn Ahab toward his destruction.

This first view of the Dead Sea is lost as the travelers descend the tower and continue their winding pilgrimage through the mountain wilderness, but the impression has been created of the desert as a field set up by the two polar concentrations of evil, Jerusalem and the Dead Sea. The pilgrims come out of the mountains just short of Jericho; from there they will continue to the Jordan and then turn south for the shore of the sea itself. Canto xiv of Part II situates the reader again geographically, placing him in a context of mountains, Jerusalem behind, Jericho ahead and the Dead Sea ahead and to the right, the gorge of Achor outside Jericho just at their feet.

Jerusalem, the mountain town
Is based how far above the sea;
But down, a lead-line's long reach down,
A deep-sea lead, beneath the zone

Of Ocean's level, heaven's decree
Has sunk the pool whose deeps submerged
The doomed Pentapolis fire-scourged.
　　Long then the slope, though varied oft,
From Zion to the seats abject;
For rods and roods ye wind aloft
By verges where the pulse is checked;
And chief both height and steepness show
Ere Achor's gorge the barrier rends
And like a thunder-cloud impends
Ominous over Jericho.
　　　　　　　　　　(II, xiv, 1–15)

In the first paragraph Melville is using a "lead-line" to plumb the depths of his sea. He insists on the length of the leadline: he is plunging deep into the heart of his universe here. Thoreau had plumbed the depths of *his* sea and found it a means of communication with a benevolent oversoul—had pulled up green shimmering weeds on his anchor even in midwinter. Melville here is antitranscendentalist. At the bottom of his sea are doomed, fire-scourged cities. The pilgrims will later drag sterile calcined treetrunks from this sea. Once again it is for Melville a malevolent oversoul, "heaven's decree," that has produced this kind of universe (ll. 5–7).

The second paragraph possibly introduces a new theme into the elements connected to the Dead Sea. There is a hint here of Arthurian quest material in some form or other. A "rood" is British and Scottish for a measure of distance only slightly longer than the American "rod." This would seem a needless repetition if the word did not also bring along with it an allusion to the medieval word for cross or crucifix. The "ye," though not untypical of Melville's style in the poem generally, extends the impression of medieval literary materials in this paragraph.

More precisely the setting here is not unlike the nightmarish landscape of Robert Browning's "Childe Roland to the Dark Tower Came." It seems possible that Melville used materials and atmosphere from this poem in constructing his own. For example there are several peculiarly Melvillean words in Browning's poem: "calcine" in Stanza XI; the word "rood" itself in the sense of a measure of distance in Stanza XXV; and the word "blind" which Browning applies to the walls of his Dark Tower in Stanza XXXI, and which Melville uses frequently to describe the walls of Jerusalem. Melville's story about the bird snatching the sailor's cap, and the kind of impression the story creates, is paralleled by Childe Roland's experience in Stanza XXVII. He does not know in which direction to proceed once he has entered the heart of the wasteland:

> At the thought
> A great black bird, Apollyon's bosom-friend,
> Sailed past, nor beat his wide wing dragon-penned
> That brushed my cap—perchance the guide I sought.

These citations suggest that Browning's poem found in Melville a congenial reader; one can point to specific details in addition to the general similarity of atmosphere. For example the ironic rhyme, "mirth-dearth," appears in lines 119–20 of the present canto and in Stanza XXV of Browning's poem.

Browning's hero follows a particular sequence of landmarks into the heart of the nightmare landscape. The first is a surprisingly lively brook for such surroundings: "No sluggish tide congenial to the glooms" (Stanza XIX). He then moves on to a lone blasted tree:

> Then came some palsied oak, a cleft in him
> Like a distorted mouth that splits its rim
> Gaping at death.
>
> *(Stanza XXVI)*

Melville uses the same sequence of landmarks at the end of his canto. The party passes along the frightful gorge of Achor and suddenly comes upon a beautifully gurgling spring, its rivulets "much like children whose small mirth / Not funeral can stay" (ll. 119–20). Immediately they too come upon a blasted tree, though Melville has changed its gender (and the significance of the presence of the feminine at the core of evil impresses the reader once again):

> One old humpbacked tree,
> Sad grandam whom no season charms,
> Droops o'er the spring her withered arms.
>
> *(ll. 21–23)*

The point of this is that the Dead Sea was first introduced on page 118 of *Clarel* as a menacing and ominous yet surprisingly magnetic center toward which the pilgrims are drawn. They will still not arrive at the sea itself until page 240. But here at a canto on pages 185–89 they already seem to have stepped into its more immediate sphere of influence. Even though they are still at a distance from the Dead Sea its atmosphere thickens, congealed largely it seems by the allusions to the nightmarish landscape of Browning's poem.

With these two stages of intensified feeling for the Dead Sea already passed, the party enters its immediate environs. " 'Tis Pluto's park," Melville says (II, xxviii, 1), a place of slime and stunted vegetation, another notch (at least) below Browning's landscape. A bitter mist sweeps over them, heightening their sense of being engulfed by what Melville here calls for the first time the "Bad Sea":

> In deeper dale
> What canker may their palms assail?
> Spotted they show, all limp they be.
> Is it thy bitter mist, Bad Sea,
> That, sudden driving, northward comes
> Involving them, that each man roams
> Half seen or lost?
>
> *(ll. 39–45)*

The sea seems to be reaching out for them with its mists, to transform and corrupt them. They are spotted by it, their energy is drained, and they seem separated and isolated from one another.

Melville's next step in defining the Dead Sea appears to me a risky one. He introduces one of the most beautiful lakes of the English romantic writers and uses that lake as a basis of comparison more than contrast: both have the same lovely contours, Como is discernible in Sodom:

> The legend round a Grecian urn,
> The sylvan legend, though decay
> Have wormed the garland all away,
> And fire have left its Vandal burn;
> Yet beauty inextinct may charm
> In outline of the vessel's form.
> Much so with Sodom, shore and sea.
> Fair Como would like Sodom be
> Should horror overrun the scene
> And calcine all that makes it green,
> Yet haply sparing to impeach
> The contour in its larger reach.
> In graceful lines the hills advance,
> The valley's sweep repays the glance,
> And wavy curves of winding beach;
> But all is charred or crunched or riven,
> Scarce seems of earth whereon we dwell;
> Though framed within the lines of heaven
> The picture intimates a hell.
>
> *(II, xxix, 1–19)*

The passage is one of the clearest examples of Melville's theme of the evil universe, a glimpse into his patterns of imagination at their deepest level. The focus is on the Dead Sea, but Como is not introduced in order to shed some light on Sodom's shore and sea. The lines of force flow in the opposite direction: the Dead Sea can show in clearer outline the real nature of Lake Como, and that real nature is just the reverse of what the romantic writers had seen. The most convenient model for explicating this passage is found in its own metaphor of Platonism. Melville sets up this system of metaphor in the first six lines: the contours of the eternal and real vase are still visible after centuries of aging and fading and destruction. So also with Lake Como: it may seem beautiful to the superficial romantic gazer, but its most basic structural outlines, "the contour in its larger reach," reveal the evil and demonic in its basic nature, "the picture intimates a hell." Melville is polemically antiromanticist here. He uses two typical romantic objects, the Grecian urn and Lake Como; he agrees that objects of beauty can be used to reveal the true nature of ideal beauty, of transcendent reality, but the agreement stops there, and Melville reverses the qualities of the nature which is thus revealed. The real is demonic, hellish, evil, malevolent in the final accounting.

We are here at the second major focal point in Melville's symbolic universe. The canto continues with a listing of the horrors that surround "the liquid waste" or are associated with it in biblical lore: dead branches stranded, no motion but that of the sea, no bramble, weed, nor trees, a gritty breeze, jackal and vulture, places connected with stories of killing and destruction. One major exploratory probe into the depths of the Dead Sea must be noticed. It involves legends about the cities the sea had flooded. Arab wizards say they are preserved intact at the bottom of the sea.

> Astarte, worshiped on the Plain
> Ere Terah's day, her vigil keeps
> Devoted where her temple sleeps
> Like moss within the agate's vein—
> A ruin in the lucid sea. . . .
> Nay, further—let who will, believe—
> As monks aver, on holy eve,
> Easter or John's, along the strand
> Shadows Corinthian wiles inweave:
> Voluptuous palaces expand,
> From whose moon-lighted colonnade
> Beckons Armida, deadly maid:

Traditions; and their fountains run
Beyond King Nine and Babylon.
                    (*II, xxxvii, 8–12, 24–32*)

There is a quiet sinister beauty in this preserved city gleaming in the moonlight under the waves. Astarte was worshiped in a temple there and still "her vigil keeps"—an active presence on the scene. She was the Canaanite goddess of love and fertility, to whose worship (which included ritual prostitution) the Israelites were constantly tempted in Old Testament times. Astarte was associated with the moon, much as the Roman and Greek goddesses of love were. Here she looks over the scene from above and has control over the effects produced there: "Her ray can bid / Their beauty thrill along the lane / Of tremulous silver." In the depths of the sea lurks a sister temptress. She is the evil Armida, who was in the service of the devil to help lure Rinaldo away from his mission to capture Jerusalem. The story is in Tasso's *Jerusalem Delivered*, where she is described as having a palace at the bottom of the Dead Sea. Melville singles out "deadly" for her epithet. Part of the evil in both women comes from their sexuality. This is obvious in the case of Astarte because of the kind of ritual she inspired. Around Armida, Melville clusters such words as "wiles," "voluptuous," "moonlighted," "beckons." These two seductively evil women control the sunken city from above and from its depths as from the two poles of this core of the evil universe. It is their city which in the next canto rises and changes fantastically in a dream to lure Nehemiah, the most purely innocent character in the story, to his destruction. He rises up to enter into this vision, which appears to him now like the new Jerusalem of the Apocalypse. He sleepwalks into the Dead Sea and is drowned.

These two cantos follow immediately the one in which Clarel listens to Mortmain's theories that woman has a position very close to the heart of evil in the universe. The cantos seem to confirm this view, although Mortmain is usually taken to be considerably more cynical than the narrator.

Melville, then, appears in *Clarel* to have abandoned his general pattern of using the sea as universe, as the exploring grounds for the searching imagination. It is here reduced and compressed, still an important center of the universe, though other things are now allowed to group themselves around it. It is here in this compressed sea that the evil of the universe is most concentrated. The evil again is associated with the personal, the destructive, death-in-life, the feminine.

III

CLAREL: THE DYNAMICS OF THE SYMBOL

I go forward with the isolated feeling of my
existence, amidst the inert phantoms
of all things.

Matthew Arnold, Essays in Criticism
(Marked by Melville in his copy)

I probe the circle's center.

Mardi

ONE OF THE qualities of *Clarel* that emerges from my analysis of the major static symbols is the highly emblematic landscape. This is a new venture for Melville: not even in *Mardi* does physical description of place so mirror universal realities as they impinge upon the consciousness of narrator and character. For a Christian in the nineteenth century the most attractive way of looking at the Holy Land was through apocalyptic literature. One could thus think of it as a land flowing with milk and honey, filled with memorials to the actual operations of a benevolent God among men, and crowned by a city which had been idealized by Saint John to represent the heavenly goal of every good man. What was one to think, then, if the opportunity for a pilgrimage should arise, and one should be surrounded by the physical realities of the place: a dry and sterile land, filled with ruins and filth, infested with bandits? Piety was not long in supplying a theological reason why this should be so: of course the Holy Land was a depressing place; it was cursed for rejecting the emissary of God. This is the line of thought developed, for example, in a theological travel book of Melville's day, issued by one of his publishers, *The Land of Israel, According to the Covenant with Abraham, With Isaac, and With Jacob* by Alexander Keith.[1] Keith argues that the Hebrews finally rejected the covenant established between God and their fathers and, as a result, their land was accursed. The book is actually a travel guide through the Holy Land; at each point in the pilgrimage Keith cites scriptural passages of former grandeur and then points out to the traveler evidences of present decay. The thesis is potentially a powerful one, but it was still to be worked out imaginatively in a popular work of literature.

Surely the most famous American pilgrimage to the Holy Land was that undertaken by Mark Twain in 1867, ten years after Melville's trip, with the other Innocents aboard the *Quaker City*. Twain edited the dispatches he had sent from abroad to the *Alta California* newspaper, and the result was *The Innocents Abroad* which appeared in July of 1869. Whatever relationship there was between Twain and Melville is, so far as I have been able to determine, devoid of written record. Neither seems to have mentioned the other; nor is Melville known to have owned or borrowed any of Twain's books. The notion must be dismissed that Melville could have been unaware of such an internationally famous writer. Jay Leyda conjectures that Melville began work on *Clarel* in 1870,[2] and the strong presence of Twain's book adds probability to this conjecture. Twain's work stands as direct link between

Keith's book and Melville's, and as catalyst for the latter. *Innocents Abroad* suggested the possibilities for the precise attitude which Melville took toward the Holy Land materials, attitudes which had already begun to crystallize in the journal he kept during his trip.

Mark Twain's subtitle, *The New Pilgrim's Progress*, suggests an authorial stance that is repeated in the subtitle Melville finally gave to his poem, *A Poem and Pilgrimage in the Holy Land*. Twain can be seen jockeying for a tone, somewhere between irreverent and ingenuous, throughout. When he arrives at the Holy Land, the book becomes most interesting for our present purposes. Twain and his party had approached Jerusalem from the north, instead of east from Jaffa, as Melville had done. Chapter 43 begins:

> We had a tedious ride of about five hours, in the sun, across the Valley of Lebanon. It proved to be not quite so much of a garden as it had seemed from the hill-sides. It was a desert, weed-grown waste, littered thickly with stones the size of a man's fist. Here and there the natives had scratched the ground and reared a sickly crop of grain, but for the most part the valley was given up to a handful of shepherds, whose flocks were doing what they honestly could to get a living, but the chances were against them. We saw rude piles of stones standing near the roadside. . . .[3]

Twain's party has reached Nazareth and is visiting the grotto of the Annunciation: "I could sit off several thousand miles and imagine the angel appearing, with shadowy wings and lustrous countenance, and note the glory that streamed downward upon the Virgin's head while the message from the Throne of God fell upon her ears—any one can do that, beyond the ocean, but few can do it here." The sentiments are to become Clarel's, a much more tormented speaker.

Toward the end of Chapter 52 these elements in the story begin to thicken. "The further we went the hotter the sun got, and the more rocky and bare, repulsive and dreary the landscape became. . . . We longed to see Jerusalem . . . but disappointment always followed:—more stupid hills beyond—more unsightly landscape—no Holy City." Melville would have found the greatest concentration of these feelings in this chapter. The compact density of the homes in the city and their peculiar dome-shaped roofs are noted. "The streets are roughly and badly paved with stone, and are tolerably crooked—enough so to make each street appear to close together constantly and come to an end about a hundred yards ahead of a pilgrim as long as he chooses to walk in it." Clarel also experiences this sense of being hemmed in and caught in the streets of

the city: "Jerusalem is mournful, and dreary, and lifeless." Verbal simi-
larities with passages from *Clarel* are obvious. For instance Clarel's
sense of sacrilege at the Church of the Holy Sepulchre is shared by
Twain: "The place is otherwise scandalized by trumpery gewgaws and
tawdry ornamentation." Twain's party continues on to the Dead Sea and
follows the route to Mar Saba earlier taken by Melville and followed
also by Clarel. The reader of Chapters 52–56 is again struck by germinal
impressions that would flower in *Clarel*. Twain has too much cultural
weight repressing him, as well as his responsibility here to popular
journalism, to maintain a consistently skeptical attitude. In two short
paragraphs that end Chapter 56 he slips from a Keith-Melville attitude
to a conventional Christian sentiment without seeming to sense the
contradiction.

> Palestine is desolate and unlovely. And why should it be other-
> wise? Can the *curse* of the Deity beautify a land?
> Palestine is no more of this work-day world. It is sacred to poetry
> and tradition—it is dreamland.

To appreciate the influence of these two stimuli, Keith and Twain, is
to account only partially for the reality created in *Clarel*. In Melville's
hands the Holy Land becomes an immense and vivid symbol whose
total force has yet to be assimilated into our sense of the American
literary culture.

The *dynamic* elements of this symbol must now be considered. They
give a sense of extension in time and movement through a patterned
series of actions. The first consists of several theories of history which
Melville tests before settling upon his own composite theory. The sec-
ond combines references to the pastoral mode, to Eden, and to the life
of Christ, which are scattered throughout the poem. Melville's treat-
ment of history is complex and extensive, a thread that weaves in and
out of the narrative and the debate throughout the poem. Melville treats
history in three ways: in an early and striking image of the "layers" of
history; in examples of the progressive decay in history: in religion, in
American history, in recent European history, and in the "demytholo-
gizing" process which was being carried on; and finally in his inquiry
into the basic nature of history and time, and the causes of its constant
downward trend. It should be emphasized that history is always seen
as a dimension of the city-landscape-sea concatenation studied in my
Chapter II—as part, that is, of the great evolving symbol which is the
poem.

Clarel's early rambles with the mystical Nehemiah give him, among other things, a sense of the antiquity of the Holy Land. His realization of history brings with it a sense of decline as an inevitable characteristic of history:

> Days fleet. They rove the storied ground—
> Tread many a sight that rues the ban
> Where serial wrecks on wrecks confound
> Era and monument and man;
> Or rather, in stratifying way
> Bed and impact and overlay.
> The Hospitalers' cloisters shamed
> Crumble in ruin unreclaimed
> On shivered Fatamite palaces
> Reared upon crash of Herod's sway—
> In turn built on the Maccabees,
> And on King David's glory, they;
> And David's on antiquities
> Of Jebusites and Ornan's floor,
> And hunters' camps of ages long before.
> So Glenroy's tiers of beaches be—
> Abandoned margins of the Glacial Sea.
>
> (I, x, 1–17)

Each archaeological level has its own story, each is under a curse ("ban"), each "confounds" the hopes of particular men in a particular era: history itself is the record of decay. Melville was living in an age when evolution was widely discussed. He certainly rejects here any optimistic theory of evolution. Nor is it precise to say that he finds in the facts of history and archaeology evidence for a continuing linear decline, a pessimistic theory of evolution. Melville seems instead to see history as repetitive and cyclic. Each of the archaeological strata reveals some different culture which left its imprint and then passed away, and each represents enormous human effort and ingenuity, then crashes and falls to ruin.

Melville alludes again quite soon to this aspect of the Holy Land. In a narrator's section he advises a ramble through the old city to observe various scenes of homely domesticity there: women grinding corn, groups chatting, a "mild matron pensive by her son, / The little prattler at her knee" (I, xvi, 31–32). The picture suddenly opens out:

> Under such scenes abysses be—
> Dark quarries where few care to pry,
> Whence came those many cities high—

> Great capitals successive reared,
> And which successive disappeared
> On this same site.
>
> *(ll. 33–38)*

The "abysses" and the "dark quarries" reinforce the sense that the buried layers of history hold more of menace for man than of hope.

Among the examples of the decay which characterizes history, the largest number concern religion. Early in the poem the Italian hunchback Celio is meditating at the Arch of Ecce Homo. He is one of those fascinating mirror images of the main character, whose temperament and problems threaten to overshadow those of the main character, and whom Melville discards early—like Bulkington in *Moby-Dick*. Celio's thoughts run along the contrast between the story of Christ which the mind tends to reject as too fantastic, too miraculous, and the teachings of Jesus which the heart embraces instinctively as good and true. He then thinks of the gulf between that pure teaching and the later strife among the creeds which claim to derive from it. "History / Shows there a gulf where bridge is none!" (I, xiii, 81–82). The processes by which the decline of religion takes place are mysterious, though the fact is undeniable:

> By what art
> Of conjuration might the heart
> Of heavenly love, so sweet, so good,
> Corrupt into the creeds malign,
> Begetting strife's pernicious brood,
> Which claimed for patron thee divine?
>
> *(I, xiii, 86–91)*

There are several emotionally operative words here: conjuration, corrupt, malign, pernicious—words which we have found before applying to history generally and to each item of the complex city-landscape symbol. The history of religions thus shows aspects characteristic of the symbol generally.

The phenomenon of warring Christian creeds is not merely an ancient one. In the midst of their journey the pilgrims briefly meet a Dominican priest, a man thoroughly adept at the art of nineteenth-century rationalist apologetics. One of the points he scores is the fragmentation of Christianity after the Reformation: "Sects—Sects bisected —sects disbanded / Into plain deists underhanded" (II, xxv, 106–7). To him at least this is a clear example of decline in religious history.

Rolfe tangles directly with this phenomenon, as he does with most in the course of the poem. After a lyric description of Jesus' life among men, filled with pastoral imagery, he notes the contrast:

> But worse came—creeds, wars, stakes. Oh, men
> Made earth inhuman; yes, a den
> Worse for Christ's coming, since his love
> (Perverted) did but venom prove.
> *(II, xxi, 85–88)*

"Creeds" is a word presented with negative values and connotations, and Melville finds that the major religious event in western history has actually injected a "venom" into man's life stream. Rolfe tries to decide why this should be so, but finally gives it up with a characteristically Melvillian statement: "Best skim, / Not dive" (ll. 104–5).

Ungar, the Confederate officer, also tries his hand at explanation of religious decay, but can come up only with a set of contrasts which illustrate decline. He mentions the things which characterized the faith of the Middle Ages (he himself has Catholicism in his family background), when Christendom was an actual fact: religious mottoes found everywhere; business documents and contracts written within a framework of religious belief and practice; soldiers sealed by religious rites before battle; kings aware more of their humble station before God than of their exalted position before men, and reminded constantly of this by the religious emblems in their crowns. Derwent, the modern churchman,[4] objects on the grounds that those ages are universally acknowledged to be the "dark" ones. Ungar replies: "If night, it was no starless one"; he argues that their art is still admired beyond contemporary works, and their vices though real were less than modern man's. Derwent dismisses him by a comment aside to the others about Ungar's madness appearing again. Ungar hears this and flares up:

> "What's overtaken ye pale men?
> Shrewd are ye, the main chance ye heed:
> Has God quite lost his throne indeed
> That lukewarm now ye grow? Wilt own,
> Council ye take with fossil-stone?
> *(IV, x, 163–67)*

Ungar cites "lukewarm" as the basic quality of contemporary religion; an example of it is the fact that men now look down to fossils as their source of knowledge about the nature of reality. The church has become a sociological phenomenon, institutional, "as worldly as the state." He acknowledges the presence of the old majestic forms of religion;

but they are mere survivals from the past, "stranded on a scene how alien."

Melville cites at length several other examples of the decline of religion. One is in his early canto describing the huts of the Jerusalem lepers. He describes the care the church once took to see that the lepers were fed and housed and also to see that they were spiritually consoled by a ritual created especially for them. The church even inspired several saintly women to live among them and minister to their sickness. The canto is ended with the reflection that leprosy still afflicts multitudes in the East, but that there is no concern for them any more:

> [Now] the Syrian leper goes
> Unfriended, save that man bestows
> (His eye averting) chanceful pence
> Then turns, and shares disgust of sense.
> *(I, xxv, 89–92)*

Melville finds the reason for the decline in a loss of faith:

> Bonds sympathetic bind these three—
> Faith, Reverence, and Charity.
> If Faith once fail, the faltering mood
> Affects—need must—the sisterhood.
> *(ll. 93–96)*

The second series of examples of the downward trend in history is taken from more recent times, the decline of democracy and the American ideal. The subject is touched upon several times in the course of the poem, and it comes up for extended treatment twice, once in the case of Nathan, Ruth's father, and once with Ungar. These characters have most been hurt by the American experience and have rejected it most thoroughly.

In Part I a long canto is devoted to Nathan's background previous to emigrating from America to Palestine. Melville quickly sketches the flow of history which produced him. The pilgrims had erred in their course for Virginia and landed in a cold, constricted wilderness. They were "austere, ascetical, but free" (I, xvii, 2). Their freedom allowed their children to spread out to warmer and lighter and more spacious areas:

> More bred more;
> At each remove a goodlier wain,
> A heart more large, an ampler shore,

With legacies of farms behind;
Until in years the wagons wind
Through parks and pastures of the sun,
Warm plains as of Esdraleon:
'Tis nature in her best benign.

(*ll. 12–19*)

Nathan was born here, in this prairie spaciousness, while the nation was still cresting toward its greatness. He took over the farm that his father had cleared, and he kept his faith, mostly for his mother's sake. The specific tenets of Christianity inspired only doubt, even though he grew up religiously, mystically in contact with the natural objects of rural life. In the midst of religious doubt he came upon a book which influenced him greatly and which may have been Paine's *Age of Reason* or possibly Ethan Allen's *Reason the Only Oracle of Man.*

The blunt straightforward Saxon tone,
Work-a-day language, even his own,
The sturdy thought, not deep but clear,
The hearty unbelief sincere,
Arrested him much like a hand
Clapped on the shoulder.

(*ll. 116–21*)

The young Nathan sits up all night reading the book; first he experiences a great deal of fear as the most basic assertions of his education are set aside; then

Came acquiescence, which though dull
Was hardly peace. An altered earth
Sullen he tilled, in Adam's frame
When thrust from Eden out to dearth
And blest no more, and wise in shame.
The fall!

(*ll. 138–43*)

Nathan's religious nature briefly reawakens in the course of his farming life: "Such mental food / Need quicken, and in natural way, / Each germ of Pantheistic sway, / Whose influence, nor always drear, / Tenants our maiden hemisphere" (ll. 157–61). But the death of his mother, plus the shallow and slightly disreputable lives of some members of a Christian sect who live nearby, cause doubt again.

Up to this point Melville recapitulates the American experience in Nathan. He has found the pattern of history: from stern puritanism, to its mellowing as the early colonies expanded, to deism, to the "Pantheism" of the transcendentalist movement, to the mid-nineteenth-century crisis of belief. That it is a decline, and not merely an evolution, seems clear from the many references to the Fall and Nathan as Adam. Nathan's later life is irrelevant, at this point, since Melville has brought him up to the present, historically, and his conversion to Judaism was but one of many contemporary options.

The possibility of a Fall as the crucial event in the history of a whole nation is interesting. Melville is attracted by the notion, as if the history of a country could parallel the story of a man. He returns to the idea in the second of his two extended treatments of American history. His expatriate Confederate officer locates the Fall of America in the Civil War, as Melville himself had finally done in *Battle-Pieces*. It is that event which soured the sweet promise of the American Eden. The narrator explains "the rankling thing in Ungar's grief":

> That evil day,
> Black in the New World's calendar—
> The dolorous winter ere the war;
> True Bridge of Sighs—so yet 'twill be
> Esteemed in riper history—
> Sad arch between contrasted eras;
> The span of fate; that evil day.
>
> *(IV, v, 75–81)*

Rhetorical emphasis is achieved by the repetition of "that evil day" and brought to a peak by the inverted meter of *"that day"* (l. 92). The day of course begins the Civil War. The passage emphasizes the place that the Civil War holds as watershed in American history. Before and after are "contrasted eras." The central importance of the war as a link between the two eras is stated in three synonyms: "bridge," "arch" and "span." Melville says *"span of fate,"* thus obliquely alluding to one of the possibilities he considers among the moving or controlling forces in history.

A third example of progressive decay in history is taken from recent events in Europe. The major spokesman for this view is Mortmain, himself a disappointed revolutionary. He spent much of his life working on various revolutionary projects in France, but his political idealism has been blackened by his experience of corruption and betrayal in his fellow revolutionaries. Every project that he worked on has turned out to bring more harm and suffering into the world than good. He is a dark bitter figure among the pilgrims for most of their trip; his name ("Death Hand") and the black skull cap he wears help to keep him sharply in focus. *Mortmain* is also a British legal term with a long history. It is used to denote lands held in perpetuity by an organization such as an ecclesiastical corporation or a college. The possessions were inalienable as long as the organization existed. In discussing the origin of the term in his *Commentaries* (I, xviii), Blackstone speculates that such lands were held as in a dead hand since the owner was not a living person, nor could the organization legally dispose of the land. Melville undoubtedly chose the name primarily for its grim etymologies, but is quite possible that there is also some nod in the direction of the legal history of the word, for it is applied to a man who is indeed in the grip of fate beyond his control. There is a canto devoted to a profile of the man and his story, much like the one devoted to Nathan. Rolfe tells the story to Derwent; he has it from an unnamed chance acquaintance who knew Mortmain well. The narrative technique here is complex: x reports to y who reports to z, about M. Mortmain is remote and distant, isolated in his present monomania; and the narrative technique helps emphasize the distance.

According to Rolfe, Mortmain is a Swede, well born but illegitimate. His mother married later and showed this child little love. His father provided for his upbringing and education, but at a distance, never acknowledging him as his son. "Thus isolated, what to bind / But the vague bond of human kind?" (II, iv, 24–25) He left the north and came to Paris, full of "warm desires and schemes for man" (l. 30). The only method available for the improvement of society seemed to be the violent overthrow of existing structures. He fitted in with other revolutionaries, though always with a high ideal in mind: "That uncreated Good / He sought, whose absence is the cause / Of creeds and Atheists, mobs and laws" (ll. 49–51). Melville juxtaposes apparent opposites, after the manner of the eighteenth-century satirists. But the few lines of wit also add the final important stroke to the character analysis of Mortmain: so thoroughly an idealist was he that he would seek a single revolutionary solution to all human ills—overly institutionalized religion as well as total absence of religion, overly rigid law as well as total absence of law.

Thus mounted to ride for an inevitable fall, Mortmain discovers within his own revolutionary movement that "the vain, foolhardy, worthless, blind, / With Judases, are nothing loath / To clasp pledged hands and take the oath" (ll. 55–57). As a result "experience with her sharper touch / Stung Mortmain" (ll. 60–61). Rolfe constructs a soliloquy for Mortmain at this point, which shows his efforts to find a solution at the most critical point of his life. Melville is also at work analyzing the tumultuous events of recent European history.

Oh, now dispense!
The world is portioned out, believe:
The good have but a patch at best,
The wise their corner; for the rest—
Malice divides with ignorance.
And what is stable? Find one boon
That is not lackey to the moon
Of fate. The flood weaves out—the ebb
Weaves back; the incessant shuttle shifts
And flies, and wears and tears the web.
Turn, turn thee to the proof that sifts:
What if the kings in Forty-Eight
Fled like the gods? even as the gods
Shall do, return they made; and sate
And fortified their strong abodes;
And, to confirm them there in state,
Contrived new slogans, apt to please—
Pan and the tribal unities.
Behind all this still works some power
Unknowable, thou'lt yet adore.
That steers the world, not man.

(II, iv, 88–108)

Several themes converge here. First there is the conviction that good
and evil are closely entwined in the world's events, but that evil by far
outweighs the good: "The good have but a patch at best, / The wise
their corner." Second, there is a repetition of the cyclic nature of time
and history, expressed in the image of the ebb and flow of the tide[5] and
the alternations of the shuttle. It is important to note that "tide" carries
with it no notion of progress, but only of repetition, and that the shuttle,
in Melville's peculiar use of the analogy, actually "wears and tears" the
fabric upon which it operates. Melville applies the cyclic view to current
history: kings may be deposed for a time but they will return; and the
old slogans will be replaced only by new ones, again appealing to gen-
eralities and the lowest common denominator. But behind these events
of history there is something more basic, controlling the events them-
selves. "Behind all this still works some power / Unknowable." There is
no hint that it may be a benevolent power. In any event it will dominate
man and reduce him to a servile position: "thou'lt yet adore. / *That*
steers the world, not man." And it is hardly possible that this controlling
fate can be benevolent, since the development of states in the flow of
history is compared to "crazy rafts" (l. 109) striving with billows. His
intellectual and spiritual crisis has brought Mortmain an insight into

the nature of history and his reaction is to dissociate himself as much as possible from the processes of history. It is this decision which leads him to the desert where he meets the other pilgrims.

Melville has given considerable thought to the processes of history. We have already noted his allusion to two theories for an explanation of historical data: a cyclic theory which demands an inevitable fall of a culture after its origin and rise to a certain level, and a theory of some suprahuman malevolent Fate driving history into ever more complex and corrupt forms. There is also evidence in *Clarel* that Melville was interested in a third theory of history, the Marxist. Three brief allusions in his works seem to derive from Karl Marx or possibly from journalistic accounts of his work. The first allusion is put in the mouth of a jovial Mexican, a friend of Derwent's, a man who had fought for Mexican independence but who has since turned skeptical of all such causes and who wanders semidetached, in a state of good-humored cynicism. Derwent asks him why he did not remain in London. Don Hannibal answers: "Oh, too much agitation; yes, / Too proletarian it proved" (IV, xix, 39–40). The conjunction of *London, agitation,* and *proletarian* alerts the reader. Ten pages later Ungar and Rolfe are discussing whether there can be progress or not in civilization. Ungar presents arguments for the eventual resurgence of America as a civilization, even after what he considers to be the disaster of the Civil War; he concludes: "The vast reserves—the untried fields; / These long shall keep off and delay / The class-war, rich-and-poor-man fray / Of history" (IV, xxi, 94–97). The "class-war" chimes with the word "proletarian" to raise the question of Melville's interest in Marxism.

Only one other allusion to a Marxist explanation of history occurs in Melville. In the 1891 *Timoleon* volume there is a poem called "The New Zealot to the Sun."[6] Melville here assumes the persona of a new kind of zealot, ridiculing man's dying religious affections, but himself engulfed in overenthusiasm for the new messiah Science. This delusion is not revealed until the last stanza. The first five stanzas develop the idea that religion began as sun worship and, just as the sun daily pursues its course from east to west, so in the course of history the gods of the sun "westward they rolled their empire far" (l. 17). This religion, the new zealot asserts, has been the source of man's bondage and lack of progress. In the fourth stanza the zealot addresses the sun:

> Chemist, you breed,
> In orient climes each sorcerous weed
> That energizes dream—
> Transmitted, spread in myths and creeds,

> Houris and hells, delirious screeds
> And Calvin's last extreme.

The thought and image are the same as one of Marx's most famous sayings. The stanza seems quite clearly a variation on the statement that religion is the opiate of the masses; the sorcerous orient weed is obviously opium. The last three lines list a sampling of the religious "dreams" it has generated. Because he has created a fictitious spokesman for this poem, Melville cannot be credited with either acceptance or rejection of the idea. Nor is there enough evidence from these three citations to say more than that he had read about Marxist theory with interest, found it representative of one of the lines of nineteenth-century thought, and used it for its contemporaneity in his poetry.

Of the three theories of history Melville considers in *Clarel*, one (the Marxist) does not seem central, and the other two seem of equal significance. However, a theory of malevolent fate driving history and a cyclic theory of history need not be mutually exclusive. Melville manages a synthesis of the two theories, and of most of his other observations on history, in a remarkably complex and beautiful passage delivered by his major spokesman, Rolfe. Because it compresses so much of Melville's thought on the nature of history the passage must be quoted in full. Rolfe, Vine, and Clarel are sitting on a hill overlooking Jerusalem from across the Kedron Valley, the site believed to be the place where Jesus wept over the city and its fate. The group comments on the appropriateness of Jesus' feelings. Rolfe's remarks then move from the present-day decay of the city to the modern erosion of faith also, and some speculations on what history must be like to produce such change.

> All now's revised:
> Zion, like Rome, is Niebuhrized.
> Yes, doubt attends. Doubt's heavy hand
> Is set against us; and his brand
> Still warreth for his natural lord—
> King Common-Place—whose rule abhorred
> Yearly extends in vulgar sway. . . .
> Since thus he aims to level all,
> The Milky Way he'll yet allot
> For Appian to his Capital.
> Then tell, tell then, what charm may save
> Thy marvel, Palestine, from grave
> Whereto winds many a bier and pall
> Of old Illusion? What for earth?
> Ah, change irreverent—at odds

With goodly customs, gracious gods;
New things elate so thrust their birth
Up through dejection of the old,
As through dead sheaths; is here foretold
The consummation of the past,
And garish dawning of a day
Whose noon not saints desire to stay—
And hardly I? Who brake love's fast
With Christ—with what strange lords may sup?
The reserves of time seem marching up.
But, nay; what novel thing may be,
No germ being new? By Fate's decree
Have not earth's vitals heaved in change
Repeated? some wild element
Or action been evolved? . . .
And this without effecting so
The neutralizing of the past,
Whose rudiments persistent flow,
From age to age transmitting, own,
The evil with the good—the taint
Deplored in Solomon's complaint.
Fate's pot of ointment! Wilt have done,
Lord of the fly, god of the grub?
Need'st foul all sweets, thou Beelzebub?
                    (I, xxxiv, 18–62 passim)

The passage seems to proceed in three movements: the older sense of meaning and of wonder is disappearing because of the modern "demythologizing" mentality (ll. 18–35); in their place new things are springing up, which may eventually prove as beautiful and satisfying as the old (ll. 36–46); but there is really nothing new: good and evil flow together through the ages, merely changing the forms by which they are manifested. (ll. 47–62).

Barthold Niebuhr (1776–1831) was a German historian whose masterpiece was a three-volume history of Rome. He is considered the first modern historiographer, winnowing out fancy and legend to present as factual a history of Rome as possible, though he was not entirely emancipated from finding parallels between Rome and Prussia. Melville's point is that "Zion" too is now seen as demythologized or desupernaturalized, just one geographical and political entity among many. He sees in this trend the workings of "Doubt's heavy hand," but that image is dropped for another: King Common-Place extending his vulgar sway ever more and more, removing the romance from life. (At the beginning of Part

II Melville self-consciously patterns his pilgrims' departure from Je-
rusalem on the Canterbury pilgrims in Chaucer's general Prologue.
There he quickly remarks a contrast though: this is now "another age,
and other men, / And life an unfulfilled *romance*" [II, i, 12–13; italics
mine].) This movement of history would probably be looked upon as
an advance, since it proceeds from "illusion" to a more realistic knowl-
edge. But for Melville it is another incontrovertible instance of historical
decline affecting old legends of Atlantis and Cathay, the composition
of the moon and the stars, Palestine, and the whole earth itself.

In the second section of this passage (ll. 36–46) he tests the idea that
this might possibly be progress, as many would hold, and not decline.
It may be an "irreverent" overturning of the gracious old certitudes, but
it is also "elate" and may be the "dawning" of a new era which the best
of men ("saints") would hardly wish to hinder. Melville is testing a
concept that Yeats would later develop at length: "Who brake love's
fast / With Christ—with what strange lords may sup?" The new cycle
will produce figures parallel with those of the old cycle. But even in this
section the notion of progress seems unlikely to pass the test: "garish" is
not a neutral word.

The third section rejects progress. The cyclic understanding of time
is retained, however, and Melville brings about the synthesis of his
theories of history: that it is cyclic and that a malevolent Fate drives
it. The universe is conceived as self-enclosed: no new forces can enter
it. Hence all apparent change is really just rearrangement of elements
already present in it from the beginning. The whole is effected "by
Fate's decree." "Solomon's complaint" is difficult to identify. Many books
were attributed to him in antiquity, including Proverbs, Ecclesiastes,
Wisdom, and the Song of Songs, as well as various noncanonical writ-
ings. Bezanson says that the "ointment" image which immediately fol-
lows "would seem to come from Ecclesiastes 10:1: 'Dead flies cause
the ointment of the apothecary to send forth a stinking savour'" (p.
582). Melville is shortly to make the allusion to the Golden Bowl and
the broken Pitcher, which we have quoted earlier, from the same bibli-
cal source. It seems quite possible then that the whole book of Eccle-
siastes, with its overwhelming preoccupation with the shifting and
changing of a world in which man himself finds his existence tainted
by impermanence and incertitude, is taken here to be "Solomon's
complaint."

The passage ends dramatically. Line 58 speaks of "the evil with the
good," as if they were mixed in equal proportions. Then "the taint"
is focused on, as if it predominated. Finally the true god of the universe

is disclosed, Beelzebub, fouling "*all* sweets." Baal-Zebul was one of the honorific titles of the Baal, the god of the Canaanites, whose worship was a constant source of temptation to the Israelites during their early years in the Promised Land. The title meant *Baal, the Prince,* and was ridiculed as early as II Kings 1:2 by a slight change to Baalzebub, "Lord of the Flies." This is the only mention of the god in the Old Testament, but the pun is continued in the New Testament, where each of the synoptics reports the charge of the Pharisees that Jesus received his power to cast out demons from the prince of demons himself, Beelzebub (Matt. 12:24). The figure gains much of its power from Milton's later treatment. In the early books of *Paradise Lost* Beelzebub stands second only to Satan himself for power and malice. It is he who proposes Satan's program for the harassment and destruction of man at the infernal conclave in Book II. Melville's main interest in Beelzebub is the corruption stemming from the translation, lord of the *flies*. The lines rise in a crescendo: the Fate driving the cycles of history, the God whose "caldron" history is, Beelzebub "Lord of the fly, god of the grub." Rolfe is *Clarel's* most persuasive and persistent spokesman. His view of history early in the poem does much to influence our response to the remainder.

The massive city-landscape-sea-history symbol develops with a slow thoroughness throughout the poem. The four parts are carefully interlocked at many points. The symbolic universe thus created is one where evil far outweighs good, where energies decline and full blossom goes on to decay, where perception always discloses a menacing personal evil.

There remains one profound element still to be analyzed in *Clarel*, also dynamic, involving a particular narrative line which gives life and direction, a temporal dimension, to the poem. It is also complex, involving several related items: edenic, pastoral, and christological.

Melville's exploration of the pastoral mode in *Clarel* is involved. He seems at many points in the poem to be attempting to *locate* pastoral material, to find its source, to determine what areas or feelings it corresponds to. His most extensive application of the pastoral mode is to the figure of Christ, though he looks for it in several other areas as well.

A pastoral setting offers an immediately obvious contrast to the sterile rockiness of Palestine. Melville uses it thus in many places, but usually with more than just this single intention of contrast. Toward the end of Part II he gives a narrator's description of the barren setting of the Dead Sea. The passage continues:

But disenchanters grave maintain
That in the time ere Sodom's fall
'Twas shepherds here endured life's pain:
Shepherds, and all was pastoral
In Siddim.
        (*II, xxxvii, 33–37*)

Here the pastoral contrast also reinforces a major symbolic motif, the decline of history. But Melville will not allow even this much easy simplification. The decline of history he imputes to "disenchanters," as if only the maliciously cynical could insist upon such contrasts. A further complication ensues since even in a pastoral setting the shepherds "endured life's pain," suggesting that perhaps the difference between pastoral and nonpastoral existence is not great. It is not easy, Melville seems to be saying, to locate the archetypally pastoral.

Occasionally the pilgrims find traces of the edenic in the present actualities of the Holy Land. For example a gushing fountain in a desolate landscape has power of suggestion:

There, by the cliffs or distance hid,
The Fount or Cascade of the Kid
An Eden makes of one high glen,
One vernal and contrasted scene
In jaws of gloomy crags uncouth—
Rosemary in the black boar's mouth.
        (*II, xxix, 44–49*)

The lines describe the pilgrims' first view of the Dead Sea—all is desolate, decaying, menacing. The one pinpoint of brightness comes from the Fount or Cascade of the Kid. Bezanson (p. 607) says that the travel book upon which Melville relied heavily calls this the Spring of the Wild Goats. One's curiosity is aroused when an author modifies his sources: why does Melville say "fount" instead of "spring" and "kid" instead of "wild goats"? Melville's copy of Horace was part of the Harper's Family Classical Library.[7] The work was in two volumes, of which the first was a translation by Philip Francis and the second was an anthology of other poets' translations of selected poems. This second volume offers three versions of the famous Ode XIII of Book III, "*O Fons Bandusiae.*" The interesting point is that all of these versions prefer to call the spring a "fount" or "fountain" and to translate "*haedo*" as "kid" rather than "goat." The ode presents a spring as pastoral refuge. It is a "green retreat" where a "verdant holm" or "nodding oak" presides over "the cavern deep" of "moss-grown rock," in the versions that Philip Francis has collected. One sees that Melville is constructing his own description of the Holy Land spring against the background of these versions of Horace. In Horace the speaker stands in the immediate presence of the spring; it is, one seems to sense, very much *his* spring. Melville's spring is remote, cut off: "by the cliffs or distance hid." Horace's spring is "verdant"; Melville suggests some relationship by calling his "vernal." But Horace's "cavern deep" or "moss-grown rock" is for Melville something quite different: "the jaws of gloomy crags uncouth." The "tender kid" which dominates the second section of Horace's poem becomes, for Melville, the ugly menacing image of "the black boar's mouth." Two important points stand out: first of all, Melville finds in the Dead Sea landscape only one small point of pastoral "Eden"; and second, there is no question but that even this small edenic point is thoroughly dominated by the menacing evil of the rest of the landscape.

There are several other areas where Melville momentarily presents the pastoral mode: the Pacific, the plains of mid-America, the Roman Church, youth, and women—particularly in the relationship between Clarel and Ruth. He had begun to transform the Pacific into an imaginative object as early as the idylls in *Typee* and *Omoo*. The transformation became thorough and complete in *Mardi*, so much so that the Pacific could stand for the cosmos itself, with all its enigmas. In *The Encantadas* the demonic aspects of this imaginary Pacific were given full symbolic expression. Afterward the Pacific continues to have interest, but subsides into subordinate position in Melville's symbolic universe, while he was occupied with the exploration of the Holy Land as symbol.

The interest continues in *Clarel*. The events of Rolfe's early manhood parallel Melville's own. Late in the poem the pilgrims are comparing their impressions of Bethlehem. Rolfe has the Pacific strongly in mind:

> "For me," Rolfe said,
> "From Bethlehem here my musings reach
> Yes—frankly—to Tahiti's beach."
> "Tahiti?" Derwent; "you have sped!"
> "Ay, truant humor. But to me
> That vine-wreathed urn of Ver, in sea
> Of halcyons, where no tides do flow
> Or ebb, but waves bide peacefully
> At brim, by beach where palm trees grow
> That sheltered Omai's olive race—
> Tahiti should have been the place
> For Christ in advent."
>
> *(IV, xviii, 35–46)*

The lines are related to later passages embodying edenic qualities in those places most closely associated with Christ in the Holy Land. Here the process is reversed: the Pacific is recalled as edenic and therefore should be associated with Christ. It is a place of continuous spring ("Ver"). The lines "where no tides do flow / Or ebb, but waves bide peacefully / At brim" must be read by one sensitized, at this late stage in the poem, by dozens of allusions to the same image in "Dover Beach": Melville makes one major aspect of his edenic Pacific the obverse of Arnold's problem of receding faith. The passage also occurs late enough in the poem to gather in the edenic associations of the Mar Saba palm tree, which can thus strengthen the meaning of the "beach where palm trees grow." Finally the word "halcyon" and the "Ver-verdant" variation should be noted as typical edenic terms for Melville.

The Pacific of the imagination, then, can be drawn upon to furnish an edenic pastoral vision, yet Pacific as symbol contains the demonic as well. *Mardi* and *The Encantadas* had both demonstrated as much. The menacing aspect of this possible Eden is present in *Clarel*, too. Mortmain finds it in a simile he uses to explain the hiddenness of evil in deeds which men would have appear good: "hate, which under life's fair hues / Prowls like the shark in sunned Pacific blue" (II, xxxvi, 38–39).

Melville's central use of the shark appears in "The Maldive Shark," and there is little doubt of its general symbolic meaning. His name is capitalized the only time it appears. The pilot fish who swim before him are said to find "an asylum in the jaws of the Fates." His attributes are peculiarly similar to those of the iceberg, the subject of a poem which occurs only a few pages later in *John Marr*. He is the "phlegmatical one," "pale sot," with "white triple tiers of glittering gates" (these are the teeth of the shark, but could just as easily describe the jagged sides of the iceberg), "the dotard lethargic and dull." Both objects are the hulking, whitish, powerful menaces lurking in nature for man's destruction. The same attributes of the shark can be found in *Mardi* and in *Moby-Dick*. In *Clarel* "the shark untired" swims ready to devour the mariner who falls from the masthead after the devil (bird) has stolen his soul (hat) (III, xxvii, 34). Earlier in the poem Celio had been protesting the ironies of life, the inextricable confusion of good and evil, though the God who is responsible for all is held to be good. He summarizes: "the shark thou mad'st, yet claim'st the dove" (I, xiii, 71).

Curiously this menace which appears within the pastoral Eden of the Pacific also appears in the landscape of the Holy Land under the same guise. Early in their journey the pilgrims come upon territory which is dangerous because of the bandits who infest it. Their own armed guards make them comparatively safe; at one point they actually see signs of a bandit group, but it is too small to attack them:

> "Look!" one cried. Behind
> A lesser ridge just glide from sight—
> Though neither man nor horse appears—
> Steel points and hair-tufts of five spears.
> Like dorsal fins of sharks they show
> When upright these divide the wave
> And peer above, while down in grave
> Of waters, slide the body lean
> And charnel mouth.
>
> *(II, ix, 94–102)*

The incident marks Clarel's discernment of "something dubious in the Holy Land" (l. 105).

Melville then is finding it difficult to locate aspects of the pastoral edenic in its pure form. The Holy Land will not furnish it, nor will the remembered Pacific. The prairies of mid-America are next tested. We have already looked at the background narrative for Nathan, whose family had traveled west and found the prairie lands there at first a new Eden. But it did not remain so for Nathan: finally he had to leave and seek something better, eventually in the Holy Land. Ungar's story has also been considered, and his view that the untouched spaces of the New World had been possibly an Eden—though the sin of the Civil War had led to the nation's Fall. It is a curious parallel that Clarel, at the beginning of the story, had felt that he was coming into an American prairie Eden as he traveled from the harbor town of Jaffe across the plains to Jerusalem:

> "The plain we crossed. In afternoon,
> How like our early autumn bland—
> So softly tempered for a boon—
> The breath of Sharon's prairie land!"
>
> *(I, i, 35–38)*

But contrary impressions soon occupy the major part of his psychological awareness.

Still another locus for the pastoral edenic is "the Latin usage" or the Roman Catholic rite. The whole party is greatly moved by the first sight of the River Jordan. Something must be done to celebrate their view of the place, where "the halcyon Teacher waded in with John." Rolfe remembers that Chateaubriand had knelt and sung the "Ave Maris Stella" when he had been here. And pulling out a vellum-covered book, he suggests that they celebrate the occasion in the same way. Chateaubriand had "caught a fortunate / Fair twinkle starry under trees" of Jordan (II, xxiv, 8–9), and had "dropped on reverent knees, / Warbling that hymn of beauty blest" (ll. 11–12). They all join in, delighting "in spirits glad," all happy as brothers "to joy with Rome" (ll. 32, 34). Even Vine relaxes his customary reserve, "marking them in cheery bloom / Of turf inviting."

> Fraternal thus, the group engage—
> While now the sun, obscured before,
> Illumed for time the wooded shore—
> In tribute to the beach and tide.
> *(ll. 45–48)*

The passage seems a variation of pastoral simplicity: fraternal joy in a natural and beautiful setting. The canto is the first of three in which Roman Catholicism is discussed at length. Even Derwent is sympathetic to some aspects of it. But the general agreement is, finally, that it is too authoritarian for modern man and its institutions are out of date.

The final locus for the pastoral edenic in this series is developed in an interesting little dramatic movement involving youth, woman, and finally the young Ruth. I do not mean movement in the sense that the whole drama fits into one canto, but rather that the items seem to connect even though they are spread throughout the entire poem.

Youth suggests a possible locus for the pastoral edenic. The prospective son-in-law of the Greek banker is a flippant youth full of spirit and life. As the party travels past Olivet from Jerusalem to Bethany, he breaks out in a song full of erotic pastoral imagery derived from the Song of Solomon:

> "She's handsome as a jeweled priest
>   In ephod on the festa,
> And each poor blade like me must needs
>   Idolize and detest her.
>
> "With rain-beads on her odorous hair
>   From gardens after showers,
> All bloom and dew she trips along,
>   Intent on selling flowers.
>
> "She beams—the rainbow of the bridge;
>   But, ah, my blank abhorrence,

> She buttonholes me with a rose
> This flower-girl of Florence.
>
> "My friends stand by; and, 'There!' she says—
> An angel arch, a sinner:
> I grudge to pay, but pay I must,
> Then—dine on half a dinner!"
> *(II, v, 54–69)*

As a technical achievement this is remarkable for Melville, whose variety never ceases to delight. But the inappropriate song offends everyone. The boy is out of place in the group, and no one mourns overmuch when he leaves the pilgrimage early.

The edenic is also suggested in the "sympathies of Eve" which the sad Clarel evokes in a group of women he encounters while strolling the streets of Jerusalem.

> The worn Greek matrons mark him there:
> Ah, young, our lassitude dost share?
> Home do thy pilgrim reveries stray?
> Art *thou* too, weary of the way?—
> Yes, sympathies of Eve awake;
> Yet do but err. For how might break
> Upon those simple natures true,
> The complex passion? might they view
> The apprehension tempest-tossed
> The spirit in gulf of dizzying fable lost?
> *(I, v, 212–21)*

No sooner does the hope of edenic sympathy arise than it disappears. The women are too simple to understand and comfort his "complex passion." Granted, their simplicity is from the fact that they are Greek peasants; but the lines also suggest that they are too simple because they are women.

The possibilities of Eden appearing in youth and in woman converge in Ruth. Clarel first sees Ruth amid a group of girls performing a ceremony at the Jerusalem Wailing Wall:

> Among the maids those rites detained,
> One he perceived, as it befell,
> Whose air expressed such truth unfeigned,
> And harmonies inlinked which dwell
> In pledges born of record pure—
> She looked a legate to insure

> That Paradise is possible
> Now as hereafter. 'Twas the grace
> Of Nature's dawn: an Eve-like face
> And Nereid eyes with virgin spell
> Candid as day, yet baffling quite
> Like day, through unreserve of light.
> A dove she seemed, a temple dove,
> Born in the temple or its grove,
> And nurtured there.
> *(I, xvi, 158–72)*

Here indeed is the hope of a pastoral Eden offered him, if he can obtain it. And it is an Eden specially suited to his particular needs. The first attribute mentioned is "truth unfeigned." Clarel considers his problem one of knowledge. His immediate impulse is to feel that she will help greatly in resolving his doubts. Rather than representing the necessity of abandoning his religious life, she links him closer to it; she is a "legate" directly from paradise to him. Ruth offers reconciliation of the two disjointed worlds of physical reality and religion, or nature and grace: in her he finds "the grace of Nature's dawn." The idea is repeated in the line "a dove she seemed, a temple dove." Pastoral Eden in its general terms is here; here also are the particular specifications of it most needed by Clarel at this time.

Here too something is wrong:

> But deeper viewed,
> What was it that looked part amiss?
> A bit impaired? what lack of peace?
> Enforced supression of a mood.
> Regret with yearning intertwined,
> And secret protest of a virgin mind.
> *(ll. 172–77)*

Three questions, three attempts to answer. All is not well in Eden. Ruth has her own problems: frustrations, yearnings, protestings that may be as strong as Clarel's. But none of this completely nullifies the "redemption" and the wholeness she seems to offer him. Ruth is a friend of Clarel's companion Nehemiah, and through him he gets to know her and her parents. The romance can grow. Eden can be recaptured bit by bit. At least the possibilities seem quite real:

> Clarel and Ruth—might it but be
> That range they could green uplands free
> By gala orchards, when they fling

Their bridal favors, buds of Spring;
And, dreamy in her morning swoon,
The lady of the night, the moon,
Looks pearly as the blossoming;
And youth and nature's fond accord
Wins Eden back, that tales abstruse
Of Christ, the crucified, Pain's Lord,
Seem foreign—forged—incongruous.
                                    (I, xxviii, 1–11)

Melville as narrator has taken a subtle and precise stance here. The incautious reader may look to this as a passage of actual description. But the fact is that the narrator has cast the whole into an ideal subjunctive with the "might" and the "could" of the first two lines. All the pastoral elements are here: green uplands, gala orchard, bridal favors, buds of spring. But they are removed and unreal, they exist only in a realm defined by the double subjunctive. The subsequent syntax is uncertain. The subjunctive at first seems to introduce a conditional kind of structure: if only they could enter this Eden, then . . . , but the "then" is never expressed; instead we have the curious "that" in line 9. The syntax expresses an impossible wish: if only they *could* enter that Eden—an Eden of such intensely real bliss that it blocks the reality of Christ's pain which would otherwise force itself upon their consciousness at every turn in the Holy Land. The Ruth-Clarel relation seems to offer initially an escape into unreal pastoral, but circumstances will not allow it. "Restrictions of that Eastern code" forbid their free roaming and limit Ruth's ability to spend much time alone or in public with Clarel, who must content himself with a few short visits to Ruth's family and ramblings with her friend, Nehemiah.

Toward the end of Part I, just before Nathan's death and Ruth's complete seclusion for the required period of mourning, Melville devotes a complete fifty-line canto to "Clarel and Ruth." It is the climax of their falling in love, the point at which the relationship seems completely right to everyone, just before the catastrophe which sets them apart—only temporarily, they think. In the next-to-last line of the canto, the narrator asks: "Could heaven two loyal hearts abuse?" Even this early in the poem, the reader has been educated to respond affirmatively. Melville's response is to put off an answer to the question; his last line for the canto reads: "The death-moth, let him keep his bower."

The progression of romantic love toward the edenic is by no means linear. The two lovers are abruptly separated and Clarel goes on pilgrimage. Many of his thoughts on the trip are attempts to evaluate this edenic possibility. Other means to its achievement also intrude. With twentieth-century clarity and nineteenth-century delicacy Melville deals with Clarel's impulse towards homosexual love as a means to fulfillment. The title of the canto, "Vine and Clarel," parallels the one just considered—"Clarel and Ruth." Clarel is always influenced by the person he has most recently talked to (or, more usually, listened to). Rolfe, as the intellectual and vocal inquirer, impresses him most often. But he has also been attracted by the silent reserves of Vine, and he asks Vine for his observations on the people in the party:

> As were Venetian slats between,
> He espied him through a leafy screen,
> Luxurious there in umbrage thrown,
> Light sprays above his temples blown—
> The river through the green retreat
> Hurrying, reveling by his feet.
>
> *(II, xxvii, 11–16)*

Melville is clearly dealing with elements of the erotic pastoral here: the Venetian slats, the leafy screen, luxurious, umbrage, the light sprays above his temples blown, the green retreat. Vine speaks for the first time. He shows a talent for close observation of the natural objects around them and for allegorizing them into moral comments on human life. Clarel finds the pastoral edenic mood building:

> Pure as the rain
> Which diamondeth with lucid grain,
> The white swan in the April hours
> Floating between two sunny showers
> Upon the lake, while buds unroll;
> So pure, so virginal in shrine
> Of true unworldliness looked Vine.
> Ah, clear sweet ether of the soul
> (Mused Clarel), holding him in view.
> Prior advances unreturned
> Not here he recked of, while he yearned—
> O, now but for communion true
> And close; let go each alien theme;
> Give me thyself!
>
> *(ll. 58–71)*

Clarel seems momentarily swept away by the new and unexpected possibilities for fulfillment. Vine, however, appears not to notice

"Clarel's thrill / Of personal longing" (ll. 74–75) and continues to ramble. He pauses and Clarel's mind is again revealed:

> How pleasant in another
> Such sallies, or in thee, if said
> After confidings that should wed
> Our souls in one:—Ah, call me *brother!*—
> So feminine his passionate mood
> Which, long as hungering unfed,
> All else rejected or withstood.
>
> (*ll. 106–12*)

The time seems ripe for words, "some inklings he let fall." But Vine silently withdraws back into himself. Clarel tries to understand this experience; and as he does so, he seems to have passed this crisis successfully. Vine appears to be saying:

> Lives none can help ye; that believe.
> Art thou the first soul tried by doubt?
> Shalt prove the last? Go, live it out.
> But for thy fonder dream of love
> In man toward man—the soul's caress—
> The negatives of flesh should prove
> Analogies of non-cordialness
> In spirit.
>
> (*ll. 123–30*)

Clarel's sudden realization fills him with disgust: "sick these feelings are" (l. 141). He thinks of Ruth and his loyalties to her. Something in Vine's wordless gentle manner, however, shows understanding and calms him. Clarel has found shocking and unsuspected aspects of himself, and still another door to the ideal world has been closed to him.

Romantic love has not proved to be the real locus for the edenic. Woman's promise to man is not or cannot be fulfilled. In fact, as the poem progresses, woman's potential instead for demonic destructiveness becomes clear—definitely for the bitterly cynical Mortmain—and at first possibly and then probably so for Clarel.

On the shores of the Dead Sea the group speculates on the nature of the transgressions serious enough to bury the cities beneath the sea. Mortmain soliloquizes on the degrees of evil. The easiest to explain is the transgression of clear and explicit laws, but there is a deeper evil, he says, "things hard to prove," a malice which may work greater evil while keeping intact the letter of the law. His speculations go even deeper: there is some principle of evil abroad in the universe, as pervasive as the noxious gasses exhaled by the Dead Sea itself. Noticing some bubbles at the edge of the sea he says:

> "Be these the beads on the wives'-wine,
> Tofana-brew?—O fair Medea—
> O soft man-eater, furry–fine:
> Oh, be thou Jael, be thou Leah—
> Unfathomably shallow!—No!
> Nearer the core than man can go
> Or Science get—nearer the slime
> Of nature's rudiments and lime
> In chyle before the bone. Thee, thee,
> In thee the filmy cell is spun—
> The mould thou art of what men be:
> Events are all in thee begun—
> By thee, through thee!—Undo, undo,
> Prithee, undo, and still renew
> The fall forever!"
>
> *(II, xxxvi, 91–105)*

The passage is admittedly complicated and obscure. Tofana brew (*aqua tofana*) is a form of arsenic; it is interesting that Melville calls it "wives'-wine." Medea's deeds are well known. Jael (Judges 4:18–21) drove a tent peg through the head of Sisera while he was sleeping securely under her protection. Leah participated in the duping of Jacob, who worked seven years for Rachel but was given Leah instead. The fifth line seems to say that no matter what the woman's name may be, she is "unfathomable" though appearing simple. "Chyle" is a fluid which develops late in the process of digestion, expediting the transfer of emulsified fat globules directly from the small intestine to the veins. Melville seems to take it as being close to the "key" to life, one of "nature's rudiments," a substance more fundamental even than bone. Woman, he says, operates at this level, closer to the core than either man or science can penetrate. The metaphor then shifts from digestion to gestation. The priority of woman is shown because she is the one who spins the filmy cell which develops into man, and is the mold into which man is cast during the period of gestation. Woman is the source of evil in Mortmain's view. She is the "soft man-eater," the seductress and destroyer, the one who through gestation continues or "renews" the fall of man forever.

The view is Mortmain's, but woman's stock has begun to decline for Clarel, too. His next ordeal in this series is a momentary temptation to celibacy. He is wandering about the environs of the monastery at Mar Saba. His thoughts are on Ruth and how she is "strange involved / With every mystery unresolved / In time and fate" (III, xxx, 4–6). He feels that she is necessary to his peace of mind, but " 'twas Ruth, and oh, much more than Ruth" (l. 12). He begins to realize that he will still want much more once he has won her. At this point Clarel comes upon a celibate in something like a vision. The man is feeding the St. Saba doves, which "from hand outspread / Or fluttering at his feet are fed. / Some, iridescent round his brow, / Wheel, and with nimbus him endow" (ll. 35–38). The man seems beatified by the setting: "so pure he showed— / Of stature tall, in aspect bright— / He looked an almoner of God, / Dispenser of the bread of light" (ll. 43–46). Pastoral imagery fills the scene; we again find the word "vernal." Clarel is attracted to this life, but first he must submit his main objection to the monk:

> "Father, if Good, 'tis unenhanced:
> No life domestic do ye own
> Within these walls: woman I miss.
> Like cranes, what years from time's abyss
> Their flight have taken, one by one,
> Since Saba founded this retreat:
> In cells here many a stifled moan
> Of lonely generations gone;
> And more shall pine as more shall fleet."
> *(ll. 86–94)*

He would miss the domestic life he has learned to love with Ruth and her mother; the solitude would be too painful. The monk seems not to utter a single word. Instead he gives Clarel a pious compilation of churchly antifeminist tales, biblical figures led to woe by women. It also contains "lustral hymns and prayers . . . / Renouncing, yearnings, charges dread / Against our human nature dear" (ll. 116–18). The book is too stern and ascetic for Clarel, yet he finds it hard to resist. He stands overlooking the gorge down from Mar Saba. There he notices Mortmain, Vine, and Rolfe. Each has found a separate niche for contemplation. Each is unseen by the others, though Clarel can see them all. Each seems fixed and isolated in his own private world of pain as in levels of a Purgatorio. Clarel experiences a momentary return of the homosexual urge as he sees Vine. But the canto tapers off inconclusively; neither Ruth, nor Vine, nor the life of celibacy can offer much hope of redemption. The canto ends: "Apathy upon the steep / Sat one with Silence and the Dead" (ll. 164–65).

The final stage of the exploration of the possibilities for romantic love as the locus of the pastoral edenic occurs as the travelers approach Jerusalem at the end of the pilgrimage. Clarel suddenly realizes with new clarity Ruth's importance to him. She can save him from the religious madness which destroyed her father and brought mother and daughter so much suffering. But immediately one of his frequent waverings sets in. Perhaps it is all a mistake for him to take Ruth as a wife. Mortmain may be right, and the book the monk had given him:

> Are the sphered breasts full of mysteries
> Which not the maiden's self may know?
> May love's nice balance, finely slight,
> Take tremor from fulfilled delight?
> Can nature such a doom dispense
> As, after ardor's tender glow,
> To make the rapture more than pall
> With evil secrets in the sense,
> And guile whose bud is innocence—
> Sweet blossom of the flower of gall?
>
> (*IV, xxix, 92–101*)

His hesitation expresses itself in three questions. The first one suggests depths in womanhood of which an individual woman may herself not be aware. The depths ("mysteries") are surely evil ones. He next worries about sexual love bringing too much joy, to the detriment of idealistic love. Clarel apparently is concerned about the possible coarsening, or actual destruction, of his ideal love. The fear is expressed more fully in the third question. The experience of love actually becomes an initiation into evil, the "evil secrets in the sense." Such rapture as he would find in love would actually lead into a greater despair than he had ever known. The underlying figure of the last two lines is that of the plant and its bud or blossom. The qualities of the bud-blossom are innocence and sweetness; those of the plant are guile and gall. Melville thus sums up Clarel's fears: the experience of love may seem to be characterized by sweetness and innocence; actually it grows from a source of bitterness and evil.

Clarel is so close to Ruth at this point that he cannot allow such thoughts to gain control. The interior monologue continues:

> Nay, nay: Ah! God, keep far from me
> Cursed Manes and the Manichee!
> At large here life proclaims the law:
> Unto embraces myriads draw

Through sacred impulse. Take thy wife;
Venture, and prove the soul of life,
And let fate drive.

(ll. 102–8)

He rejects the previous line of thought, but not because it is untrue that sexuality is evil at the root. Instead it is because "life proclaims the law" of marriage and begetting. Clarel (and Melville) drops the search for the edenic in romantic love. Married love is to be undertaken because it is one of the fundamental life processes, subject to the "fate" that drives history as a whole. Its evil root, then, seems not to have been a mistaken perception, but instead still another glimpse into the way things are in Melville's evil universe.

Melville has successively tested the Holy Land, the Pacific, the American prairies, the Roman Church, youth, woman, and married love with Ruth as possible loci for the pastoral edenic. One other source is tested at several points in the poem. This is the Christ story.

Jesus was "the halcyon Teacher" (II, xxiii, 198). In his time he shed a pastoral aura about the people and places associated with him. The village of Bethania can evoke a mood of serene beauty in the pilgrims. Derwent says of the town as they approach it: " 'How placid! Carmel's beauty here, / If added, could not more endear' " (II, vi, 16–17). Clarel looks at it and thinks:

> But, ah, and can one dream the dream
> That hither through the shepherds' gate,
> Even by the road we traveled late,
> Came Jesus from Jerusalem,
> Who pleased him so in fields and bowers,
> Yes, crowned with thorns, still loved the flowers?
> Poor gardeners here that turned the sod
> Friends were they to the Son of God?
> And shared He e'en their humble lot?
> The sisters here in pastoral plot
> Green to the door—did they yield rest,
> And bathe the feet, and spread the board
> For Him . . . ?
>
> *(ll. 23–35)*

Melville casts Clarel's reconstruction of the pastoral Christ as a "dream." The "ah" seems a wistful desire for something acknowledged as unreal. There is something of the remote and sentimental in his image of the "poor gardeners" and the Jesus who loved the flowers even when crowned with their thorns. Still the "pastoral" is achieved, largely with the help of Wordsworth's phrase "green to the door" (from "Tintern Abbey"), and it is Christ who is at the center of it.

It is Rolfe who, in another place, paints the most striking picture of the pastoral Christ as a genial Pan:

> "Whither hast fled, thou deity
> So genial? In thy last and best
> Best avatar—so ripe in form—
> Pure as the sleet—as roses warm—
> Our earth's unmerited fair guest—
> A god with peasants went abreast:
> Man clasped a deity's offered hand;
> And woman, ministrant, was then
> How true, even in a Magdalen.
>   *(II, xxi, 65–73)*

Rolfe is a nineteenth-century intellectual, knowledgeable in comparative religion and willing to explore the "avatars" through which the God-idea progresses. His comparisons with ripeness, sleet, and roses make Christ a nature god, one who comes to share a close intimacy with man and woman. But once again the dream status of this pastoral edenic is discovered. "Disenchantment" gains and overcomes them. Matthew Arnold's image once again is brought into play: "Back rolled the world's effacing tide" (l. 80). After the disenchantment, "worse came—creeds, wars, stakes" (l. 85); we see once more Melville's idea of the downward curve of history overtaking an era. The world is actually worse off for the presence of Christ in it: "Oh, men / Made earth inhuman; yes, a den / Worse for Christ's coming, since his love / (Perverted) did but venom prove" (ll. 85–88). Melville's deepest convictions reverse those of the optimist: always evil will eventually come out of good.

The edenic Christ theme culminates at Bethlehem. This is near the end of their travels for the pilgrims, though the place is associated with the beginning phases of the Christ story. Bethlehem is pastoral Eden because of its close association with Christ: "oliveyards and vineyards fair," "a theater pale green of terraces," "fragrance sweet," "grasses fair" (IV, vi, 19–21, 36–37). The Dale or Valley of the Shepherds seems to the pilgrims to be the center of this pastoral atmosphere. Here they easily imagine the shepherds watching their sheep by night. The scene begins to glow as the story of the angelic manifestation unfolds for them again in imagination: "Sparkling in scintillant ray— / [the shepherds] Beheld a splendor diaphanic— / Effulgence never dawn hath shot, / Nor flying meteors of the night" (IV, ix, 32–35). Somehow the religious meaning of Bethlehem radiates more intensely for them from this scene than it does from the marble enslabbed shrine of the cave and manger. Rolfe even remarks that old legends place the location of the original Eden somewhere nearby (l. 87), and he notes the appropriateness of this legend since it is thus "A link with years before the Fall" (l. 90). This is the closest the pilgrims have come to the pastoral among sublunary actualities.

Melville's final reading of the Christ story is diffused throughout the concluding cantos. The pilgrims arrive back at Jerusalem on Ash Wednesday. Clarel is stunned by the death of Ruth and Agar. His friends are loath to leave him in his mourning, but they have other obligations and within the week all have had to leave him. Clarel stays to spend Lent alone in the Holy City. Weeks pass and the processions of Palm Sunday only remind him of the funeral processions he had passed when leaving Ruth. He sees now that he should have taken it as an omen. On Good Friday he imagines that the dead walk, and sees all the dead of the poem pass as if in review: Nehemiah, Celio, Mortmain, Nathan, Agar, and finally Ruth—who looked "how estranged in face" (IV, xxxii, 99), as she passed by the eye of his mind wreathed in funereal vapors.

We now come to Easter. The temptation for Melville must have been immense at this point to end on some apocalyptic note, some revelation that would finally leave his protagonist at peace. All Jerusalem now celebrates the resurrection of Christ; why cannot some parallel be found for the formal close of the poem? Just as immense, of course, must have been the temptation in the opposite direction: a large nineteenth-century audience could have been found to appreciate the closing of all possible doors to the transcendent and the supernatural.

Melville's solution in the last three cantos is more complex. He finishes the Christ story by reporting the Easter celebrations in the Holy City. The Resurrection seems like a folk festival, the ritual commemoration of events remote and legendary:

> Nor blame them who by lavish rite
> Thus greet the pale victorious Son,
> Since Nature times the same delight,
> And rises with the Emerging One;
> Her passion-week, her winter mood
> She slips, with crape from off the Rood.
>
> (*IV, xxxiii, 25–30*)

The Resurrection of Christ parallels nature rituals. The pun on Son-sun helps this. Melville has never consistently capitalized words referring to Christ; but here all words referring to Christ or to nature are capitalized. Nor has he ever, in the course of the poem, referred to the historicity of Christ's Resurrection as a fact demanding belief. Melville considered Christ a creator of a momentary Eden, a teacher of possibilities. The Resurrection, when it is handled, is remote and mythic, an acting out of a particular stage (spring) in the endlessly repeating cycle of the natural year.

The lack of correspondence between actual human life and the pattern of nature—indeed the irrelevance of the natural pattern to man—is noted at length:

> But heart bereft is unrepaid
> Though Thammuz' spring in Thammuz' glade
> Invite; then how in Joel's glen?
> What if dyed shawl and bodice gay
> Make bright the black dell? what if they
> In distance clear diminished be
> To seeming cherries dropped on pall
> Borne graveward under laden tree?
> The cheer, so human, might not call
> The maiden up; *Christ is arisen:*
> But Ruth, may Ruth so burst the prison?
> *(ll. 56–66)*

Thammuz (or Tammuz) was an ancient Babylonian nature deity, associated with the fertility goddess Ishtar. The prophet Ezekiel records that one of the "abominations" shown him by the Lord was the sight of the women of Jerusalem weeping for his annual autumnal demise (Ezekiel 9:14). His rebirth with the spring was also celebrated. Melville compares this celebration with the one observed for Christ outside of Jerusalem: neither can do much for "heart bereft." The passage becomes more cynical as he notes the similarity between the festive costumes dotting the landscape and the fruit that drops haphazardly from a tree onto a "pall" which is being carried to a graveside. The pattern of nature is at best indifferent to the pattern of human experience, and Christ's resurrection is meaningful only as analogue of nature's pattern. For Clarel Christ's resurrection can do nothing to restore to him the lost Ruth. The canto ends quickly with the image of the town depopulated after Easter by the exodus of the pilgrims.

The setting for the next-to-the-last canto, "Via Crucis," is the street

traveled by Christ on his way to the crucifixion, and the time is Pente-
cost Sunday. The point is that, whatever the truth about Christ's res-
urrection may be, man still is situated in an earlier phase of Christ's
pattern, forced to submit to the carrying of his cross. Melville describes
the panoramic *comédie humaine* visible in Jerusalem at Whitsuntide:
beggars and sick people, the lonely, the tired, the bereaved, the impover-
ished, the sad. "In varied forms of fate they wend— / Or man or animal,
'tis one: / Cross-bearers all, alike they tend / And follow, slowly follow
on" (IV, xxxiv, 41–44). Fate once again dominates the forces of life.
Ironically Melville set these lines in his canto on Pentecost, the day
when presumably the Christian meaning of pain should become clear.

The Christ story had also seemed promising to Melville as a locus
for the pastoral edenic and as a pattern for man's hopes, but with the
unreality of the final Resurrection phase of the story, it too proves to be
more promise than fulfillment: another idol or illusion for man to hope
in temporarily. Clarel merely disappears: the last line of this next-to-
last canto says that he "vanishes in the obscurer town" (l. 56). Melville
has thoroughly tested the pastoral-edenic-Christ materials as a pattern
that might possibly be incorporated into his symbol. But the pastoral
mode proves to be only a construct of the imagination. It cannot be lo-
cated anywhere among the realities of this world. And the pattern of
Christ's life shows much the same limitation. Melville was to explore
the same pattern again in *Billy Budd*. There as well as here the good
man can embody and emanate temporary bliss and harmony. But the
good man is finally crushed by evil. Any attempt to extend the pattern
beyond death to some kind of resurrection and apotheosis is just as
unreal as the memory of a man in a ballad (*Billy Budd*) or the distant
formalities of an alien liturgical celebration (*Clarel*). The pastoral
edenic and the Christ myth, as antitypes to Melville's massive and de-
pressing symbol, have all the more dramatic an effect for their failure
to be incorporated.

Has Melville actually been building here a symbol for the whole uni-
verse? Does the Holy Land, with Jerusalem and the Dead Sea as its polar
points, stand as a pattern of the imagination for the whole of reality as
Melville sees it? The question has been urging itself with increasing
intensity in the course of this chapter. It is answered affirmatively at
several points in the poem. One striking example occurs in Part IV as
the pilgrims are returning to Jerusalem at night through an increasingly
dismal landscape, "rounding the waste circumference" (IV, xxix, 12).
They come up to the city through the valley of Hinnom, each oppressed

by the events of the pilgrimage and looking forward to taking up life again. The moon lights their way and the menace of the city grows: "Thence uplifted shone / In hauntedness the deicide town / Faint silvered" (ll. 129–31). Their route passes the place where two "glens" converge, "those two black chasms which enfold / Jehovah's height" (ll. 143–44). The landscape conveys the sense again of concentrated evil in Jerusalem. The canto ends:

> The valley slept—
> Obscure, in monitory dream
> Oppressive, roofed with awful skies
> Whose stars like silver nail-heads gleam
> Which stud some lid over lifeless eyes.
> *(IV, xxix, 151–55)*

We have already seen sleep and dream associated with visions of reality. The significance suddenly opens out: Jerusalem is put in the context of the universe. The skies and all the stars furnish a setting that intensifies the pilgrims' impressions of the city. The skies are "awful." The word can be neutral: one's response to something powerful, larger than oneself, but colloquially it is the response to something horrible or terrifying. The final two lines introduce a new and dramatic image—stars like elegant nail-heads studding the lid of a coffin. Melville implies that the pilgrims have the impression of living in a land of death, that the world is dead and the stars are like the nails of the coffin in which it lies. Melville takes quite literally the ancient Christian linking of sin and death. Saint Paul speaks frequently of this body of death, of death as the wages of sin, of death entering man's world through sin. "This star of tragedies, this orb of sins" is dead because its life is vitiated by evil. What Melville has not logically conveyed at the level of plot or theme—the final nature of the universe—becomes overwhelmingly clear at the level of symbol.

Just as this passage provides one of the strongest statements in the poem concerning the total corruption of nature or man's universe, so also another passage must now be investigated for its explicit statement about the total corruption of man himself. The canto on man's corruption is also a "narrator's passage." It is called "prelusive" and introduces the sections attempting to define the nature of the evil all the pilgrims experience at the Dead Sea. Melville opens the canto by describing a series of prints by Piranesi. He probably refers to a series of pictures of fantastic dreamlike architecture called *Carceri d'Invenzione*.[8]

In Piranezi's rarer prints,
Interiors measurelessly strange,
Where the distrustful thought may range
Misgiving still—what mean these hints?
Stairs upon stairs which dim ascend
In series from plunged Bastiles drear—
Pit under pit; long tier on tier
Of shadowed galleries which impend
Over cloisters, cloisters without end;
The height, the depth—the far, the near;
Ring-bolts to pillars in vaulted lanes,
And dragging Rhadamanthine chains;
These less of wizard influence lend
Than some allusive chambers closed.

(II, xxxv, 1–14)

Melville here establishes his model: visual patterns of nightmare quali-
ty, suggesting complexity and horror, torture (the "ring-bolts") and the
terror of death (Rhadamanthus was the stern judge of the Greek under-
world), and the even more terrifying unknown in "allusive chambers
closed." This is not capricious fancy playing to no serious end. In-
stead Piranesi's pictures are a model of "truth" produced by the
"Imagination":

These wards of hush are not disposed
In gibe of goblin fantasy—
Grimace—unclean diablery:
Thy wings, Imagination, span
Ideal truth in fable's seat.

(ll. 15–19)

Here is one of Melville's rare statements of his own esthetic. Imagi-
nation is the primary faculty by which the artist works; its product is
truth presented in an imaginative way, "in fable's seat." Piranesi's draw-
ings are not the sneers or mockery ("gibe") of a twisted fancy, but
direct insights into the heart of reality. Immediately Melville draws his
parallel:

The thing implied is one with man,
His penetralia of retreat—
The heart, with labyrinths replete.

(ll. 20–22)

Man's heart is symbolized in these drawings, full of explicit horrors,
with hidden recesses "allusive" of even greater horror. Another source

is then called in to explain further: "In freaks of intimation see / Paul's 'mystery of iniquity'" (ll. 23–24). Saint Paul uses the phrase in II Thessalonians, 2:7, to express the power of wickedness abroad in the world, restrained for a time by the Lord, but eventually to manifest its power. The phrase appears twice in *Billy Budd*. As Captain Vere and the "drumhead court" are deliberating Billy's case after the testimony has been given, one of the members alludes to "what remains mysterious in this matter." The text continues:

> "That is thoughtfully put," said Captain Vere; "I see your drift. Ay, there is a mystery; but, to use a scriptural phrase, it is a 'mystery of iniquity,' a matter for psychologic theologians to discuss. But what has a military court to do with it?"[9]

The iniquity then is nothing imputed or mistaken, not a judgment that can be wrongly made by the clumsy and imprecise laws of men. It is evil at a deeper level, working darkly, the kind of reality handled jointly by psychology and theology.

The reader must focus his attention upon these etchings and their import. One has the sense of being at one of the centers of the poem, forced by the author not to miss the point:

> Dwell on those etchings in the night,
> Those touches bitten in the steel
> By aqua-fortis, till ye feel
> The Pauline text in gray of light;
> Turn hither then and read aright.
> *(ll. 33–37)*

Melville asserts, then, that the heart of man is truly symbolized by the labyrinths of horror in Piranesi and that Saint Paul's phrase further defines the nature of that evil which is located in the heart of man. The passages taken together point to total corruption of the created universe, including both man and nature.

There remains a final series of statements concerning evil. They point to a more explicit metaphysical explanation of why man and the universe are as Melville sees them. To explain his metaphysics of evil Melville several times uses the word Calvinism. There is no evidence that Melville ever read Calvin's *Institutes*.[10] Therefore Melville's "Calvinism" should be taken in a general sense, standing for a fairly well-defined outlook on man and the nature of the universe. Melville had long been interested in the attractive power of a Calvinistic outlook.

Before he had written *Moby-Dick* he set down the famous passage in "Hawthorne and His Mosses," which says at least as much about the work he was to do as it does about Hawthorne:

> For spite of all the Indian-summer sunlight on the hither side of Haw-thorne's soul, the other side—like the dark half of the physical sphere—is shrouded in a blackness, ten times black. But this darkness but gives more effect to the ever-moving dawn, that forever advances through it, and circumnavigates his world. Whether Hawthorne has simply availed himself of this mystical blackness as a means to the wondrous effects he makes it to produce in his lights and shades; or whether there really lurks in him, perhaps unknown to himself, a touch of Puritanic gloom—this, I cannot altogether tell. Certain it is, however, that this great power of blackness in him derives its force from its appeals to the Calvinistic sense of Innate Depravity and Original Sin, from whose visitations, in some shape or other, no deeply thinking mind is always and wholly free. For, in certain moods, no man can weigh this world, without throwing in something, somehow like Original Sin, to strike the uneven balance.

A number of important items cluster about the phrase "the Calvinistic sense." There are comments here both about man and about the nature of the universe, as well as some indication of how such a world view could dominate a mind like Melville's. Innate depravity and original sin describe man's innermost nature. In a Calvinist frame of reference they signify a total vitiation of man's powers. Not only can man accomplish no lasting good, but the product of all his actions is actually sin, moral evil.

With regard to the universe itself (or Nature, to put it into more transcendentalist terms), Melville's first image is a "physical sphere," the globe of the world. Half of it is dominated by "a blackness, ten times black," a "mystical blackness." Melville will not decide whether Hawthorne uses such blackness merely for esthetic effect (to emphasize the light) or whether it comes from some deeper personal view of the world. Equivalently, however, a decision is made later when he contrasts a real evaluation of Hawthorne with the popular opinion of him as "harmless" and mild, a writer of jolly stories: "This black conceit pervades him through and through."

Melville switches to the image of sunlight and thunderclouds. Melville sees "the blackness of darkness beyond." Switching the metaphor slightly, he declares that the brightness is merely some light playing on the fringes of thunderclouds. The menacing quality of evil and the comparative impotence of good is emphasized.

All these items are important in understanding Melville's conception of Calvinism. Both the inner nature of man and the universe at large are dominated by evil. Melville adds that such a world view can become obsessive—actually that no thinking mind can be entirely free from entertaining the possibility of such a view.

The essay had been published in 1850, but it seems almost programmatic for the speculations that emerge in *Clarel.* When Melville asks questions about the metaphysical foundations for his universal symbol he returns to the same conception of Calvinism, twice through his major spokesman Rolfe, and once through Ungar.

Rolfe's first view of the meek Nehemiah is that he is a man whose spirit has been broken by misfortune. He tells the story of a sailor of his acquaintance whose life followed the same supposed pattern. The mariner was a "hardy" man, "sanguine and bold, / The master of a ship" (I, xxxvii, 24–25). He would often discuss serious topics with his mate, "a man to creed austere resigned" (l. 29). But "the master ever spurned at fate, / Calvin's or Zeno's. Always still / Manlike he stood by man's free will / And power to effect each thing he would, / Did reason but pronounce it good" (ll. 30–34), even though the mate would humbly hold out for the idea "that still heaven's overrulings sway / Will and event" (ll. 36–37). The master's ship comes to disaster on a hidden rock and all hands take to the boats. By the time they are rescued he is the only one alive. When asked how he survived such an ordeal he responds, "I *willed* it" (l. 74). He sets out again, captain of another ship. This time "a whale / Of purpose aiming, stove the bow" (ll. 83–84). Owners now lose confidence in him; even his wife looks at him as one particularly ill-fated; no one will give him charge of a ship a third time. He finally can get a job only as night watchman, watching the bales till morning hour.

> Never he smiled;
> Call him, and he would come; not sour
> In spirit, but meek and reconciled;
> Patient he was, he none withstood;
> Oft on some secret thing would brood.
> He ate what came, though but a crust;
> In Calvin's creed he put his trust;
> Praised heaven, and said that God was good,
> And his calamity but just.
>
> *(ll. 97–105)*

The man has been convinced by the most compelling evidence, the weight of his own experience. So completely broken in spirit is he that he will not even register bitterness. His spirit is totally subdued to "Calvin's creed" which must mean belief in a malevolent fate crushing man's instincts for freedom and self-determination. In the end the mariner even accepts the paradoxical statement of Jonathan Edwards— that God is good even though he seems to mete out punishment and reward without reason or justification.

The story is offered by Rolfe as an explanation of the kind of mentality which could lead to a meek submission like Nehemiah's. But the mariner found his experience so persuasive that Rolfe's hearers—and the reader—must also weigh its probability. Vine, Rolfe, and Clarel ponder the story:

> From the mystic sea
> Laocoon's serpent, sleek and fine,
> In loop on loop seemed there to twine
> His clammy coils about the three.
> *(ll. 115–18)*

Laocoon's situation was not unlike the mariner's. He had warned the Trojans of his fears about the wooden horse that the Greeks had left. This action angered one of the gods who supported the Greek cause, and he retaliated by sending the two sea-serpents (Melville reduces them to one) to strangle the priest and his two sons. The powers of the universe once again punish the man who acts independently. These lines tend to broaden the applicability of Rolfe's story about the mariner. It is not merely the notion of one broken man that a malevolent fate crushed man's free spirit; all three of the main characters now feel entwined in the same "clammy coils."

Rolfe's second attempt to find a metaphysical explanation of the evil universe in Calvinism comes in the middle of Part II, when the pilgrims have come through the mountain wilderness to the gorge of Achor outside of Jericho. They are impressed by its grimness. Nehemiah, who once again stimulates Rolfe's thoughts on Calvinism, points out the fact that the gorge is fit setting for the grim biblical events that took place there. He tells the events recorded in the Book of Joshua, Chapter 7. Shortly before Joshua successfully fought the battle of Jericho, his army had run into a strange reversal. A raiding party of his had been routed and several of them killed by the natives of the region, even though Joshua's party should have been large enough for victory. It subsequently appeared that the Lord was angry with Joshua's people and had used this reversal as punishment. A man named Achan had appropriated spoils of a previous battle, directly contrary to the orders of the Lord. When Joshua found this out he had the man and his whole household, including family and servants and cattle, stoned to death and burned in compliance with the Lord's command. The story once again is about the vengeful destructiveness of the controlling powers of the universe.

Derwent responds by deprecating Nehemiah and the "austere school" of spiritual ideals he has chosen to follow. Rolfe, however, is more perceptive:

> "But here speaks Nature otherwise?"
> Asked Rolfe; "in region roundabout
> She's Calvinistic if devout
> In all her aspect."—
>
> *(II, xiv, 47–50)*

Again he links a malevolent vengefulness of the Deity with Calvinism and finds also a religious tone to the conception. Nehemiah is following no artificially conceived "school," but nature's own way.

The final explicit mention of Calvinism in the poem is Ungar's. In the canto entitled "Of Wickedness the Word," a long section of which has already been discussed, Derwent and Rolfe have been talking about Ungar's pessimism. Derwent, true to character, says that it could easily be melted away if luck would change for him: "The icicle, / The dagger-icicle draws blood; / But give it sun!" (IV, xxii, 7–9). Rolfe interprets Derwent's subtle figure: "You mean his mood / Is accident— would melt away / In fortune's favorable ray" (ll. 9–11). Ungar breaks in: "What incantation shall make less / The ever-upbubbling wickedness! / Is this fount nature's?" (ll. 17–19). He uses the common romantic image of Nature as a fountain, continuously pouring forth life. But the life in this antiromantic case is "wickedness." Ungar speculates whether Nature itself might be so corrupt as constantly to feed evil into the life stream of the world. When asked to explain his notion of wickedness, Ungar passionately recites the list discussed earlier: wickedness is something which leaves no one "whole"; it is not default, nor mere vice, nor even Adam's fall in paradise. It is something deeper and worse, evil enough to evoke in man's imagination the need for a hell to punish the evil he sees in himself. Finally, Ungar says, it is man's perception of the pervasiveness of this evil that "gave in the conscious soul's recess / Credence to Calvin" (ll. 39–40). Calvin's formulation, once it had been articulated, seemed right to many. For a third time in the poem an adequate metaphysical explanation of evil can be stated only in terms of Calvinism. The whole of created nature, including man, is so corrupt that all its products and actions can only be evil and lead to further evil.

THE EPILOGUE

The Epilogue to *Clarel* has caused many problems, best typified in Hyatt Waggoner's recent reactions. "We cannot tell quite what to make of its apparent affirmations. . . . The resurrection images of the final lines come to the reader as a complete surprise. Reading them, we wonder whether we have missed something that would serve as a basis for this final burst of hope."[11]

The Epilogue consists of six verse paragraphs of unequal length. The first is only two lines long:

> If Luther's day expand to Darwin's year
> Shall that exclude the hope—foreclose the fear?
>
> (*IV*, *xxxv*, 1–2)

The meter has been expanded to pentameter, giving a more leisurely (or perhaps more tired) quality to the lines. "Luther's day" may mean a momentary flourishing of piety or Christian faith, and "Darwin's year" seems to indicate the rule of science over men's minds. This is corroborated later in the Epilogue. The present dominance of a scientific mentality need not exclude hope. The last three words are cryptic. The dominance of science need not "foreclose the fear" either. Melville seems to be saying that no matter what the patterns of thought are, or the sources of knowledge—whether science or religious faith—still life will continue to be a mixture of hope and fear. This is a highly ambivalent note to sound where one may expect a resolution. The poet says that both faith and fear are constants.

The second paragraph expands the two categories of faith and science:

> Unmoved by all the claims our times avow,
> The ancient Sphinx still keeps the porch of shade;
> And comes Despair, whom not her calm may cow,
> And coldly on that adamantine brow
> Scrawls undeterred his bitter pasquinade.
> But Faith (who from the scrawl indignant turns)
> With blood warm oozing from her wounded trust,
> Inscribes even on her shards of broken urns
> The sign o' the cross—*the spirit above the dust!*
>
> (*ll.* 3–11)

This is a small scenario with three characters: the Sphinx, Despair, and Faith. The Sphinx, ultimate ambiguity, still presides from her obscure temple despite all the claims to clarity made by science. Despair reacts to this riddle by scrawling a bitter lampoon ("pasquinade") on her brow. But Faith—badly injured though she is—responds to the riddle by asserting a higher reality, a transcendent reality expressed in the italicized phrase. But the ambivalence is maintained. A quick reading may yield the impression that faith holds the final answer, but faith is actually the weaker of the two responses, bleeding as she still is from her "wounded trust" and with her urns now empty and broken into "shards." Despair's "bitter" cynicism is stronger.

The third verse paragraph rearranges the conflicting forces again:

> Yea, ape and angel, strife and old debate—
> The harps of heaven and dreary gongs of hell;
> Science the feud can only aggravate—
> No umpire she betwixt the chimes and knell:
> The running battle of the star and clod
> Shall run forever—if there be no God.
>
> *(ll. 12–17)*

Science, "Darwin's year," is now tested as possible mediator or judge between the conflicting elements in man's experience and is found inadequate. The wisdom of his own age, Melville intimates, is not sufficient for answering the profoundest questions. They shall always remain unanswered: the battle "shall run forever." The condition he states at the end of this sentence, "if there be no God," does not imply either affirmation or denial of God's existence. Melville is setting up a structure here in which problems will ultimately be answered if there is a God and which will remain under debate if there is not.

In the fourth paragraph Melville focuses on the contemporary response or reaction to the problem of ambiguities:

> Degrees we know, unknown in days before;
> The light is greater, hence the shadow more;
> And tantalized and apprehensive Man
> Appealing—Wherefore ripen us to pain?
> Seems then the spokesman of dumb Nature's train.
>
> *(ll. 18–22)*

There is no real accumulation of wisdom then to help modern man solve the conflict. He only sees it more clearly, in more degrees and with a starker contrast between light and shadow, because of the new knowledge he has gained. Modern man's response is merely to echo, to talk about, the problem Nature presents him, to be "the spokesman of dumb Nature's train." The position brings him no peace or satisfaction, but leaves him tantalized, apprehensive, appealing. The question "Wherefore ripen us to pain?" must be taken as parenthetical, an editorial comment to the effect that more knowledge about the problem only causes severer discomfort in the absence of any answer. The word "ripen" is an interesting compression. It is an address to something or someone: wherefore *do you* ripen us. . . . The word is also metaphorical. As the sun brings fruit to ripeness, so Something is bringing man toward his peak of "pain." For the first time in *Clarel* Melville is addressing the malevolent deity directly.

The next verse paragraph comes closer to linking the generalities of the Epilogue with the poem it concludes:

> But through such strange illusions have they passed
> Who in life's pilgrimage have baffled striven—
> Even death may prove unreal at the last,
> And stoics be astounded into heaven.
>
> *(ll. 23–26)*

The second line recalls the subtitle of the poem: "A Poem and *Pilgrimage* in the Holy Land." There have been bafflement and illusions in their journey, and after witnessing the deaths of two pilgrims, Clarel has been pushed to a deeper and more excruciating level of conflict by the death of Ruth. The narrator offers the slim hope that "death *may* prove unreal at the last." With the subjunctive mood Melville once again backs away from affirmation.

The final verse paragraph is the one where Waggoner and others have found the "resurrection images."

> Then keep thy heart, though yet but ill-resigned—
> Clarel, thy heart, the issues there but mind;
> That like the crocus budding through the snow—
> That like a swimmer rising from the deep—
> That like a burning secret which doth go
> Even from the bosom that would hoard and keep;
> Emerge thou mayest from the last whelming sea,
> And prove that death but routs life into victory.
>
> *(ll. 27–34)*

The first two lines offer only the advice to keep the ambiguities clearly before him, even though resignation to the fact of their existence has not yet come. Clarel is left with the tensions and contradictions that have been exposed in the course of the poem; he should focus on them and hope for resignation to them. Then, as an eventual result, "thou mayest" reach some point of reconciliation and fulfillment. The images which build up are indeed resurrection images, but the verb that controls the last two lines is again the subjunctive, again indicating only a possible resurrection. And still another retrenchment from affirmation occurs in the last line of the poem. The word "prove" usually means to establish the truth of something beyond a doubt. In this sense Clarel would be encouraged to keep up the struggle because he will eventually find out that the forces of good are proved dominant. But "prove," closer to its Latin origins, can also mean to test something in order to ascertain its nature or even its existence. And in this sense the line means that Clarel is to keep searching to find out *whether* "death but routs life into victory."

Melville then refuses to answer, verbally, at the thematic level, the question of whether good or evil finally dominates in the universe (though his nuances lean in the direction of evil as dominant). The Epilogue thus forces us back to the body of the poem and its symbolic level, the level where the results of artistic imagination most properly occur, and where Melville's answer is unequivocal.

IV

JOHN MARR AND
OTHER SAILORS

After twenty years nearly, as an outdoor
Custom House Officer, I have latterly come
into possession of unobstructed leisure,
but only just as, in the course of nature,
my vigor sensibly declines.

Melville to Archibald MacMechan,
December 5, 1889

Oh! there is a fierce, a cannibal delight, in
the grief that shrieks to multiply itself.

Mardi

Why did the old Persians hold the sea holy?
Why did the Greeks give it a separate deity,
and own brother to Jove?

Moby-Dick

TWELVE YEARS were to pass between *Clarel* and Melville's next venture into publication, the *John Marr* volume of 1888. The book was printed privately, in a small edition of twenty-five copies, to be used mainly as gifts for friends. Publication was possible since the Melvilles were now at last financially comfortable because of recent bequests. The book gathers the firstfruits of Melville's leisure after his retirement from the Customs Office in December 1885. It is a slight gathering when one considers the many fine poems he had available, but the volume is a deliberately organized one. Melville seems to have intended filling out the picture of his literary career, should any future generation be interested in an author who was by now very nearly forgotten by his contemporaries. He was to publish still another carefully arranged volume of poems three years later and to leave other poetic sequences in various stages of development. These are fascinating materials from a period of Melville's life about which very little is known.

Several poems in *John Marr* have the ring of newness—the musings of an old man—though it is likely that poems such as "The Berg" and "The Maldive Shark" are many years older. The volume was conceived as a whole. Melville divided the collection into four parts, based mostly on the length of the poems: each section contains progressively shorter poems: "John Marr and Other Sailors," the first section, contains four recollections of sailors known and idealized, or simply imagined, from the years at sea some four decades earlier. Each of these poems is preceded by a prose headnote. The second section, "Sea-Pieces," contains two long and peculiarly Coleridgean pieces. The poems in Part III, "Minor Sea-Pieces," show the greatest diversity, though the majority of them are concerned with some aspect of the ominous sea. Finally the short epigrammatic "Pebbles" conclude the volume and perhaps hint at some resolution of the conflicts suggested by the other poems. Each of the poems in *John Marr* can stand by itself, but Melville's careful arrangement suggests that he himself attempted to order the collection so that the poems might mutually illuminate one another. Their common subject, in each case, is some aspect of the sea, and the reader gradually comes to realize that the real subject of the volume is Melville's exploration of the vast sea-as-universe metaphor.

The volume opens with an Inscription Dedicatory to William Clark Russell, a British writer of sea stories. His best-selling *Wreck of the Grosvenor* (1875) is praised by Melville here. Russell had dedicated his 1881 novel, *An Ocean Tragedy*, to Melville and a correspondence ensued which may have given Melville the necessary sense that he still had an appreciative readership. Melville's inscription shows the same artificiality and circumlocutions that characterize all of his prose between *The Confidence-Man* and *Billy Budd*. One feels that Melville had been badly hurt by the loss of his audience and that he offered his prose only gingerly, from behind a brittle and mannered facade, even to such a limited readership as the twenty-five published copies of *John Marr* would find. The praise of Russell is genuine and detailed, but one catches the tone of companionable *bonhomie* rather than real warmth or intimacy. Melville was obviously touched and flattered to find that he still had a reader, but there would never again be as ideal a reader as Hawthorne had been, nor would Melville commit himself in writing so freely to another correspondent as he had to Hawthorne. The dedication is worth mentioning since it suggests a theme that links the four poems of the first section with one another. The poems are written as dramatic monologues. Each poem enters into the mind of a sailor near the end of life, who is aware of vanished brothers and who strives to cope with the absence of those who had given life a context and a meaning. All four poems are attempts to ransack memory for the patterns one's life has had, as that life seems about to end.

The long prose introduction to the first poem develops the situation of a sailor who has married and moved inland, lost wife and child, and at the end of life finds himself marooned with staid farmers who know nothing of his former profession. In its detailed treatment of landlocked "hereditary tillers of the soil" the introduction suggests the same kind of background from which Ruth's father came. Also, in the description of the rotting and forgotten mailbox, it presents the only item from the famous "Agatha" story which Melville ever cared to salvage. Finally it contains some descriptive lines comparing the midwestern prairies to the sea, a similarity that also connects the poem with *Clarel*. But the main function of the introduction is to point to the "void at heart" experienced by John Marr in his final exile among well-meaning but unsympathetic people. His last resort is reverie, the vivid summoning of those shipmates who had been intimate companions at one time. In the midst of a staid and moralistic people he remembers companions of the past as "barbarians of man's simpler nature" (l. 36). The theme of the pagan edenic past will recur in *John Marr* and the word "barbarian" will develop and become useful in characterizing *Billy Budd*. For John Marr these shipmates are all irrevocably dead: not even the "trumps" of the last judgment will bring back these figures of memory. They live only at the summons of his "heart-beat at heart-core," but not in a way that he can "clasp, retain" them. The poem is a clearheaded study of crushing isolation, one of the major concerns of Melville's late poetry.

In another poem Melville has written "an art of memory is . . . to forget," but in the first section of *John Marr* he plies its other art. "Bridegroom Dick" is the monologue of another ex-sailor, a mellow and jovial old fellow enjoying the companionship of his aging wife. He also finds himself compulsively reshaping the past. The tone of the poem is similar to the one that Melville would try to strike in parts of his unpublished collection *Weeds and Wildings*. A surface of "cheeriness" is presented to the reader, though one easily catches clues to panic and despair beneath the surface. Bridegroom Dick is really attempting to relive, through reverie, the excitement and male companionship of his sailor days. His thoughts, too, like John Marr's, veer toward the tragic: these lives of dash and exuberance exist now only in the fragile tissues of an old man's dying memory. If he forgets, they no longer exist. But unlike John Marr, Dick is prevented from melancholy, from full development of the tragic aspects of his reveries, by loyalty to the companion who is still with him. His wife is a simple and sentimental person— "old lassie," "old auntie." She alone has any claim on him, needing him to show himself jolly and "mellow." Curiously many of the poems of *Weeds and Wildings*, the only book which Melville ever dedicated to his wife, seem to come out of the same kind of husband-wife relationship. The notion is given more substance by the fact that Melville seems, at least partially, to identify himself with Bridegroom Dick here: they are about the same age, and Dick admiringly recalls Guert Gansevoort (1. 82)—a beloved cousin whom Melville frequently recalled and whose memory would surface again in *Billy Budd*.[1]

The third monologue of this first section describes a "grizzled petty-officer," still a sailor, dying in his hammock, "attuning the last flutterings of distempered thought" to the rhythms of an old song, "Ladies of Spain." The title presents the sailor's name, Tom Deadlight, which initiates a pun that runs through the poem. A deadlight can be a storm shutter fastened over a porthole, and Tom complains about the fading light. He speaks now of the necessity of sailing by "dead-reckoning"; this is good enough when one is sailing for "the Deadman." This is the sailors' term for Dodman's Point, an English coastal landmark, but in his feverish thought it becomes also an allegorized figure of death. The dying sailor has a grand vision of judgment, in stanza six, stated in terms of a naval review with the "Lord High Admiral" looking on. But then he reduces himself in stature for the last pitiful requests: a bit of tobacco in his mouth and no "blubber" from his shipmates at his burial. The theme of dying alone, with none of those present who filled the remembered life, occurs again.

The final poem of this section, "Jack Roy," may also be taken as a monologue, though the title figure is not the speaker of the poem. Jack Roy is remembered from a point in time many years later, when only the highlights of his personality and a few details remain. Without the first six lines the poem is a lyric re-creation of a life of sheer joy and exuberance: "Vaulting over life in its levelness of grade, / Like the dolphin of Africa in rainbow a-sweeping." But the opening lines put the poem in the same funereal setting as the other three:

> Kept up by relays of generations young
> Never dies at halyards the blithe chorus sung;
> While in sands, sounds, and seas where the storm-petrels cry,
> Dropped mute around the globe, these halyard-singers lie.
> Short-lived the clippers for racing-cups that run,
> And speeds in life's career many a lavish mother's-son.

The song may go on but the singers, one by one, drop into oblivion. The word "but" which begins line 7 would seem to exempt Jack Roy from the common annihilation, but lines 8 and 9 state only that he "should" be exempted. Melville's skeptical subjunctive reappears from the Epilogue to *Clarel*.

The first part of *John Marr and Other Sailors* is Melville's version of "*Où sont les neiges d'antan.*" A swarm of faces come up momentarily— ghosts from Melville's actual or imagined past. But the only existence they have is in his memory, and the only permanence will be their existence in his lines. Melville's four poems are attempts to fix and preserve a youthful vision whose existence depends on him alone. And the corollary of this is just as important—one is left, finally, with nothing but the resources that have developed within himself.

"SEA-PIECES"

The second section of *John Marr and Other Sailors* contains two of Melville's longer poems. They are linked together by their genesis in romantic imagery, though thematically each poem is finally more characteristic of late rather than early nineteenth-century thought.

The first, "The Haglets," develops the story of a ship's compass distorted from true north by a shift in captured swords which are stored in a cabin directly beneath the helm. The miscalculations which result bring the ship to disaster on the rocks. The ironies of the story appealed to Melville: the apparent victor is finally vanquished, and by the weapons of his enemy, long after he had thought the conflict decided. The story has a long history. Melville first heard it on his 1856–1857 trip to the Mediterranean. He recorded these details in his journal: "In the evening Captain told a story about the heat of arms affecting the compass. . . . Arms taken down into cabin after being discharged."[2] Penciled in later, showing that Melville had come back to his original note, is the phrase, "Cap. T's Story of arms."

The first use of the story appears to be a balladlike poem called "The Admiral of the White."[3] Melville never published the poem himself, probably because he felt the materials could be more fully realized. "The Admiral of the White" contains some of the elements which appear in "The Haglets": an English ship is sunk by the arms it has captured from a defeated enemy. They cause the compass to spin, leaving the ship directionless and headed for the rocks. The final stanza, like "The Haglets," creates the image of the admiral and his crew, now suspended and timeless, asleep " 'neath the billows loud."

The story is next told in *Clarel* (III, xii) by an old timoneer who joins the group of pilgrims at the monastery of Mar Saba. Timoneer means nautical pilot, but suggests Timon also, whose career of hardship resulting in bitterness parallels the present instance significantly. The timoneer tells his story to Rolfe. He had pitied a Moor who was fleeing from the plague in Egypt and let him and his chest aboard. Unknown to him the chest contained swords which the Moor was smuggling out of Egypt. The theme becomes a betrayal of personal trust, though the outlines of the narrative are the same. Some details are added which will become important in the final version: the storm at sea with lightning and corposants on the yardarms, "three gulls" following the ship to its doom, the timoneer's designation of the agent of their destruction as "the black lieutenant of Lucifer."

Melville had come close to a final version of the poem, "The Haglets," by May 1885, the date a shorter version of the poem was printed in the *New York Daily Tribune*. Several sections of powerful description are dropped in this version, leaving only the high points of the narrative for the newspaper audience. On the same day, the *Boston Herald* published the complete poem, but still with the old title "The Admiral of the White," and some minor details in this version would still be changed before Melville was satisfied. The history of "The Haglets" is a small window into the more hidden years of Melville's life and evidence against the theory of a long sterile desert between *Clarel* and *Billy Budd*.

The stanzaic form used in the body of "The Haglets" is a variation of the stanza used by Spenser in his *Epithalamion* and *Prothalamion*. Melville's favorite line is tetrameter, which he uses instead of pentameter, with the final line of each stanza a pentameter, not an alexandrine. Melville's pentameter again has all the effects of an alexandrine line. Spenser's stanza is broken into three parts by short lines; Melville breaks his stanza into three parts by using longer lines. One can still see Melville, in manuscript, in galley and page proof, fighting with his printer to indicate these breaks by indentation also.[4] Finally the rhyming in Melville and Spenser is similar, though Melville's is more regular.

In the final version the "gulls" are elevated to the title role and become central figures. They are precisely named. "Haglets" may be just the ornithological *Puffinus major*, but they are also three "small hags." (The reader is reminded of Melville's other references to the three weird sisters in *Macbeth*.) They are the fates and they are also demonic lieutenants of Lucifer as the timoneer had perceived it. Sharks also join the pursuit. The universe becomes remarkably concentrated in its fell purpose: "With one consent the winds, the waves / In hunt with fins and wings unite." Tracking the ship even as it shifts course, the three haglets do not leave until they have actively participated in its final disaster. The rigging, at the climax of the poem, is described as harpstrings where the storm winds moan. Then it becomes a loom where the haglets, now even more explicitly the fates, finish their work of weaving:

> Like shuttles hurrying in the looms
> Aloft through rigging frayed they ply—
> Cross and recross—weave and inweave,
> Then lock the web with clinching cry
> Over the seas on seas that clasp
> The weltering wreck where gurgling ends the gasp.

This conclusion recalls the spinning and weaving chapter (47) in *Moby-Dick*, just as the harp image looks forward to the next poem.

"The Haglets" is a framework poem. The opening lines describe a memorial chapel in terms that recall an earlier romantic idiom: sea-beat walls, lichened urns, "a form recumbent, swords at feet." At the end it is clear that this chapel is deep "in liquid night" at the bottom of the sea. "The wizard sea" holds the admiral and his men "where never haglets beat." The "life" in this city beneath the sea is similar to that described in Poe's poem, and similar also to the description in *Clarel* (II, xxxvi–xxxviii). This last stanza is a small compendium of Melville's imagery, describing a middle kingdom, a limbo, where the dead sleep amidst fantastic creatures:

> On nights when meteors play
> And light the breakers dance,
> The Oreads from the caves
> With silvery elves advance;
> And up from ocean stream,
> And down from heaven far,
> The rays that blend in dream
> The abysm and the star.

Meteor imagery is rare in Melville, but one recalls the hanged John Brown likened to a meteor, as a portent of the destruction that was to sweep over the lovely Shenandoah Valley. The "breakers" are those waves which destroyed the admiral's ship, though now they present an aspect of joy and innocence. Melville's "elves" are here, too; he may have known of the etymological theory that links the word to the same root from which develop such words for *white* as the related Latin word *albus.* The chapter on whiteness in *Moby-Dick* should be recalled here, as should the white monsters of evil found throughout Melville's works. The elves are "silvery," and the light that comes both "up from ocean stream / And down from heaven far" has a ghostly quality to it. The two sources of light are repeated in the last line of the poem, where the word "abysm" appears. It is a rare form of abyss, used because the rhythm of the line would not tolerate "abyss." But six lines into the next poem, "The Æolian Harp," one realizes that Melville was reading *The Tempest.* The play's influence is at work here too. Early in the first act (ii, 46ff.), Miranda recalls fragments of her early years "rather like a dream." (In the lines quoted above, Melville ends *his* story rather like a "dream.") Prospero questions her: "What seest thou else / In the dark backward and abysm of time?" The statement aligns itself naturally with Melville's theory of time and history and with the exercise of memory which characterizes the first section of *John Marr.* The poem is another of Melville's emblems for the world in miniature. A natural disaster is described in a swiftly paced narrative, with the active agents of evil clearly indicated; and the final stanza presents a frozen and time-less image of their triumph. Something very much like peace and joy pervades the scene of man destroyed by the universe. Melville will look for similar clues to the Real in the next poem, "The Æolian Harp."

In addition to the many connections already noted between the two poems in this "Sea-Pieces" section, one might add the fact that both are conceived as framework poems. There is even an interesting kind of symmetry here: "The Haglets" begins with one framing stanza and ends with two; "The Æolian Harp" begins with two and ends with one. Melville seeks a "hint" of the nature of reality from one concrete occurrence in "The Æolian Harp at the *Surf Inn*." Another exercise in memory, the poem is also a major statement in Melville's lifelong argument with romanticism and the transcendentalist view of nature.

The harp itself had been an instrument that functioned in the romantic imagination as proof, in a poetic sense, of an immanent benevolent deity or oversoul. Strings, sometimes made of grass, were stretched over a sounding board or box and the instrument was placed in a window to vibrate as the wind passed across it. The instrument thus functioned as a receiver and amplifier for whatever messages, sweet or powerful, the wind was communicating. Shelley seems to have this image behind stanza 5 of his "Ode to the West Wind": "Make me thy lyre . . . ." One recalls the spirit-wind ambivalence as ancient as the *ruah* of the Book of Genesis and the Latin "*spiritus-Spiritus.*" Shelley's wind is both the meteorological phenemonon and the deity.

Coleridge's poem "The Eolian Harp" describes the instrument as a means of discovering "the one Life within us and abroad," the "one intellectual breeze, / At once the Soul of each, and God of all." And in "Dejection: an Ode," the æolian harp matches his moods, which he is able to bring from sobbing and moans, through agony, to final innocence and joy. Coleridge had dismissed the "agony" phase of his process as merely "reality's dark dream" (l. 95), showing that Coleridge and Melville (in lines 6 and 7 of the present poem) are concerned with the same issue, though Melville is not impelled to find the same resolution.

This wind-harp imagery is pervasive in the nineteenth century. Mrs. Frances Ridley Havergal, a well-known poetess and writer of hymns, had a poem on the subject. A landscape by the American painter Homer D. Martin was called "View of the Seine"; but the fact that its main feature was a line of regularly spaced trees justified its subtitle, "Harp of the Winds."[5] Thoreau also has a poem called "Rumors from an Aeolian Harp," which describes a kind of platonic heaven where all innocence, beauty, and virtue originate and to which they all return. The message of Melville's poem, "less a strain ideal," may be taken as still another of his answers to Thoreau. Perhaps even more in the center of Melville's attention is Emerson's essay "Inspiration," where the æolian harp is a frequently repeated image.

"Ariel" also is a multifaceted word in this poem. Primarily it suggests the fairy in *The Tempest* who arranges the wedding masque for Miranda and Ferdinand. He conjures a scene of edenic beauty and health, without scarcity or want, without even winter between harvest and spring. This seems to be the "rendering of the real" to which Melville objects. But Ariel also appears in Milton, an author equally a favorite of Melville. He is one of the angels in league with Satan during the war in heaven (*Paradise Lost*, VI, 371). Melville's intent here may be that the visions created by Shakespeare's Ariel were demonically deceptive, and that Ariel is also one of the "black lieutenants of Lucifer" found in the history of the poem "The Haglets." Finally, and closer in history, Ariel was also the name of the boat which carried Shelley to his death in the Mediterranean.

Behind the poem, then, is a rich literary history of image and idea. Primarily, to reassert the focus intended by the title, the poem offers evidence to counter the romantic view of reality conveyed by the many poems involving the same image. The major piece of evidence is the derelict hull, waterlogged and drifting. It is more dangerous than shoals, since it cannot be charted, more dangerous than other ships met in the fog, since it tolls no warning bell. The hull has been in the sea for so long—its sides are "oozy as the oyster banks"—that it may be considered one of the ocean's creatures, as an oyster bank is. Bleached, sluggish, dangerous, it has affinities with the iceberg and the shark, to which Melville shall shortly devote separate poems.

The hull is also compared with the "kraken" in line 18. This should be a sea monster existing only in Norwegian legends, but in Chapter 59 of *Moby-Dick* Melville speculated that stories about its appearance might have come from actual sightings of the giant squid. The monster was still on his mind the month the book was published. He wrote to Hawthorne in November of 1851 that both of them should now go on "growing" and writing more: "So, now, let us add Moby Dick to our blessing, and step from that. Leviathan is not the biggest fish;—I have heard of Krakens." The presupposition here is that Melville will go on to search for an even richer symbol, a more adequate "pasteboard mask," for the lurking evil in the universe. The description of the giant squid in Chapter 59 is relevant here: "A vast pulpy mass, furlongs in length and breadth, of a glancing, cream-color, lay floating on the water. . . ." One may break off the description here, and it applies just as well to the derelict hull of the present poem. We shall see more of these sluggish white carriers of destruction very shortly. The present poem molds the reader's feelings for them in *John Marr*. The Æolian Harp's message of "the Real" is terrifying, its music communicates "thoughts that tongue can tell no word of!"

One further note must be added to "The Æolian Harp at the *Surf Inn.*" The name of the ship which sights the hull is the *Phocion.* This may be simply the word needed to rhyme with "ocean" in line 13. On the other hand Melville's admiration for Plutarch's *Lives* is well known; it is, for example, one of the sources for his meditation in "Timoleon." Phocion, the fifth-century Athenian general and statesman, is mentioned at the beginning of Plutarch's life of Timoleon and is given his own fuller biography later on. In the first sentence of his biography of Phocion, Plutarch introduces the metaphor of the ship of state, more precisely the phrase is "shipwrecks of the commonwealth." A few lines later one reads that "Phocion's was a real virtue, only overmatched in the unequal contest with an adverse time, and rendered, by the ill fortune of Greece, inglorious and obscure." A few lines further Melville could have read: "Yet thus much, indeed, must be allowed to happen in the conflicts between good men and ill fortune, that instead of due return of honour and gratitude, obliquy and unjust surmises may often prevail, to weaken, in a considerable degree, the credit of their virtue."[6] The sentiments match Melville's frequent theme of the good man in an evil universe; they match also his feelings of rejection after he had ceased to consider himself a professional writer, feelings which he may have been externalizing explicitly in "Timoleon." But the lines just quoted from Plutarch also suggest larger meanings for the present poem. The *Phocion,* which in this one instance is able to sight the object which could have destroyed it, may be taken allegorically—on the basis of Plutarch—for the commonwealth or the good man, very much in danger of shipwreck in a hostile universe. There may be more here. Emerson was also a great admirer of Plutarch and used Phocion several times as an example of one rising above "external evil" by a stoic heroism.[7] This is quite different from the meaning found in the Phocion story by Melville, and one wonders just how consciously he is here once again arguing with the optimism of the older transcendentalists.

It is likely that "The Æolian Harp" was written quite late in Melville's life. The title indicates that at least the finishing touches were put on it within the few years before it was published. The Melvilles spent some time on Fire Island during the summers of 1885, 1887, 1888, 1889. The favorite place to stay was a well-known resort hotel called Surf House. The Melvilles stayed there at least during the summer vacation of 1889, but Melville seems to have disliked the place and would stay for only a part of the vacation with his wife and daughters. The reference to "the *Surf Inn*" in the title quite possibly links the poem to the place, and it also shows that Melville was still working on the poem during his last years.[8]

The controlling image of this poem, the lyre or wind harp, had been used by Melville in the Preface to his *Battle-Pieces:* "Yielding instinctively, one after another, to feelings not inspired from any one source exclusively, and unmindful, without proposing to be, of consistency, I seem, in most of these verses, to have but placed a harp in a window, and noted the contrasted airs which wayward winds have played upon the strings." The simile is the traditional one of the poet in the grip of forces higher than himself which authenticate the truth of his message. But in *Battle-Pieces*, as we have seen, and in this poem, the larger Reality is not a benevolent Oversoul, nor is it Shelley's wind, creative as well as destructive. The final reality is sheer terror and disaster for wandering man. Finally one realizes that the two long poems in this section, "Sea-Pieces," come to the same thing.

"MINOR SEA-PIECES"

All the poems in the third section of *John Marr* deal with the sea, and all but a few of them take a tragic view of it. Otherwise there is little unity in the section, little evidence of any principle of arrangement, yet the poems all continue to explore the metaphor of the sea as universe set up earlier in the book. From this vantage point, two magnificent poems dominate the section. The first of these is "The Maldive Shark." It is important to note that the Maldive Sea is in the same general area, geographically, where the kraken was spotted in *Moby-Dick*. The name also combines Melville's favorite word, "dive," with *mal* (evil).

THE MALDIVE SHARK

About the Shark, phlegmatical one,
Pale sot of the Maldive sea,
The sleek little pilot-fish, azure and slim,
How alert in attendance be.
From his saw-pit of mouth, from his charnel of maw
They have nothing of harm to dread,
But liquidly glide on his ghastly flank
Or before his Gorgonian head;
Or lurk in the port of serrated teeth
In white triple tiers of glittering gates,
And there find a haven when peril's abroad,
An asylum in jaws of the Fates!

They are friends; and friendly they guide him to prey,
Yet never partake of the treat—
Eyes and brains to the dotard lethargic and dull,
Pale ravener of horrible meat.

The true focus of the poem is on the pilot fish. The shark itself is slightly offcenter throughout. The pilot fish are the grammatical subject of the first sentence and continue to be spoken about for the rest of the poem. It is as if the shark is so horrible, so Medusa-like ("Gorgonian"), that the poet does not allow the reader to look at it directly. The analogues suggested in the chapter on *Battle-Pieces* are necessary for a full appreciation of this poem.

In exploring the sea-as-universe metaphor, Melville discovers several centers of power. They all have characteristics in common: whiteness or paleness, which has a ghostly unearthly quality; a dull lethargy apparently amounting to stupidity; a certain clumsy brutal strength; an appearance that strikes horror in the beholder, the apprehension of instant destruction. The qualities can apply equally to whale, kraken, derelict hull, shark, or (in the next poem) iceberg. One may add to this list, oddly enough, "Milan Cathedral" and probably also "the sphered breasts" of woman in *Clarel* (IV, xxix, 92). All of them, in short, are "pasteboard masks" for the single demonic reality behind them.

The first epithet applied to the shark is "phlegmatical." Melville's interest in the ancient theory of the four humors is well-known, as is his careful reading of Burton's *Anatomy of Melancholy* (Sealts, #101–2). Phlegm was considered to be the cold and moist humor; if it predominated, its subjects were dull, pale, sluggish. Each of the humors was aligned with one of the four elements. The phlegm was identified with the element of water, not inappropriately for Melville's purpose here. Burton's concern was mainly melancholy, but he anatomizes its peculiarities as it happens to combine with one or other of the remaining three humors. He describes the influence of phlegm on the melancholic disposition thus:

> For example, if [Melancholy] proceed from phlegm, (which is seldom and not so frequently as the rest) it stirs up dull symptoms, and a kind of stupidity, or impassionate hurt: they are sleepy, saith Savanarola, dull, slow, cold, blockish, ass-like, *Asininam melancholiam*, Melancthon calls it, "they are much given to weeping, and delight in waters, ponds, pools, rivers, fishing, fowling, etc.". . . They are pale of colour, slothful, apt to sleep, heavy; much troubled with head-ache, continual meditation, and muttering to themselves; they dream of waters, that they are in danger of drowning, and fear such things.[9]

Melville goes on to describe his shark in terms of the phlegmatic disposition, in several instances using exactly the same words that Burton used in the context from which the passage above was quoted: *pale* (twice), *sot, ghastly, white, dotard, lethargic, dull.* Burton does not go as deeply as Melville needs to go here, but among his categories phlegmatic melancholy takes Melville farthest along his way.

To increase the sense of horror associated with the shark, Melville also suggests cannibalism or, more precisely, necrophagy. A charnel house, the shark's throat, is the place where remnants of old burials were stored. The phrase from the fifth line, "from his charnel of maw," must be remembered when the last line is read: "Pale ravener of horrible meat."

A significant metrical feature of the poem is obscured by the way Melville had the poem printed. The rhyme shows that the poem is actually four quatrains. So also does the syntax: full-stop punctuation—periods, semicolon, and exclamation point—appears only at the end of every fourth line. The point might be merely academic, except that the logical climax of such a metrical form—the end of the third stanza—dramatizes the one word "Fate!" Melville has also chosen a lilting anapest as his major metrical foot: "The sleek little pilot-fish, azure and slim." The meter suggests a foolish little ditty. Indeed the "Ditty of Aristippus" in *Clarel* shows the same preponderance of anapests. Here the lightness of the metrical form nicely contrasts with the horror of the subject, just as the beauty of the pilot fish holds the Gorgonian head of the shark slightly off the center of focus.

Though Melville has put two poems between them, one may conveniently go on to "The Berg" at this point.[10] One finds the iceberg and the shark linked, for example, in the central thematic chapter of *Moby-Dick*, "The Whiteness of the Whale." Among the examples of whiteness that strike horror Melville asks the reader to "witness the white bear of the poles, and the white shark of the tropics; what but their smooth, flaky whiteness makes them the transcendent horrors they are?" A footnote develops the shark's particular horror:

> As for the white shark, the white gliding ghostliness of repose in that creature, when beheld in his ordinary moods, strangely tallies with the same quality in the Polar quadruped. This peculiarity is most vividly hit by the French in the name they bestow upon that fish. The Romish mass for the dead begins with "Requiem eternam" (eternal rest), whence *Requiem* denominating the mass itself, and any other funereal music. Now, in allusion to the white, silent stillness of death in this shark, and the mild deadliness of his habits, the French call him *Requin.*

Icebergs appear later in the chapter, where one reads of their effect on the sailor, "beholding the scenery of the Antarctic seas; where at times, by some infernal trick of legerdemain in the powers of frost and air, he, shivering and half shipwrecked, instead of rainbows speaking hope and solace to his misery, views what seems a boundless church-yard grinning upon him with its lean ice monuments and splintered crosses." The scene has its own power in context, but one seems to sense that the iceberg as poetic symbol has not yet reached its full maturity in his imagination.

Coleridge is also mentioned several times in this chapter in *Moby-Dick*, and one may look to the ice floes in "The Ancient Mariner" for some similarities with Melville's poem. But the aspect of the bergs which most terrifies the mariner is their thundering noise, whereas Melville's poem maintains almost entirely the utter silence of an actual dream. With the subtitle Melville explicitly places his poem within the dream vision tradition. The genre uses the device of a dream for allegorical representation of a truth or a view of reality. One finds it in the dreams of the Pharaoh in Genesis 40–41, as well as in the visions recorded in the Book of Daniel. It achieves full development in the Middle Ages. Melville has used the genre before, in "America" in *Battle-Pieces*, where it is an obvious vehicle for allegory. In the present poem he labels the genre unmistakably with the subtitle "A Dream," alerting his readers at the beginning to the possibility of allegory.

Structurally the poem is developed by a thematic progression embodied in one repeated phrase or incremental repetition: "the infatuate ship," "the stunned ship," "the impetuous ship in bafflement." The verb "went down," which follows each of these phrases, has its own climax in line 34, "*go* down."[11] Reduced to its simplest terms, the poem depicts the clash between an object made by men—and carrying men—and an object produced by nature itself. The outcome of the clash is decisive and total, simple and almost instantaneous. The iceberg is white, sluggish and powerful, destructive. As the narrator recalls it, in his meditations at the end of the poem, it is "lumpish . . . a lumbering one— / A lumbering lubbard loitering slow." The poem adds another feature—a malevolent personal quality. There is a hint of a "self" here, in line 29. It exhales a "dankish breath." It is referred to as "thou" and "thy," and the vaguely personal qualities of "lumbering" and "lubbard"[12] are perceived in it. It is finally capable of "indifference."

A source for this poem, and some likely evidence for dating it, appears in the Duyckincks' *Literary World*, No. 284 (July 10, 1852). Melville was interested in the *Literary World* during the 1840s and 1850s. He was a close friend of the Duyckinck brothers, attended their parties for writers and reviewed several books for the paper.[13] This particular issue carried a prominent advertisement for *Mardi*. The article which especially caught his interest and which is the source for "The Berg" is the second half of an account of a polar expedition to rescue the explorer Sir John Franklin. Its leading sentence might have elicited a shock of recognition from Melville: "The year 1850 was eminently disastrous." (Melville had spent the last half of that year rewriting *Moby-Dick* according to his own personal and, as it turned out, relatively unmarketable insights.) The article continues:

> No less than nineteen ships were totally destroyed, and twelve badly injured. On the 19th of June a gale sprang up; the skies grew black, the wind howled loudly through the rigging, and voices were heard in wild confusion as the different crews were securing their ships; but more fearful was the advance of a wall-like front of grinding, crashing ice. Slowly it came; it reached the ships, and then ensued a scene of destruction painful to describe: falling masts, the crushing in of vessels' sides, the ice rearing and tumbling on their decks until they sank beneath its weight, the disorder heightened by a thousand men striving to save boats, clothing, and provisions. With all this, it is a remarkable fact that no lives were lost, the ice, the element of destruction, affording an easy means of escape.

The description is vividly presented. The image of the *"wall*-like" advance of the iceberg is found in both, as is the crushing effect of the ice "tumbling on their decks." The correspondent's description of the ice as "the element of destruction" would have evoked a particular response from Melville's imagination.

The second paragraph of the article in the *Literary World* begins with these two sentences: "We pushed our way slowly along; our minds occupied with the work before us, or during leisure hours in contemplating the many objects of interest around. In shore rose a wall, the sea front of a vast glacier, which extends throughout the length of Melville Bay." The coincidence of seeing one's own name in print in an unexpected place might make any reader stop to ponder the context in which it had appeared and the possible associations it might evoke. Evidence for this conjecture multiplies as the article proceeds. Words and sentiments appear that eventually were transformed from journalism to poetry. The details of the seals and the waterfowl, for example, follow shortly in the article, as does the image which Melville took over entirely of "Towers undermined by waves."[14] Perhaps even the subtitle of the poem and the dream vision convention are suggested by the dreamlike quality of the scene described in the article shortly after the mention of Melville Bay: "The effect of atmospheric refraction was marvelous in the extreme. Objects beyond the horizon would suddenly seem suspended in air, undergoing a variety of strange shapes; they became inverted; the lower parts would descend to the horizon, while the upper, stretching out laterally until they touched, would grow in appearance to an arched bridge."

The writer allows himself a moment of fancy: the scene seems to him "a fit place for the genii of the North." The statement corresponds to Melville's own vague feelings of the personal and the preternatural qualities of the berg in the last paragraph of his poem. One feels very close, here, to the moment when "The Berg" began to form itself in Melville's mind, though it is impossible to say what transformations took place between his reading of the article in 1852 and publication of the poem thirty-six years later.[15]

It seems quite evident that both "The Maldive Shark" and "The Berg" were written sometime in the late 1840s or early 1850s. The two poems are of the same intense emotional quality and symbolism that characterize Melville's other works during these years. It becomes interesting to speculate why Melville included them in a book of poems published forty years later. The fact argues to his conviction of the permanent validity of his view of a universe with powerful symbolic centers of evil. In their own context, in *John Marr*, they fit precisely into the exploration of the sea-as-universe theme.

In a corner of Melville's sea universe there is a paradise, contrasting with the terrors generally described in *John Marr*. But the terrors are real and present, whereas the paradise exists only as a re-creation of memory. "To Ned" is a poem embodying the *ubi sunt* theme; it is a lament for a glorious and vanished past, as well as a statement contradicting nineteenth-century Darwinian optimism.

The remembered paradise is the world of *Typee*, and "Ned" is the Toby of that book. It is also clear that a sufficient number of years has passed since the Typee days for the direction of history and man's evolution to be discernible: "But scarce by violets that advance you trace" (l. 24). When Zeus changed Io into a white heifer in an attempt to evade Juno's jealous eye, he caused violets to spring up wherever she went, compensating her at least with sweet food. The advance of modern man is not similarly favored. In line 20 the poet remembers the island paradise "in violet-glow," but the signs of divine favor have been withdrawn. Melville undertakes to be his own literary critic in this poem, evaluating the effect of *Typee*. The book had published the discovery of "Marquesas and glenned isles," "our Pantheistic ports," but the very act of disclosure had laid open the way for exploitation and destruction by Paul Pry, cruising with Pelf and Trade. Another Eden is lost, another door closed to "young lads" searching as they were. The poem ends with a religious stoicism: one will marvel if he finds a paradise ahead to match the one long past.

It is perhaps the paradise to come that is the subject of "The Enviable Isles." The typical furniture of an Eden is here: greenery, rainbows, palms and the cypress, glades and flocks. One reaches them only "through storms"—the sea-of-life metaphor underlies this poem also.

The poem is Melville's version of "The Lotus-Eaters." One can find the same key words in Tennyson's poem, published more than fifty years earlier. But where Tennyson seems to consider the subject of his poem as a possible state in life or attitude toward life, Melville is creating a possible state of being after life. The quality of life, however, is very nearly the same in each case. Melville adds some pastoral details not found in Tennyson: "green," "rainbowed dew," the cypress, "flocks"; and his poem seems to be based on an early Christian opinion that the souls of the just sleep for the period between their deaths and the Last Judgment. At any rate the prospect of slumber is not presented here as the temptation that it was for Ulysses and his men in Tennyson. The purpose rather is the creation of a place in the mind's geography, out of space, out of time. As it stands, there is only one flaw in the blissful picture: the slumberers are "unconscious" of the loveliness of the setting. Melville builds a paradise and then destroys it.

The subtitle ("From 'Rammon'") hints that there is a larger work projected, of which this poem is a part. The manuscript evidence shows that the poem was first completed as it stands; Melville then attempted to develop a prose framework for it; finally he decided to print the poem by itself in *John Marr*, with the subtitle to indicate that it still needed a setting. The surviving prose section of *Rammon*[16] shows that Melville was experimenting with the kind of thought that could have developed if a newly founded Buddhism had influenced Hebraism during the world-weary period of skepticism in the years following Solomon. A discrepancy of several centuries in the dates of Buddha and Solomon makes the proposed confluence impossible for anyone but a poet; Melville notes at the beginning of the prose manuscript that he is taking "a certain license" here. Central to this prose frame is the figure of Rammon, a fictitious son of Solomon. He is a prince but not the ruler, and thus has leisure for his "despondent philosophy" as well as access to foreign visitors to the court. Rammon is puzzled by the evil which taints all reality: "Evil is no accident." But he is even more interested in the question of immortality. For the melancholy prince "cessation of being was the desired event." (The question of "annihilation" was a longstanding one with Melville, as Hawthorne noted in his report of their next-to-last conversation.) At this point in the development of Old Testament theology there was no firm doctrine on the question of an afterlife. Rammon was free to hope and speculate and to look to what sources he could find for enlightenment. One of the sources is the Buddhist thought introduced into Solomon's court, according to Melville's fiction, by the well-traveled Queen of Sheba. As Rammon tries vainly to come to some conclusion on the subject, a foreign poet arrives at the court. Rammon attempts to engage him in conversation on the question of immortality and the doctrines of the "terrible" Buddha, who he thinks affirms the afterlife of the soul. But soon finding that his visitor is a shallow man with little interest in the unanswerable questions, Rammon asks instead for one of his poems. The poem recited by the visitor is the one we have under consideration.

It now becomes clear why Melville rejected this prose introduction to "The Enviable Isles" and decided to print the poem by itself. The poem *is* a solution to the tensions created by a desire for annihilation and the terrible fear of immortality existing in Prince Rammon. As Melville saw this, he would have had to recast the last part of the introduction, characterizing the foreign poet as something other than a frivolous man of the world. As it stands, the poem presents a resolution to the apparent either/or dichotomy of annihilation or immortality. One can have both, the poem says. The key phrase in the poem, and one that seems to have been present in it from the beginning, is "the trance of God." The Buddhist background is complicated here, as is the shifting and evolving doctrine of Nirvanah. At one point, for example, the whole of reality is conceived as a dream of one of the Gods. Fairly constant, though, is the use of the trance as a technique of removal from the less real to the more totally real.

The famous description of the death of the Buddha, as a process of ascending to the final trance, may have been known to Melville. The following translation was available to him:

> Thereupon The Blessed One entered the first trance; and rising from the first trance, he entered the second trance; and rising from the second trance, he entered the third trance; and rising from the third trance, he entered the fourth trance; and rising from the fourth trance he entered the realm of the infinity of space; and rising from the realm

of the infinity of space, he entered the realm of the infinity of consciousness; and rising from the realm of the infinity of consciousness, he entered the realm of nothingness; and rising from the realm of nothingness, he entered the realm of neither perception nor yet non-perception; and rising from the realm of neither perception nor yet non-perception, he arrived at the cessation of perception and sensation.

Thereupon the venerable Ānanda spoke to the venerable Anuruddha as follows:—

"Reverend Anuruddha, The Blessed One has passed into Nirvana."

"Nay, brother Ānanda, The Blessed One has not passed into Nirvana; he has arrived at the cessation of perception and sensation."

Thereupon The Blessed One rising from the cessation of his perception and sensation, entered the realm of neither perception nor yet non-perception; and rising from the realm of neither perception nor yet non-perception, he entered the realm of nothingness; and rising from the realm of nothingness, he entered the realm of the infinity of consciousness; and rising from the realm of the infinity of consciousness, he entered the realm of the infinity of space; and rising from the realm of the infinity of space, he entered the fourth trance; and rising from the fourth trance, he entered the third trance; and rising from the third trance, he entered the second trance; and rising from the second trance, he entered the first trance; and rising from the first trance, he entered the second trance; and rising from the second trance, he entered the third trance; and rising from the third trance, he entered the fourth trance; and rising from the fourth trance, immediately The Blessed One passed into Nirvana.[17]

The "trance," then, seems to have been the core from which Melville developed first the poem and then the introductory *Rammon*. The real meaning of the poem must have become clear to Melville only as he tried to create an appropriate speaker for it. The importance of "The Enviable Isles," for Melville, was that it gave at least one solution to the question of whether death were annihilation or the beginning of immortality. The poem affirms that neither is precisely true: individual consciousness is annihilated, or rather absorbed into more general being; there is immortality, but no self-consciousness.

"PEBBLES"

Melville concluded his volume with a series of seven epigrammatic statements. They are similar to the later-published "Fragments of a Lost Gnostic Poem of the Twelfth Century" and to some of the short verses at the end of *Battle-Pieces*. The "Pebbles," however, are all related to the sea, and they seem intended as a culmination of the sea-as-universe statements of the whole book. The fifth "Pebble" is spoken by the sea itself: "Implacable I, the old implacable sea." In the proof sheets Melville changed the lower case to a capital for "Sea" here, further intensifying the personification. This Sea takes sadistic delight in its destructiveness: "Pleased, not appeased, by myriad wrecks in me."

The first of the "Pebbles" opposes mere human technique to the more fundamental will in nature:

> Though the Clerk of the Weather insist,
> And lay down the weather-law,
> Pintado and gannet they wist
> That the winds blow whither they list
> In tempest or flaw.

Man is not a natural part of the universe; his knowledge of nature is merely clumsy supposition. The short last line, ending in "flaw," seems to cut off the word "law," the only word which rhymes with it. The first of the two thematic cycles in *Battle-Pieces* is recalled here, and the conclusion that reason's attempts to discern law in the operation of the universe are futile.

The theme progresses in the second "Pebble":

> Old are the creeds, but stale the schools,
> Revamped as the mode may veer,
> But Orm from the schools to the beaches strays,
> And, finding a Conch hoar with time, he delays
> And reverent lifts it to ear.
> That Voice, pitched in far monotone,
> Shall it swerve? shall it deviate ever?
> The Seas have inspired it, and Truth—
> Truth, varying from sameness never.

"Creeds" here, presumably in the sense of fundamental and traditional wisdom, is opposed to "schools," the shifting and evolving rationalizations with which men try to elaborate explanations of these creeds (l. 2). Melville uses his favorite distinction between head and heart. Orm, the medieval writer whose metrical commentaries on the Gospels belabor the obvious at great length, can find Truth only when he leaves "the schools" and listens to Nature in an attitude of reverence.[18] The Truth, here, is inspired by the sea; the conch shell becomes an amplifier of Nature just as the Æolian harp had been.

The progression to be noted in the third "Pebble" is that this sea is to be taken as more concentrated evil reality. The mountains, in spite of their wavelike patterns, cannot produce the same despair:

> In hollows of the liquid hills
>   Where the long Blue Ridges run,
> The flattery of no echo thrills,
>   For echo the seas have none;
> Nor aught that gives man back man's strain—
> The hope of his heart, the dream in his brain.

Puns can yield truth. The fourth "Pebble," in its entirety, reads thus:

> On ocean where the embattled fleets repair,
> Man, suffering inflictor, sails on sufferance there.

Two warring fleets are unaware of a third presence there, equally the enemy of both. Man's role ("suffering") and the conditions of man's existence in the universe ("on sufferance") reinforce one another.

The sixth "Pebble" brings into this concluding section the South American materials suggested by "Crossing the Tropics" in Part III. It also repeats the word used for the Maldive shark—"ravening." This penultimate work in *John Marr* presents the oppositions of the world—destruction and redemption, evil and innocence—in a frozen stasis, with no attempt to dispute or resolve the contradictory forces:

> Curled in the comb of yon billow Andean,
>   Is it the Dragon's heaven-challenging crest?
> Elemental mad ramping of ravening waters—
>   Yet Christ on the Mount, and the dove in her nest!

What resolution there is in the volume comes in the last "Pebble," the final lines of the book. There is acceptance and healing here, even praise ("laud") for the way things are. The explanation for the repeated word "healed" must be that one has faced, recognized, accepted the dangerous reality described at length in *John Marr*.

> Healed of my hurt, I laud the inhuman Sea—
> Yea, bless the Angels four that there convene;
> For healed I am even by their pitiless breath
> Distilled in wholesome dew named rosmarine.

The phrase "the inhuman Sea" appears in *Clarel* (IV, xiii, 7); there it is the force that has schooled the old Timoneer to a sad passivity. Here there is a more active perception of it, a willed acceptance. Like the redeemed Ancient Mariner the poet now blesses the destructive element. This can only be because he now trusts his own perceptions of it. The breath of the presiding angels, the wind that had caused the Æolian harp to shriek in agony, is "pitiless," yet it is at the same time "wholesome." The sea is the destroyer, the element which had turned the tuft of kelp bitter; but the same element, once it is "distilled," is also a refreshing sea spray (*ros marinus*). One can live in a terrifying universe by recognizing it as such, not by hoping and pretending that it is something else.

V

TIMOLEON, ETC.

Shakespeare acquired more essential history
from Plutarch than most men could from the
whole British Museum.

*T. S. Eliot, "Tradition and the
Individual Talent"*

Truth rolls a black billow through thy soul.

Pierre

IN THE FINAL year of his life Melville managed to see through the press still another volume of his poems. *Timoleon, Etc.* was published in a small edition, as *John Marr* had been three years earlier. There is bitterness in such a gesture: one thrusts oneself into print knowing there will be no public. As late as 1921 there were still enough copies remaining in the possession of the family for one to be used as a gift.[1]

Melville roughly divided the book in halves. Twenty-two poems follow the title poem; then there is a blank page and a page with the section title "Fruit of Travel Long Ago," followed by eighteen poems. The book concludes with a separate poem, "L'Envoi." The poems in "Fruit of Travel Long Ago" follow exactly in reverse the itinerary Melville used in his 1856–1857 tour of Europe and the Mediterranean. There are still to be seen among his manuscripts folders entitled "Egypt and Greek Pieces" and "Greece." This last one has "Looked over March 23 '90" penciled across the front of it. The folders as they are now contain only a couple of poems each, which Vincent has collected under "Unpublished or Uncollected Poems."[2] The indications are, then, that Melville rifled these two developing sequences for the second part of *Timoleon.* One puzzle arises from this arrangement: there are several poems in the first part of the book which also concern Mediterranean subjects: "The Ravaged Villa," "Magian Wine," "The Garden of Metrodorus," "The Weaver," "The Age of the Antonines."

Timoleon can also be described according to thematic concerns. For example several poems touch on theoretical questions of esthetics and the activity of the artist—a fairly rare subject for Melville. Several other poems can be called introspective, in the sense that they are concerned with the exact description of subjective psychological states. These include "Timoleon," "After the Pleasure Party," and "In a Bye-Canal." There are historical poems also, in which Melville returns to his lifelong questions about the pattern and sense of history. Many of these are found in the "Fruit of Travel Long Ago" section, where the poet is again a passionate pilgrim recording the insights of his Mediterranean trip.

Timoleon carries the dedication "To My Countryman Elihu Vedder." In a letter to Mrs. Melville, after Melville's death, Vedder acknowledged the dedication gratefully but in tones that seem to indicate that he was not personally acquainted with the family,[3] though Melville had known Vedder's paintings for over twenty-five years. "Formerly a Slave" in *Battle-Pieces* has this subtitle: "An idealized Portrait, by E.

Vedder, in the Spring Exhibition of the National Academy, 1865." More recently Melville had acquired a copy of *The Rubáiyát of Omar Khayyám*, illustrated by Vedder, which was published about 1886. Into this copy Melville inserted a portrait of Vedder and an 1889 review of *Letters and Literary Remains of Edward Fitzgerald.*[4]

The title poem is based on the life of the Greek soldier and statesman whose biography is recorded in Plutarch as well as in Pierre Bayle's *Dictionary.*[5] Plutarch is mainly concerned with determining the causes of Timoleon's various successes—whether they resulted from merit, fortune, "natural causes" or some combination of these three. The Corinthian's main accomplishment was the liberation of Sicily, which had become a warren of loosely confederated tyrants backed up by troops from Carthage. He gradually dislodged each of the tyrants and resettled the towns with Greek Sicilians. He lived the rest of his life in Sicily, refusing to return for honors in Corinth. Early in the essay, as a flashback, Plutarch tells how, twenty years prior to his appointment as general for the Sicilian campaign, Timoleon had been involved in the assassination of his older brother Timophanes, whom he had earlier rescued from certain death in battle. The brother had subsequently developed as a military dictator whose harsh tyranny demanded radical solution. After the assassination Timoleon was surprised to find that the Corinthians had grown cool toward him and that he was savagely denounced by his mother. As a result of this suspicion Timoleon lived in semiretirement for the next twenty years until fortune brought him forward again in the Sicilian crisis.

All of Plutarch's factual material appears in "Timoleon," although the authorial stance is different. Melville moves to the psychological drama implicit in the act of assassination and its results, exploring the conflict of loyalties tormenting Timoleon and, in Section III, the psychology of the mother who favors the ruthless strength of the older brother and would live her life through his glorious rise. But it is in Sections VI and VII that Melville's empathy with Plutarch grows strongest. Timoleon, during his twenty years of semiexile, becomes a late Victorian, going beyond the easy assignment of causes which satisfied Plutarch, to feel the kind of alienation his decisive action had imposed upon him and to wander through a morass of faith and doubt concerning the existence of a providential plan. But Timoleon's life had a satisfactory dénouement, which Melville could not see for his own story. The final section gives "some little sign" from the skies. Moods change, "Corinth recalls Timoleon," and the final phase of his career—to which most of Plutarch's prose is given—is one of public honor and recognition. Melville, unlike Plutarch, ends with a slightly disappointing pettishness or vindictiveness on the part of his hero: "But he, the Isle's loved guest, reposed, / And never for Corinth left the adopted shore."

Melville builds his sections from various numbers of quatrains with a strict rhyme scheme. For the meter he returns to tetrameter, using his own version of the alexandrine for each fourth line. Melville's pen is supple here; the emotions of a man nearly seventy years old are running high.

"Timoleon" has attracted more critical attention than most of Melville's poetry, and it has usually been handled from the biographical point of view. Thus Timoleon's relationship with his mother and his older brother have been traced, with analysis that tends toward the psychiatric, to supposed relationships in Melville's own early life. Such an approach disregards the high points of the poem to concentrate on subsidiary issues. "Timoleon" is a dramatic poem and should be read accordingly. The basic issues are outlined in the first section: the moral ambiguities latent in the unconventionally good action, and the very Plutarchian inquiry into the roles of "providence or Chance" subsequent to such an action. As the drama unfolds, Fortune's wheel turns inexorably to bring Timoleon farther and farther down into despair; but finally a reversal occurs and the hero, in the last section, is reinstated in a higher position than he formerly occupied. There are two points of special interest: the first section where the issues are stated, and the sixth and seventh sections where Timoleon's alienation and despair are most thoroughly dramatized.

Section I presents the subject of the rare and superior virtue, an act that has all of the strength and brazen self-confidence which usually characterizes evil actions. Such virtue, the poet says, is even less supportable by the masses than an equivalently evil action; it is "a strain forbid" in human life. The action leaves one on a lonely peak; "wan eclipse" ensues. Such pure goodness alienates one from his fellow man.[6] The question then arises, very much in the terms in which Plutarch poses it, as to what kind of metaphysical forces then intervene to determine results. The final quatrain of this first section introduces an analogue to intensify the kind of virtuous action Melville has in mind. The phrases "twined with thorn" and "thy garment's hem" suggest parallels between Timoleon and Christ. With this analogy established, even the phrase "cross-tide" in this quatrain becomes a complex Melvillean double entendre. The deed as Melville conceives it is unequivocally good. His point is that ordinary people cannot recognize the good in its pure form; just as the ordinary person, Captain Amasa Delano, cannot recognize the extreme of pure evil when he encounters it in *Benito Cereno*. Ordinary human perceptions cannot register at either end of the spectrum. Another "transcendent deed," one that goes beyond legal formulations of justice to achieve pure justice, will of course function brilliantly in *Billy Budd*, where even the extraordinary individual, Captain Vere, will be unable to cope with it.

Timoleon then becomes a fascinating figure because, unlike Billy Budd, he is both introspective and articulate. One finds here a character with maximum consciousness, reminiscent of the characters that Henry James was at the same time developing as the focal points of his fictions. Timoleon is able to analyze his own deed and its effect, and therefore his character is of major importance in understanding this idea of the "transcendent deed." The idea itself is central to our understanding both of Melville's later thought and of his evolving conception of his work as a whole. Thus, for example, it throws light back onto the dynamics of *Pierre*. Pierre's deeds are motivated by the purest idealism, yet they generate only hostility and his own final destruction in an uncomprehending world. The impact of the action is clear: one has done what seemed noblest and most highly motivated, only to find that the price is incomprehension on the part of those around him, and consequent isolation from the ordinary patterns of human life.

Timoleon's analysis of his situation occurs in sections six and seven, in a kind of dramatic soliloquy when the wheel of fate has brought him to his lowest point. The writing is powerful, indicating that Melville was by no means writing a mere poetic exercise. Timoleon's killing of the tyrant is interpreted solely as fratricide in "the whispering gallery of the world." If investigation of Melville's psyche is desirable, the more interesting opening would be here, where the theme of destruction of the tyrant is similar to that evolving in *Moby-Dick*. "Transcendent" is repeated from the first section of the poem, to describe the kind of virtue which is above "prescriptive morals" and hence unintelligible to ordinary mortals. The deed sets Timoleon apart, in the sense that it alienates him from his fellow human beings. As a result Timoleon is prey to doubt about his own judgment of the tyrannicide; suicide would put an end to the torment. Recoiling from this he chooses exile, "for years self-outcast."

The seventh section records the phases of his despair during the years before the wheel of fortune turns again. The center of Melville's personal interest in the story seems to be here, in the way that a man adjusts himself to a long eclipse. Timoleon's thoughts are spoken. (The manuscript shows that at one point in the evolution of the poem Melville had put quotation marks around the words he gives to his central figure; but, as in "After the Pleasure-Party," they were dropped from the published version of the poem.) Timoleon abandons the attempt to understand or justify his repudiation by fellow human beings or other "second causes." He turns to the "Arch Principals" themselves for understanding of his suffering. Timoleon's quarrel with God here rises to a peak in the sixth quatrain:

> Yea, *are* ye gods? Then ye, 'tis ye
> Should show what touch of tie ye may,
> Since ye, too if not wrung are wronged
> By grievous misconceptions of your sway.

These lines, the powerful dramatic climax of "Timoleon," were added after Melville had made his final fair copy.[7] The poem makes dramatic sense without the quatrain, though the *inquisitio dei* is then flattened out and submission seems quite easily offered. With the lines added, the poem rises to the level of a cry from the heart for the *deus absconditus* to show himself. In retrospect the poem without these lines seems like a truncated pyramid waiting to be capped by this magnificent climax.

The next poem, "After the Pleasure-Party," also has elements of the dramatic monologue. The poem is one of Melville's more frequently commented upon, and has proved to be his most misleading. An early critic of the poem believed the speaker to be a man. Another, on the basis of line 144, took the subject of the poem to be art and the creative process. Still another has left a splendid example of the biographical fallacy by interpreting the poem as a record of Melville's own seduction while on his Mediterranean trip. This was followed by Freudian speculations about Melville's supposed sexual insecurities.[8] The surest method of analysis is to follow Melville's own clues in the poem. He had originally put a "2" between lines 104–5, which was changed to the request for double-spacing in the printer's copy of the manuscript.[9] Structurally, then, the poem has two parts, dramatizing a psychosexual crisis in a mature woman's life and its aftermath. Each part contains a monologue by the woman, with an editorial introduction. The poem then ends with another nine and one-half lines of editorial comment.

It is likely that "After the Pleasure-Party" was well under way when Melville began reading Schopenhauer;[10] indeed the vividly imagined Mediterranean descriptions suggest that at least one stratum of the poem was quite old. But it is interesting to learn that the famous Chapter 44, "The Metaphysics of the Love of the Sexes," in *The World as Will and Idea*, stood on Melville's shelf as he was finishing this poem for the printer. After introducing his theme with a short poem (as Melville himself does), Schopenhauer observes that poets are principally occupied with describing the love of the sexes. He goes on to distinguish rational love from instinctive passion. The latter usually triumphs, though not to the subsequent happiness of the individual involved. Instinct works to select the best mates for producing the next generation, even if it leads to intolerable suffering for the present generation. Sexual passion thus fits into Schopenhauer's larger metaphysics since it is a clear manifestation of the universal will, which is responsible for the evil that is an inevitable part of life.

While the larger arguments of Schopenhauer and Melville are remarkably similar, it is the incidental observations which Schopenhauer makes on the nature of sexual passion which more nearly correspond to the poem. Schopenhauer describes sexual love as "a passion which exceeds all others in vehemence" which has been known to drive people "to the madhouse." He cites Plato's *Symposium* (this is the dialogue containing the myth of the androgyne, upon which Melville based lines 86–94 of his poem). Schopenhauer also speaks of the passion as "constantly introduc[ing] disturbance and confusion into the well-regulated life of man." Some of this confusion arises from what Schopenhauer calls the onesidedness of sex. It is the masculinity of the male precisely corresponding to the femininity of the woman—conditions best serving the physical and temperamental perfection of the next generation—which generates the passion.

The general will is indifferent to the "howling discord" which may result from mismatched personalities. Melville's thought is mirrored precisely in Schopenhauer's: "Nay, not only with external circumstances is love often in contradiction, but even with the lover's own individuality, for it flings itself upon persons who, apart from the sexual relation, would be hateful, contemptible, and even abhorrent to the lover." This is exactly the way Urania sees the man who has attracted her attention. Finally Melville's introductory verses on the blind Amor could easily have been inspired by the prose of Schopenhauer: "the ancients personified the genius of the species in Cupid, a malevolent, cruel and therefore ill-respected god, in spite of his childish appearance; a capricious, despotic demon, but yet lord of gods and men. A deadly shot, blindness and wings are his attributes. The latter signify inconstancy; and this appears, as a rule, only with the disillusion which is the consequence of satisfaction."[11]

Thus Schopenhauer's chapter provides one of the sources for "After the Pleasure-Party" and furnishes evidence that the poem was a product of the author's last years—or, more precisely, that this stratum was clarified only after 1888. For there are other strata in the poem which are much older, e.g., the Mediterranean setting. More immediately interesting, though, is the name of the protagonist, Urania, and her occupation as a student of astronomy. These items take one all the way back again to the first volume of the Duyckinck's *Literary World* (1847). In the issue for February 20 there is a review of a poem by Oliver Wendell Holmes called "Urania: A Rhymed Lesson." The content of his poem and Melville's are entirely different, but in view of the name of Melville's character and especially of the last two lines of "After the Pleasure-Party," the title is apt. In fact the feeling the reader has—that these two final lines do not harmonize with the tone of the rest of the poem—may be explained if they do belong to a very early stratum of the poem, before it took its final shape under the influence of Schopenhauer, and while it still had the tone of a playful cautionary tale suggested by these final lines.

One's interest in this number of the *Literary World* grows as a page is turned and there appears a review of recent scientific articles in the *Quarterly Review* and the *Westminster Review*. This passage is especially relevant:

> During an exceedingly short space of time a great planet has been found to belong to our system; an asteroid between Mars and Jupiter, another fragment of what might be termed the sphere-wrecked world, has also been added to the known bodies of the system; the great telescope of Lord Rosse has determined the question of the nebular theory. . . . The discovery of the new planet, Le Verrier, is, perhaps, the crowning glory of science,—nothing has given a more tangible proof of the nobility of the human intellect. . . . It appears that Mr. Adams, a young Cambridge mathematician, was engaged upon the perturbations of Uranus at the same time.

The penultimate phrase is immediately related to the theme of "After the Pleasure-Party." Melville found other phrases, as well as ironies, in the passage. The "sphere-wrecked world" would have particularly harmonized with his philosophy, and "Lord Rosse's monster telescope" would be remembered for the third paragraph of his sketch "I and My Chimney." In this issue of the *Literary World* Melville could have read a sonnet by John S. Kidney about a group of young girls whose innocent beauty derives from the fact that they are as yet sexually unawakened;

the poem concludes with the statement that they are "as yet uncon-
scious of the anxious thought, / Which, with another year, may to your
hearts be brought."[12] The lines are an accurate prediction of Urania
herself.

A final source which Melville used in the development of "After the
Pleasure-Party" derives from the rich tradition of British erotic poetry.
One of these poems, "Songs" by John Suckling, is so close thematically
and even verbally that Melville must have known it.

The dramatic situation of the "crafty boy" setting an "ambush" in "a
stranger land" is basic to Melville's poem. One can easily find several
other verbal correspondences.

Central to the tradition of erotic poetry is the metaphor of the bee
and the rose. Thomas Carew developed the sexual implications of the
metaphor most fully and explicitly in his poem "A Rapture" (ll. 55–78):

> Then, as the empty bee, that lately bore
> Into the common treasure all her store,
> Flies 'bout the painted field with nimble wing,
> Deflow'ring the fresh virgins of the Spring,
> So will I rifle all the sweets that dwell
> In my delicious paradise, and swell
> My bag with honey, drawn forth by the power
> Of fervent kisses from each spicy flower.
> I'll seize the rose-buds in their perfum'd bed,
> The violet knots, like curious mazes spread
> O'er all the garden, taste the rip'ned cherry,
> The warm firm apple, tipp'd with coral berry;
> Then will I visit with a wand'ring kiss
> The vale of lilies, and the bower of bliss.

Melville's Urania was aware of this tradition; she sees herself as a rose
in search of her own bee: "How glad, with all my starry lore, / I'd buy
the veriest wanton rose / Would but my bee therein repose" (ll. 77–79).
The obviously erotic lines are spoken by a woman of great delicacy,
and Melville was sensitive to the possibility of having her uncharacter-
istically cheapen herself. Just before the poem went to the printer Mel-
ville crossed this line out of his manuscript and had Mrs. Melville erase
it from her fair copy: "Tho' but a plunderer and no more!"

The bee-rose imagery, with erotic connotations, also appears in
Hindu poetry. For example, in Thomas Duer Broughton's *Selections
from the Popular Poetry of the Hindoos* (1814) there is a lyric de-
scribing a young man contemplating a beauty spot on the chin of a

beautiful girl. He feels it is a trap set to catch foolish fellows like himself, a rose set to trap a bee. The relevant stanza, as translated by Broughton (p. 121), reads:

> How that dark little spot on thy chin
> Enhances thy beauty and power!
> 'Tis a rose, and the poor bee within,
> Deceived, lies entranced in the flower.

The similarities between this poem and the lines under consideration from "After the Pleasure-Party" become interesting in the light of Hennig Cohen's discovery that Melville owned a copy of this book.[13]

Melville's "After the Pleasure-Party," then, has roots that indicate a long slow development. Placing the poem in the intellectual tradition helps to avoid the extra literary biographical voyeurism which would posit sexual ambivalences in Melville on the sole basis of such works as this. This is not to deny that the poem is vividly imagined and deeply felt: that is its greatness. But such an inquiry does avoid what Northrop Frye in his essay on Emily Dickinson has called the vulgarity of biographical conjecture.

The theme is stated in the epigraph: a kind of madness will eventually overtake one who proudly "exempts" himself from the human need for love. The theme is reflected by an earlier title given to the poem, "A Boy's Revenge." The two parts of the poem, through narrator's editorializing and Urania's monologues, show the stages of this revenge: the torment and indignity of the "awakening" within a few hours after it actually happened, and the aftermath, perhaps some months later, when the narrator views her in the process of making a critical decision in order to cope with her new emotional life. In making Urania a well-educated woman, Melville has created an articulate speaker who can find a wide range of analogues for her situation: Sappho and Vesta, Cassiopea; she can draw from Boccaccio and Plato as well as from astronomy and religion. The woman has the kind of maturity and self-possession that allows her to analyze her emotional life with some objectivity. She can even create an ironic pun on her situation in the phrase "iron-bound verge!" (l. 15) The rage which she deplores would seem to be tragic insight enough, as the dawn breaks with its disillusioning light, and its emblem of cold sterility, "yon bramble above the vale" (l. 103; cf. l. 71).

The quieter and deeper tragedy of the aftermath is still to be investigated. Urania's brief monologue in the second part of the poem focuses on a critical moment of choice between two options that seem open to a woman who has experienced the rage of passion and the need for love, yet who feels herself too old or too aloof for marriage or an affair. The options come into focus for her in the images of two women, both presented to her in works of art: the picture of the Virgin Mary, which she has contemplated in a "convent shrine," and a statue of the "helmeted" goddess, Pallas Athene, before whom she now stands. Athene's legendary birth, when she sprang fully armed from the head of her father, emphasizes her traditional masculine qualities, as does her association with war. She is also goddess of wisdom and the intellect.

The choice of alternatives, as Urania comprehends them, has already been made. The first option was submission to all that is represented in the picture of the Virgin Mary—not only belief but acceptance of the veil of a nun devoted to the values here represented. But the mood is resisted as "languid," "nerveless." Instead she chooses to be inspired by the values embodied in the "pagan" statue of Athene. The image is "less benign," mighty, "self-reliant, strong and free." The values are those of intellect. The goddess is armed, both for protection and for aggression. The image promises transcendence—removal from "sexual strife" and "peace." The price seems to be loss of femininity, possibly even a hostility toward sexuality in any form. The editorial voice concludes that such a mood is foolish. A decision such as this cannot bring permanent peace, "while Amor incensed remembers wrong." Her suffering is projected into the foreseeable future; tragedies are not permanently resolved by contemplating works of Art.

Several other poems of considerable interest remain in Part I of *Timoleon*. Some of Melville's poems on art are to be found here. (These poems are treated later along with Melville's other statements on the art of poetry.) For the rest the section seems at first to be a miscellany. It is only after careful reading and rereading that an impressive thematic unity begins to emerge. One point of entrance is provided by the theme of a lost leader. The mood is evoked of a society or an organized group from which the leader is mysteriously and unaccountably missing. The theme will immediately be seen to have theological implications.

The most explicitly theological poem in this group is called "The Margrave's Birthnight." The last two lines are so obviously sacramental that they force the reader back through the poem for hints about the identity of the Margrave and for elements of the poetic statement Melville is attempting. Phrases like "his birthnight, in mid-winter, / Kept year after year" strongly suggest Christmas. He is the "host," the "lord" and then "the good lord": were he there, his presence would be "gracious." "His people" (l. 21) were called "his vassals" at an earlier stage in the development of the poem; the change allows an ecclesiastical meaning. These items suggest that Melville is exploring the ceremony of the Christmas Mass, which he presents as having become merely a meaningless "old observance." The people are unaware that the throne has long been vacant, and they are "mindless" about the significance of this absence. Like most stories that take place once upon a time in a land far away, this poem conveys an insight valid in the present: the formalized ritual goes on long after it has become meaningless.

The same sense of loss pervades "The Night-March." An army marches in utter silence through the night. The imagery is entirely visual: "And beaming spears and helms salute / The dark with bright." The poem may have been inspired by the death of Lincoln and the loss of his influence during the rest of the Civil War; the final stanza reads:

> Afar, in twinkling distance lost,
> (So legends tell) he lonely wends
> And back through all that shining host
> His mandate sends.

But there are words like "spears" and "legions" which set the poem in ancient times and would have made it jar slightly with the rest of *Battle-Pieces*, if indeed it is that old. The parenthetical "so legends tell" introduces a great uncertainty about whether the leader actually does still guide and direct. There is something aimless now about the marching army: "Over boundless plains they stream and gleam— / No chief in view!" With the word "boundless" the poem seems to transcend earthly politics and hint at the vast empty spaces of the universe.

Continuing his exploration of this theme of the lost center, Melville develops the portraits of two modern seekers after meaning. One is called "The New Zealot to the Sun." Identification of this new zealot is easy; Melville's manuscript shows an earlier canceled title, "The Scientist," an identification which is confirmed in the last stanza.

The scientist has a sense of history and reduces the whole cultural thrust of several millenia into a few lines. One of the major convictions expressed is that, fundamentally, religion is an Asiatic invention and foreign to western ways of life. Adulation, abasement, sacrifice characterize the religious impulse, and such qualities prepare the way for the worst kind of men ("Cain") and their drive for military conquest and domination. A second conviction is that religion leads men into unreality, into the pattern of myths and "delirious" tirades, which finally resulted in the West in "Calvin's last extreme." For all its insistence on light, religion has never been able to banish "frauds and fears." Up to this point the speaker may be taken as fundamentally in agreement with Melville, for all these views can be documented in other poems. In the last stanza, however, the "zealot" finally shows his fanaticism: the parvenu nineteenth-century scientist asserts that his special kind of knowledge is about to display a power greater than religion, to illuminate the mysteries it has left unanswered, and indeed to give rational explanations for religion itself. Melville's reservations about science have not changed since *Clarel.*

The second portrait of a searcher for meaning is called "The Enthusiast." One seems to find here some of Melville's deepest struggles and triumphs, to see him speaking *in propria persona;* but the Enthusiast is a fanatic, just as much as the New Zealot is. The two poems stand as companion pieces, as portraits of two kinds of extremist. Melville's sympathies are much more with the second figure than with the first. Melville's granddaughter remembers the poet's writing desk: "and pasted on one side wall, well out of sight, was a printed slip of paper that read simply, 'Keep true to the dreams of thy youth.' " [14]

The first two stanzas propose one question, stated in several ways: when the ideals of youth die, must one inevitably become a financial being, one motivated mainly by economic desires and necessities? The question is put strongly, four different times, whether youthful magnanimity, "spirits that worship light," heart, faith, Truth, on the one hand, shall yield under the influence of "Time" to ignobility, "interest," worldliness, the "loud gregarious lies" of the marketplace. The temptation was strong for Melville throughout his life, as both his and his wife's letters show: "Dollars damn me." The question that further develops must have been personally felt: whether one who has remained idealistic shall yield to the temptation at least to envy those who have gone on to financial success, the "palterers of the mart." The Enthusiast's response in the third stanza is to resist. The mature responsibilities that fetter one are simply to be cut—an apparently hard doctrine (reminiscent of Emerson's poem "Give All for Love"). Melville's poem ends with the final heroism of which man is capable: "Though light forsake thee, never fail / From fealty to light."

Another short poem reinforces the theme of "The Enthusiast." Melville first called it "Giordano Bruno," then "Counsels," and finally took a phrase from the poem itself to call it "Lone Founts" which emphasizes the sense of isolation that pervades this volume. It is similar in some ways to the Epilogue to *Clarel* and might have been connected with that poem at one time. The unusual use of the word "foreclose" is similar in both places. "Founts" also corresponds to the extensive use of fountain imagery in *Clarel*. This poem offers only a methodology without content: look at the present from the standpoint of the past and the future. No indication is given of the "never-varying lore" that thus becomes available.

Melville is trying unsuccessfully to find the springs of vitality. In this context the skillful ditty of another poem, "Lamia's Song," takes on a special poignancy: "Descend, descend! Pleasant the downward way . . . / How pleasant the downward way!" The theme of la dolce vita is lightly touched, but it is a small flash momentarily illuminating another of life's options, making the darkness around it seem all the more dark.

The impossible fidelity to the dreams of one's youth is the theme of a poem called "C———'s Lament." An earlier version of the title spelled out the name as Coleridge, but the attempt to read the poem as an insight into Coleridge distracts one from the true lines of thought in the poem. The manuscript shows that several other names were considered. More significantly the titles are all written in pencil over an originally untitled poem in ink.

The poem is based on deep personal grief which was transformed into art. The final stanza continues the thematic exploration of loss and isolation found in this section of *Timoleon:*

> But will youth never come again?
> Even to his grave-bed has he gone,
> And left me lone to wake by night
> With heavy heart that erst was light?
> O, lay it at his head—a stone!

The poem immediately following seems intended as a companion piece. The title, "Shelley's Vision," may show some reason for the association of Coleridge's name with the previous poem. This time the manuscript shows "Shelley" or at least "S" to have been a part of the title from the beginning. Thematically the poem is an exercise in the process of transition from self-hatred to "self-reverence." The scenario calls for the speaker to pelt his shadow, his substitute self, with stones. Then in a moment of illumination the shadow self is seen to represent Saint Stephen, demanding reverence rather than contempt. Though the vision is attributed to Shelley, nothing similar can be found in his writings. One realizes again that this poem projects a thin disguise for Melville's own emotions.

Is one's philosophy determined by shifting moods within oneself, or are there objective reasons, philosophical data for such a view? The question is one to which Melville frequently turns, and he does so again in "Fragments of a Lost Gnostic Poem of the 12th Century." The poem is a restatement of the fundamental Melville philosophy.

> Found a family, build a state,
> The pledged event is still the same:
> Matter in end will never abate
> His ancient brutal claim.
>
> . . . . .
>
> Indolence is heaven's ally here,
> And energy the child of hell:
> The Good Man pouring from his pitcher clear,
> But brims the poisoned well.

The poem asserts a position directly contrary to transcendentalist optimism, indicating quite clearly one of its sources. Howard P. Vincent cites the close parallel to "Reading" from *Walden:* "In accumulating property for ourselves or our posterity, in founding a family or a state, or acquiring fame even, we are mortal; but in dealing with truth we are immortal, and need fear no change nor accident." [15] For the first two lines of his poem Melville's gnostic agrees with Thoreau; in lines 3 and 4 he disagrees: matter will *never* abate its claim. "Matter" in line 3 was at one time "Apollyon." This figure occurs in the book of Revelation (9:11); his name means originally "The Destroyer," and he is spoken of there as "the angel of the bottomless pit." In Bunyan he is the foul fiend who assaults Christian on his way through the Valley of Humiliation. The name could stand, but Melville's change focuses the poem more clearly on Gnosticism and defines the aspects of Gnosticism intended by the title. Dualism is at the basis of gnostic thought: on one side are the powers of light, beauty, goodness; these are opposed to darkness, evil, matter. Such a dualism has no place in Transcendentalism; Melville once again records his opposition. [16]

In the second quatrain or fragment Melville's gnostic thought takes on a Calvinist coloration. The preference for indolence over energy can be, ironically, derived from the theology of Calvin. Human action, because it proceeds from human nature, is always sinful; thus inaction is preferable to action. After this beginning the last two lines are initially a surprise, though the logic is unassailable. The "Good Man" may be Christ; if so, even his actions only added to the sum of worldly evil. Elsewhere (*Clarel*, for example) Melville succinctly expresses a characteristic view of the subsequent history of Christianity: the actions of Christ, which seem so beautiful, have led to endless rancor and bloodshed.

The quatrain also shows that Melville had been reading William Blake. (The first two lines could have been written by Blake.) Melville had acquired Gilchrist's famous *Life of William Blake* (1863) seven years after it was published.[17] It is likely that this date furnishes a *terminus a quo* for dating the poem. In *The Marriage of Heaven and Hell* the Devil cites the following as errors: "That Energy, called Evil, is alone from the Body, and that Reason, called Good, is alone from the Soul" and "that God will torment man in Eternity for following his energies." On the contrary, according to the Devil, the opposites are true, among them that "Energy is the only Life, and is from the Body; and Reason is the bound or outward circumference of Energy." The ironies generated by Blake's choice of speakers would have appealed to Melville.

"Fragments of a Lost Gnostic Poem" still contains one more problem. Gnosticism as a movement was dying by the third century of the Christian era. Melville may have felt that the philosophy remained as an underground movement, to emerge from time to time—as part of theories such as Calvin's, in the example he gives here. But the "12th Century" of the title points to something quite specific. One gradually comes to trust Melville's allusions as precise.

We can follow the instances of gnostic dualism throughout the history of Christian piety. The idea of supreme good and evil powers, with the creation and governance of the world in the hands of the evil divinity, has proved an attractive and persistent solution to the problem of suffering and evil. When Gnosticism as a historical movement has died out, the idea became embodied in the doctrines of the Manichees, and is still most associated with them. The Paulicians, whom Melville read about in Pierre Bayle's *Dictionary*, were the next to propose this dualism. The Paulician movement was exceptionally long-lived, enduring from the fifth century well into the Middle Ages, even though its advocates were constantly persecuted by the church. In the twelfth and thirteenth centuries the local Slavic Paulicians were called the Bogomils, and their missionaries carried the dualistic ideas into Russia and, more to our purpose, into western Europe and the south of France.

It is here, I believe, that we are to find the subject matter for Melville's poem on "gnostic" doctrines. The movement developed there among the Albigenses and was persecuted bitterly by Rome and the bishops with excommunications, executions, and a holy war between northern and southern French nobility that is said to have wiped out the flourishing Provençal civilization. In one day, in 1245, over two hundred of the heretics were burned. Most of their documents were destroyed—hence Melville can speak of "Fragments of a *Lost* Gnostic Poem." The identification of the subject matter of this poem is made complete by the phrase "the Good Man." The Albigensian movement was carried out mainly by a small corps of dedicated ascetics and preachers. They were called the *bons hommes* or *bons chrétiens*. It was these *cathari* who were considered to have achieved the highest Christian perfection. In this context of a particular gnostic movement, the poem gains in clarity and depth. The first quatrain can be seen as a statement of the implications contained in gnostic dualism, with Matter as the principle of evil continually reasserting its dominance. The second quatrain renders the inability even of the perfect man to create goodness in an evil world. One notes then the centrality of this poem in Melville's later writings. It is connected with the Christ of *Clarel* and with other achievers of the transcendent deed who culminate in *Billy Budd*.

Some justification for isolation and despair, for the dejected mood, can be found in the fact that the famous "Monody" appears in this section of *Timoleon*. The subject is Melville's lament for the death of Hawthorne.[18] The first stanza of the poem appears to have been written shortly after his death in 1864, when Melville was writing *Battle-Pieces*. The second stanza, with its reference to the word "vine" may have been written while he was developing his Hawthornesque character of Vine for *Clarel*. "Monody" thus touches Melville's life and writings at several points: it can be taken as a summary statement of his relationship to Hawthorne; it can be compared to the Civil War poems he was writing at the same time; and part of it has interesting connections with *Clarel*. Melville's final touch was to place it in this first section of *Timoleon*, and the uncertain biographical and bibliographical details assume secondary importance and merge with the more general purposes of the poem in its published context. Melville's sense of meaninglessness and decline takes the form of a lament for the kind of love that had satisfied one completely and then was lost forever.

> To have known him, to have loved him
> After loneness long;
> And then to be estranged in life,
> And neither in the wrong;
> And now for death to set his seal—
> Ease me, a little ease, my song!

By wintry hills his hermit-mound
The sheeted snow-drifts drape,
And houseless there the snow-bird flits
Beneath the fir-trees' crape:
Glazed now with ice the cloistral vine
That hid the shyest grape.

The time sequence in the first stanza compresses four movements or stages into a very short space: the long loneliness, the moment of knowing and loving, the unintelligible estrangement, and the final sealing of this stage by death. Artistry thus finds a pattern for chaotic personal emotions. Walter Bezanson has cited a letter to Duyckinck where Melville speaks of Hawthorne's works in the metaphor of the vine producing grapes.[19] Hawthorne was "the vine which is to bear grapes that are to give us the champagne hereafter." The allusion is one of the bases for finding similarities between Hawthorne and the character Vine in *Clarel.* In the second stanza of "Monody" the terms of comparison have shifted slightly. The vine and grapes are no longer Hawthorne and his works; though the comparison is not clearly worked out in the poem, it seems to be the exterior appearance ("vine") of the man hiding his "shyest" interior.

There is another allusion to Hawthorne in this second stanza: the "snow-bird" (l. 9) is from "The Snow Image." Two small children have decided to build a child out of snow to be their companion. They are not at all surprised when the image comes to life and dances and plays with them, gleaming with health and otherworldly beauty, though clothed only in white feathery garments like the snow itself. Snowbirds come to cluster about her, though they avoid the earth children, as if to attest to her preternatural character. The children believe in her without the slightest question and indeed their mother comes to believe also. It is as if this faith in the possibility of creating such a wonder has actually enabled them to do so. The villain is their father, "an excellent but exceedingly matter-of-fact sort of man," afflicted with a "stubborn materialism," who insists on dragging the lightly clad child into a warm room before the fire, where she immediately melts. Melville summons the same snowbirds to Hawthorne's grave, to attest the same otherworldly quality and to suggest an analogue for the vanished moment of rapport he found with him.

The lost moment of friendship is not the only reason for the feelings of isolation and despair. Into this section of *Timoleon* Melville put four poems on the nature of art and artistic creation. These poems—"The Weavers," "In a Garret," "Art," and "The Marchioness of Brinvilliers"—

will be discussed later. For now it might simply be noted that, according to these four poems, the very nature of the creative process itself requires long isolation and a struggle with materials that are recalcitrant and demanding. By their very nature the materials with which the artist works, the kind of knowledge of good and evil which becomes available to him, and even the creative process itself all tend to set him apart from the ordinary flow of social life. In other words these poems fit very exactly into the sequence of this section.

The section ends with a strange poem called "Herba Santa," resolving the conflicts at what appears to be an incredibly superficial level. Melville proposes pipe smoking as a cure to the world's problems, both physical and metaphysical. The tone of the poem recalls "Bridegroom Dick" and some of the poems he left unpublished in *Weeds and Wildings*, where the persona is conceived as a simple-minded reminiscer who has thoroughly stepped out of the stream of life and can barely remember its passions and doubts. The argument is that tobacco, "herba santa," can bring the sense of peace and fellowship which the teachings of Christ have been unable to accomplish. Pipe smoking is a better sacrament than the Lord's Supper. Having rejected the message once "on a higher plane," man accepts the god now in this more homely form. The tone is pompous, but playfully so. The apparent abandonment of the search for solutions to problems which have no solution, in this poem and others like it, is only a temporary strategy. The inquiry is lifelong for Melville.

FRUIT OF TRAVEL LONG AGO

Melville's trip through Europe and the Mediterranean countries in 1856–1857 furnished him with probably the most important pool of experiences for his later career. The journal he kept during the trip[20] was supplemented by extensive reading in travel literature and considerable meditation on the experience. The major result was *Clarel*, in 1876, but in his mind Melville remained a passionate pilgrim of these parts all his life. The trip was constantly reworked, and the last result is a series of poems entitled "Fruit of Travel Long Ago." Each poem can stand separately, but one should attend to the overall structure which is twofold: Melville has arranged the poems in exactly the reverse order of his itinerary of 1856–1857; the poems also handle progressively older civilizations. Geographically the section is divided into six poems on Italy, ten on Greece and the Grecian isles, and two on Egypt.

At the heart of each of the three sections is a poem investigating human attempts on the part of the culture to construct a model for the divine. The last poem, to omit for the present the concluding "L'Envoi," describes an actual epiphany, experienced in the desert of the oldest of the civilizations. There are, in other words, many reasons for saying that Melville considered this section as a whole.

The first poem, "Venice," incorporates recollections of Melville's whaling voyages in the Pacific with the more recent trip to the Mediterranean. The poem sets up a parallel between coral animals and the builders of the city of Venice. Coral is found in the Mediterranean— there had been a brisk trade in it for centuries; but Melville chose to focus on the Coral Sea in the South Pacific instead. This apparently trivial point furnishes a key to the poem. "Venice" is an investigation of the energy that drives action *wherever* it is found: in a youthful experience or in one from his mature years, in some small marine animals or in men, at one end of the world or another. Man builds in a "shallower wave" and is a "prouder agent"; but still the action is "kindred" to that of the coral anthozoa. They work in the same way and all are driven by "Pan's might," or "Pantheistic energy of will." Two streams converge. "To Ned" had identified the south sea islands as "Pantheistic ports" and described them as a now-vanished Eden. Melville also has Schopenhauer in mind, where "will" is the most fundamental component of being. For Schopenhauer this cosmic drive is evil. Both men and coral animals are its mindless instruments.

The next poem, "In a Bye-Canal," is also inspired by the ancient city of Venice. As a description of strong fear of the female and her tempting sexuality it can be compared with *Clarel* (IV, xxix, 92ff.). The episode evokes a sense of terror (though the dénouement is playful) not matched by any experience in the world of merely physical danger or even in the world of moral danger exclusive of sexuality.

The incident seems an insignificant one, an instant's glance from a lovely woman, taken to be a solicitation; but it gains power from the analogues introduced in the speaker's attempt to explore his own profound reaction: Jael, the basilisk (who destroys by a mere glance), whaling, the desert, and Ulysses. This last analogue is the most fully developed and furnishes the resolution of emotions. Jael appears in the Book of Judges, Chapter 4. She had agreed to hide the fleeing Sisera. After treating him with more hospitality than he had requested, she hammered a tentpeg through his head while he slept and brought his enemies in to look at him. Jael also appears in Melville's "The Bell Tower," a short story which has some similarities with "Venice." In *Clarel* (II, xxxvi, 91–105) her name is in a list of seductresses who have used their wiles to destroy men.

There is another parallel with the second book of *Clarel*. The speaker, a tourist in Venice, glimpses the seductive eyes "between slats." In *Clarel* (II, xxvii, 11ff.), the central figure is momentarily drawn into a relationship with Vine which has homosexual overtones. The attraction begins as the travelers are dismounted for a rest period and sitting in the shade: "As were *Venetian slats* between / He espied him through the leafy screen." One concludes that the theme of "In a Bye-Canal" concerns the possibilities for destruction of the self which are latent in an irregular sexual relationship.

From these established premises the poem proceeds to two other dangerous situations: the physical arena of whaling (ll. 17–19) and the moral "desert" where "Envy and Slander" threaten destruction. Neither of these dangers can stand comparison with the psychic dangers of casual sexuality. The poem ends with a magnificent justification of this insight: the heroic Ulysses also fled such a temptation; he must have known what he was about, since his mother was the goddess of love. (Melville rewrites Greek mythology here to make Ulysses the son of Venus.)

A second kind of moral danger is explored in "Pisa's Leaning Tower." There is a convergence of the themes of the preceding two poems—the complex beauty of the things man has built and his potentialities for moral self-destruction. This poem also has some interesting parallels to "The Bell-Tower." The same emphasis is found in the character of the master builder and the Babel temptation. The final paragraph of "The Bell-Tower" can serve also as an illuminating commentary on this series of poems about man the builder: "So the blind slave obeyed its blinder lord; but, in obedience, slew him. So the creator was killed by the creature. So the bell was too heavy for the tower. So the bell's main weakness was where man's blood had flawed it. And so pride went before the fall."

A clear pattern begins to emerge in these Italian poems at the beginning of "Fruit of Travel Long Ago." The themes of moral evil and man the builder develop and intertwine. The next two poems continue the pattern. "In a Church of Padua" recalls the American Protestant's reflections on the Roman Catholic confessional. For Melville it presents a unique situation in which some of the mysterious depths of evil can be sighted.

The poem develops through progressively shorter stanzas. The first stanza presents a remarkably compact description of the confessional box. The conditions for disclosure of one's own evil to another human being are given in the next stanza: the two parties must be mutually anonymous, not only through sight but through the sound of the voice.

"Punctured holes minutely small" serve to make the "low-sieved voice" anonymous. In the last stanza Melville returns to a favorite metaphor—that the knowledge of reality, of evil, is accessible only to those who dive. The diving bell is not the neatly engineered and comfortably out-fitted bathysphere of today, so romantic a part of our fantasies because of the films of Jacques Yves Cousteau. It is instead the huge and clumsy shell, weighted and open at the bottom, in which laborers were sent, for extra pay, to dredge in the mud at the bottom of a river or harbor. The work was dark, confining, and terrifying, and the allusion is apt.[21]

The next poem is a companion piece, almost the obverse of "In a Church of Padua." Melville contemplated the famous Duomo di Milano, and the theme of man the builder recurred. The cathedral appears as an example of man soaring toward an ideal of heavenly beauty and therefore contrasts with the diving imagery of the previous poem. The poem explores the attempts of this later Roman culture to come to a definition of the Deity.

"Milan Cathedral" demands careful reading: what Melville seems to say is not what he actually says. The cathedral is glimpsed, "through . . . a rolling sea." The signpost is familiar—we are once again in Melville's metaphysical depths, where Pip had his visions and where the pilgrims of *Clarel* imagined the weird City of the Dead to be under the Dead Sea. Materials associated with "The Berg" are also brought into play early in this poem. The impression becomes clear for the reader by line 7, where the cathedral's pinnacles "gleam like to ice-peaks." The cathedral is "old" and "White." These are qualities of the iceberg, the shark, the kraken, the whale, and the derelict hull. More similarities ac-crue. A prominent feature of the cathedral is that

> Erect upon each airy spire
> In concourse without end,
> Statues of saints over saints ascend.

Compare these lines with "The Berg":

> Along the spurs of ridges pale,
> Not any slenderest shaft and frail,
> A prism over glass-green gorges lone,
> Toppled; or lace of traceries fine,
> Nor pendant drops in grot or mine
> Were jarred, when the stunned ship went down.
>   (*ll.* 10–15)

At a sufficient distance the physical details of cathedral and iceberg merge, and they are indistinguishable. Melville's cathedral is another one of his massive white symbols for the malevolent deity. The fact is reinforced by the "forks of fire" (l. 11) which appeared earlier on the spars and rigging of the *Pequod* during Ahab's demonic baptism ceremony. In the present context the curious final line of "Milan Cathedral" is not the simple pietism it seems, but an ironic statement that fits Melville's philosophy completely. It is ironic that man himself could create one of these symbols. The others had all been the work of nature.

The Italian section of "Fruit of Travel Long Ago" closes with a long narrative poem called "Pausilippo." Superficially it looks like a poetic version of a sentimental Pre-Raphaelite painting: two beggars, a young girl and a broken man, sing a pathetic song for a group of tourists. The poem is more remarkable for the fact that it contains a song (reminiscent of Browning's "A Toccata of Galuppi's") within a skillfully paced narrative.

The key to the poem rests in the man's name, Silvio (ll. 27, 54), and in the subtitle, "In the Time of Bomba." Bomba was the nickname given to the tyrannical Ferdinand II, who suspended the civil rights of the Neapolitans in 1848. (Melville crossed out "1848" at the head of the manuscript version of the poem.) Ferdinand received the name Bomba a few years later when he bombarded rebellious cities in Sicily into submission. "Silvio" is based lightly on the historical figure Silvio Pellico, a minor Italian dramatist who was sentenced in 1822 without a trial to fifteen years of imprisonment for liberal political opinions. "Pausilippo" is really Melville's private version of the story of this man; actually Pellico spent his declining years writing and being comfortably taken care of by the Marchesa di Barolo. One of his writings was a book on his imprisonment which Melville may have known. Pausilippo, now a suburb of Naples and usually written "Posilipo," is named from the Greek meaning "easing pain."

Silvio appears in *Clarel* in a context which illuminates this poem. The pilgrims are speculating on the meek and pious docility of Nehemiah. In trying to find similar temperaments Rolfe speaks at length about a captain whose ships were twice wrecked. Though he could not find anyone to entrust him with a third and was reduced to menial labor, he never lost a rocklike trust in God, even though all joy had drained from his life. Rolfe concludes the description with another analogy:

> So Silvio Pellico from cell-door
> Forth tottering, after dungeoned years,
> Crippled and bleached, and dead his peers:
> "Grateful, I thank the Emperor."
>
> (*I, xxxvii, 106–9*)

In "Pausilippo," then, Melville is dealing with a central character who has been crushed by the fates, and yet still refuses to say "NO! in thunder." Melville has distrusted the type ever since his famous letter to Hawthorne of April 1851. He will continue to probe the mystery of such a response even in the dying words of Billy Budd. The narrative section of the poem sketches the character of Silvio along these lines: "a quelled enthusiast," "unmanned," "spiritless and spent." In this context the girl's song, which is about the older man who is now reduced to being her ward, becomes more interesting, as do the concluding five lines of the poem. The girl's song underlines the fact that, contrary to its name, Pausilippo has done nothing to ease the pain of Silvio. The last five lines extend the girl's thought with Melvillean universality: nor does heaven care much about the sufferer's pain.

The six poems of the Italian section of "Fruit of Travel Long Ago" form a unified whole, comprising a small anatomy of Melville's moral and imaginative universe, with issues of pride and sexuality, the possibility of suicide, the crushing of the defiant man—a universe presided over by still another of his massive white symbols for divinity.

These poems are followed by a Greek section composed of ten poems. The Melville papers at Harvard University still contain a folder marked "Egypt and Greek Pieces." The word "rejected" is written on the folder, and only two poems remain in it: "The Continent" and "The Dust-Layers."[22] Both are interesting examples of Melville's poetry, neither significantly above nor below his ordinary poetic skill. Their exclusion confirms the importance of finding the principles of selection and arrangement in this section.

Melville's technique in this Greek section can be described as cinematographic. The poet begins with a panoramic view from far off, then moves in to individual items and finally to details. The first two poems try to describe the individuality of the Greek landscape itself, the principle of its uniqueness. It does not have the "picturesqueness" of old Europe (Melville analyzes "the picturesque" as an esthetic quality at length in the *Burgundy Club* sketches). Instead he finds a "sculptural" purity and grace in "The Attic Landscape."

The same technique is used in "The Parthenon," a sequence of four short poetic sections depicting the beauty of the building from progressively nearer points of view. The subtlety of form, the balanced and frozen tensions of the frieze, are perfectly realized. Finally, with "The Last Tile," the judgment can be stated:

> Ictinus sat; Aspasia said
> "Hist!—Art's meridian, Pericles!"

Ictinus was the architect of the Parthenon, built during the era of Pericles. Aspasia, one of the two famous Greek courtesans mentioned in this poem, was the mistress of Pericles after he had divorced his wife. After the death of his legitimate sons, Pericles had his sons by her legitimated. The word "Pericles" is direct address: therefore the most talented people of the age are imagined as being at the scene when the Parthenon is completed, and as realizing how historic the moment is.

The final perception into the pure beauty of this landscape is recorded in the four-line "Greek Architecture":

> Not magnitude, not lavishness,
> But Form—the Site;
> Not innovating wilfulness,
> But reverence for the Archetype.

The poem is an attempt to comprehend Greek esthetics. "Archetype" recalls Plato, who is mentioned in a short poem immediately preceding, "The Parthenon": "Repose that does of Plato tell." The passionate pilgrim is an acute and thoughtful observer.

The next four poems in the Greek series dive deeper into the older themes of Melville's poetry. The first, "Off Cape Colonna," is like a miniature sonnet. The Grecian landscape is still beautiful, but ironies in it are now made manifest.

William Falconer (1732–1769) was second mate on a vessel sailing from Alexandria to Venice. The storm Melville alludes to, off Cape Colonna, killed all aboard except Falconer and two others. Falconer profited from the experience by writing an immensely popular poem, "The Shipwreck" (1762, with enlarged editions in 1764 and 1769, and numerous reprintings throughout the nineteenth century). Melville could have written the ironic ending of the man's life: the last ship Falconer was on left the Cape of Good Hope with everything in fine order and was never heard from again. In "Off Cape Colonna" the poet commemorates Falconer's first and most famous shipwreck. The idiosyncratic addition is that Grecian architecture has adorned the deadly cape and thereby furnished a reminder (massive and white) of the actions of the malevolent gods themselves.

The next two poems extend and develop the human participation in evil. In the first, "The Archipelago," the islands are seen to be uninhabited and thus

> They still retain in outline true
> Their grace of form when earth was new
> And primal.

Melville's powers are superb here. Each stanza is a dramatic construction of three rhyming lines capped by a short amphibrach. A typical pun illuminates the center of the poem:

> Each isle a small Virginia fair—
> Unravished.

The final stanza repeats the theme of "To Ned": the passionate pilgrim now allows the Grecian isles to be as strong a reminder of Eden as his favorite Marquesas:

> 'Tis Polynesia reft of palms,
> Seaward no valley breathes her balms—
> Not such as musk thy rings of calms,
> Marquesas!

The theme of the lost Eden is developed in "Syra (A Transmitted Reminiscence)." Here the loss is by sheer atttrition through man's mundane activities. The point of view is once again that of the alert tourist who recalls the history of Syra, one of the isles of the Cyclades. Settled originally by Greek fugitives from the Turks, it is another Eden turned into "a mart" by man. Melville describes a situation midway between Eden and a totally fallen world. Trade on Syra is conducted haphazardly, with informality and gusto. No real wharves or warehouses have yet been built; the rich and diverse goods are spilled in scattered piles on the beach to be haggled over at leisure. All in all the traveler receives a pleasant impression of this bazaar. The world needs these concrete reminders of "Saturn's prime" (the Greek equivalent of Eden). The poem ends:

> I saw, and how help musing too.
> Here traffic's immature as yet:
> Forever this juvenile fun hold out
> And these light hearts? Their garb, their glee,
> Alike profuse in flowing measure,
> Alike inapt for serious work,
> Blab of grandfather Saturn's prime
> When trade was not, nor toil, nor stress,
> But life was leisure, merriment, peace,
> And lucre none and love was righteousness.

Once again there is irony in the poem, accessible only through the subtitle. Even as he wrote, Melville was aware that this small Eden had now vanished. By 1875 Syra had become much more populated; business was more organized, and the island Melville was remembering was the chief commercial center in its part of the Mediterranean.

Two short poems bring this Greek section to a conclusion. "Disinterment of the Hermes" is a plea for the spiritual or the esthetic over the economic. In form the poem is another miniature sonnet, quite similar to "Off Cape Colonna." This is rare for Melville, for he makes up his own verse forms and then usually breaks the mold. The "forms divine" continue a line of allusion to Plato that can be traced through this Greek section, where the author by way of experiment tries to assume the basic ideas of Plato. Platonic idealism in its technical sense is a mode congenial to Melville. Here and in "Greek Architecture," with its "reverence for the Archetype," he experiments with Platonic concepts directly: the work of art is a concrete analogue for the eternally true; the only way that humans can know the eternal forms is indirectly, through these glimpses caught in the physical and sensible patterns. A personal stamp is put on this Platonism by Melville's directional signals in line 7. It is not "dive" here, but its counterpart on land—"to dig for these." Melville's final realities are chthonic; one gets closer to the "forms divine" at the depths of the physical universe.

The title of the final poem in this Greek section, "The Apparition," duplicates the title of the key poem in *Battle-Pieces*, though the similarities end there. A different figure dominates each of the three stanzas successively. A model is constructed in the first stanza: Constantine's total conversion caused by his vision of a concrete object in the heavens. The second stanza contrasts this with one's vision of the Parthenon, also a concrete object beheld aloft, but which cannot convert the cynic—even though it very nearly does. A key to the difference is in the word "trophy." The Parthenon is a manmade object, a "trophy"; even though it is "Adam's best," it still does not have the power to sway that the "supernatural Cross" has. It is interesting to note that Melville completely changed his mind on this point in the process of writing the poem. At an earlier stage of composition the parallel had been perfect, Parthenon and Cross both had equal power to convert; lines 7–8 had read:

> You strike with awe the cynic heart
> Convert it from disdain.[23]

The lines were reworked and then rejected. What seems to have happened was that the poet's initial enthusiasm for the Parthenon gradually faded after the experience as his more basic philosophy reasserted itself, but in its present form line 8 still justifies the final stanza. One's cynicism cannot be pure and total in view of such awesome beauty as that produced by Man. If art cannot convert, at least it may mollify one's cynicism.

The two poems of the final Egypt section are among Melville's most profoundly theological statements. The passionate pilgrim has arrived at a center, a source—at the roots of the western religious tradition. These poems recall the desert imagery in *Clarel*, but the locale is now farther south and more intensified. Both are based on the idea that western civilization received its idea of God primarily from Moses, and that Moses constructed his ideas and images of God in Egypt, which were highly conditioned by the landscape and atmosphere. The first describes the formation of the concept of "Shekinah," the visible manifestation of the presence of God.

The first stanza of "In the Desert" places the center of intelligence within the passionate pilgrim. He is strangely disoriented by "this veritable Noon." The ocean again serves as one of the analogues for the desert atmosphere. The other analogue is the long reddish gold pennon of Saint Denis, the "oriflamme," which the early kings of France bore into battle. More recent French military history is summoned to justify the traveler's sense of having arrived in a weird and awesome place, where the atmosphere is too burning and numinous to permit ordinary human life: even the soldiers of Napoleon could not stand this for long.

The last stanza begins with the "Sanctus" of the communion service, the song of the angels who stand in God's presence in Isaiah (6:3) and Revelation (4:8). The definition of Shekinah is begun: "Immaterial incandescence"—a combination of the purely spiritual with the physical. This light is "the effluence of the essence" of God. The imagery may allude to recent electrical experiments and inventions. God's presence is the unseen power, transforming the physical world into brilliant illumination at the point where the two meet. This may seem quite orthodox, a use of traditional materials such as those that Rudolf Otto was shortly to bring together in *The Idea of the Holy* (1917). One must notice, however, that the destructive aspects of this deity are emphasized throughout, making the poem fit also with Melville's particular kind of heterodoxy. Light has always been an analogy used to describe God; this poem gains its power from the inquiry into the nature of that light.

"The Great Pyramid" continues this probing of the source of the Judaeo-Christian concept of God. The manuscript shows that Melville had once considered adding a quotation from Acts 7:22 to the title of the poem: "And Moses was learned in all the wisdom of the Egyptians." He must have felt that the poem was sufficiently clear without this quotation and that a New Testament citation might have distracted the reader from the idea of God found earlier in the Old Testament.

The poem is a subtle recapitulation of much of this section and of the elements of Christian theology. The themes of man the builder and the search for the center recur; Melville's interest in the philosophy of time and history and his symbols for the divinity come to a climax here. The basic image of the first stanza is from the important nineteenth-century science of geology, so thoroughly rendered in the figure of Margoth in *Clarel*. The "strata" of the earth, visible in such mountain outcroppings as the Scottish "Grampians," were yielding data about the history of the earth and the life forms on it which required serious re-valuation of current religious opinion. So also the pyramid was built in visible "strata"; but it is a poetic insight rather than a scientific datum that these strata also yield theological information. Melville's "glaciers" come into play in the second stanza as the immensity of the pyramid manifests its ability to dwarf the human into insignificance. So also the word "blank" connects with the powerful "dumb" of the final stanza to complete the complex of feelings associated with berg and with similar massive white structures. The pyramid is another awesome, sluggish and malevolent image for the final powers in the universe. "Lording it" (l. 15) is another of Melville's complex puns which helps develop the same theme.

The fourth stanza contains a remarkable implication. The pyramid stands impervious to the sandstorms that have tried to destroy it: "You —turn the cheek." The phrase is Christ's: "whosoever shall smite thee on thy right cheek, turn to him the other also" (Matthew 5:39). The implication is that the subject of this poem is truly the origin of the notion of God—as if the God of Christian theology who is later to manifest himself in Jesus already embodies the characteristics which will there be displayed. The point is subtle, but the last stanza will show that this is precisely what Melville is saying.

In the next-to-last stanza Melville dives into the depths again, into the "rumored" passageways and chambers within the pyramid. Once one has gone too deeply into the mystery, come too close to its operational center, he is destroyed: like the Ancient Mariner he is cursed with Death-in-Life; or like Pip, goes mad—"comes out afar on deserts dead / And, dying, raves." And in the last lines it is clear that this pyramid symbol stands in Melville's imagination as the Being who has dominated western civilization through its whole course and who was defined as God in the early vision of Moses. It was men who created the symbol: "Craftsmen [who] . . . / Usurped on Nature's self with Art." But so powerful was it, so far did they reach (or so deep did they dive) that they *imposed* an idea of supreme power on subsequent civilizations by their massive construction. Melville is unmistakably clear. When Moses received the first indication of his mission to the children of Israel, from the Voice within the burning bush, he asked for the name of the speaker. The reply was, in the version used by Melville (the King James Version): "I AM THAT I AM: and he said, Thus shalt thou say unto the children of Israel: I AM hath sent me unto you" (Exodus 3:14). The unusual capitalization is preserved in this final stanza. Melville's point, then, is that Moses' idea of God was conditioned, defined, by his experience in Egypt, by the fact of his having been born and reared among these huge pyramids, already into their second millenium when he lived among them. For this particular kind of deity the author can experience awe and even a kind of reverence, but nothing like love or respect or adoration.

    Timoleon ends with "L'Envoi," a poem appropriately spoken by a returned traveler. His experience has given him more insoluble questions than answers. He has visited Kaf, the mountain in Islamic mythology which rings the world and is the abode of the powers of evil. Melville had used this same mountain as a powerful aspect of his Civil War geography in "Look-Out Mountain." Araxes is the modern Aras river originating in Turkey. Contemporary archaeologists had found canals and other traces of a large population and an ancient civilization on its banks. Ancient writers had said it flowed into the Caspian Sea, and recent research had shown that this was once true. The river passes by Ararat, the mountain where Noah's ark had landed according to legend. Until modern times its peaks were inaccessible, supposedly to protect the remains of the ark from prying eyes. In *Clarel* (I, xvi) the city of Jerusalem is immense and vaguely powerful, "an Ararat." After visiting these fabulous lands, the Sire de Nesle returns to his only center, his wife, overburdened with knowledge and experience.

    The sentiment of "L'Envoi" is reminiscent of the final stanza of "Dover Beach." Arthur Stedman, a frequent visitor in the Melville household in later years, says the poem was addressed to Mrs. Melville.[24] And this was the place to which Melville as traveler returned several times himself: the smaller more controllable universe of domestic life, the home presided over by the loving wife who in her simplicity (presumably) does not disturb herself about the larger insoluble questions which men ask. The move is a retreat, a capitulation, "one lonely good"; yet it is a good, a solid if smaller reality. The masculine characteristic—at once its strength and its weakness—is "yearning infinite," according to the premises of the poem. The traveler, on his return, feels "blest to fold but thee." Yet the reader of *Timoleon* cannot believe that the passionate pilgrim has been totally domesticated.

VI

WEEDS AND WILDINGS

Evil is unspectacular and always human,
And shares our bed and eats at our own table.

W. H. Auden, "Herman Melville"

So, therefore, that mortal man who hath more
of joy than sorrow in him, that mortal man
cannot be true—not true, or undeveloped.

Moby-Dick

WHEN MELVILLE died he left still another collection of poetry very nearly ready for the printer; but it was not actually published until 1924, in the Constable edition of his complete works. Each poem had been carefully written out and the dedicatory prose passage was finished. Four tables of contents are extant among his manuscripts, showing that conscious selection and arrangement were a necessary part of the act of composition here also.

The dedication, "To Winnefred," is obviously to his wife, Lizzie. Less obvious is Melville's reason for choosing this nickname; I believe that this is the only place where it appears in his works. Possibly etymology, a constant source of interest and verbal irony for Melville, explains the choice. "Win–" originally meant "joy" (it develops from the same root as the Roman "Venus"); for the etymology of "–fred" one need go no further than the German for the meaning "peace," though it is possible to work one's way back to the goddess "Frigg," the counterpart to the Roman Venus in the Scandinavian pantheon. Joy and Peace, then, and married love, are the concepts that are to prevail in this book of poems. It would be an effort on the author's part to achieve this, and relics of the effort are scattered throughout the manuscript. One poem is altered from a dark and tragic view of life to a joyous one by the change of merely two words (see "Profundity and Levity"). And according to Robert Ryan's studies of the four tables of contents, "In the Pauper's Turnip-Field" was not to have appeared in the final version of the book.[1] The explanation for this omission must be that it is the only other poem in the series that presents an explicitly dark view of life. This book then is atypical of Melville's work: a conscious attempt to see life through rose-colored glasses. The expression is not the usual cliché in this instance, for the last part of *Weeds and Wildings* contains about a dozen poems on the subject of roses.

What were the pressures shaping the composition of such a book? Mrs. Melville's letters to her relatives, throughout her married life, are full of wifely concern for her husband's health and mental well-being. Furthermore it seems clear from Melville's manuscripts that in later years his wife was his only secretary; it was she who prepared the fair copies of all his poems for the printer. It is quite conceivable, in view of the letters, and of her close association with all his poems, that she was able to elicit at one time a book that was consciously designed to please her alone. If one is correct in these surmises, then the presence of Melville's wife is important in this book from the beginning. She is, in a way that is explicitly stated, the ideal reader to whom the poems are addressed, just as the Hawthornes were conceived as the ideal readers for *Moby-Dick*.

One approaches this nearly completed book with the expectation of some complexity and intensity; and I will state at the outset what remains of course to be proved—that the achievement is one of considerable beauty as well. In the dedicatory preface Melville flirts momentarily with his favorite concepts of mortality and immortality; he even alludes to the likely immanence of his own death—"that terminating season on which the offerer verges." But the flirtation with death is resisted. The focus shifts instead to the re-creation of an idyll. The date is "the fourth day of a certain bridal month, now four years more than four times ten years ago." The Melvilles were married on August 4, 1847. The addition of forty-four years gives us the date of the Preface as 1891, the year of Melville's death. His premonitions turned out to be valid. The location is "Arrowhead," the farm near Pittsfield to which the Melvilles moved in 1850. The flower which dominates the Preface is a weed, the red clover, which still grows in the backyard there.

The exercise in memory is detailed: Lizzie referred to melting snowflakes on a gathered bunch of clover as "tears of the happy." Melville repeats the phrase. The mood will be totally idyllic: one finds poems only about flowers and weeds, small animals, beautiful children, and rustic celebrations. The idyll has its queen: Lizzie becomes "Madonna of the Trefoil"—the poet's humorously pretentious name for the ordinary clover. Melville mentions that he would "yearly remind you" of the fact that he had, only once, found "that rare four-leaved variety accounted of happy augury to the finder" and that this was the morning of their marriage day.

The Preface is remarkably vigorous for a man in his seventies. It shows, I believe, where the center of peace was in Melville's life, a haven to which he would return, like the Sire de Nesle, for respite from his metaphysical journeys. The Preface shows that it is now this emotional center itself which is to be explored, a center without which, perhaps, the darker explorations would have led only to personal disintegration. *Weeds and Wildings* is therefore essential to a complete understanding of Melville's universe.

The atmosphere owes much to Hawthorne's *Mosses from an Old Manse*. Indeed Melville is trying consciously to duplicate the mood of the earlier book. Melville's famous essay on *Mosses*, published in the *Literary World* in August 1850 sprang from deep within his own psyche, and the impact of the book was to remain with him. When he came to collect his own short stories, a piece was included familiarizing the reader with Arrowhead, much as Hawthorne had offered to introduce his readers to the Old Manse in his preface. Hawthorne attempts to give unity to his collection of stories and sketches by describing a setting from which they all presumably issue. The sketch is an attempt to share something very personal with the reader, a sense of the home where the Hawthornes spent the first very happy years of their marriage. Part of the atmosphere includes the birds, animals, flowers, and shifts of weather at the Old Manse—many of the same subjects that Melville includes in this selection of poems forty years later. To leaf through the *Mosses from an Old Manse* again is to realize how profound and how lasting was Hawthorne's influence on Melville, even as he was concluding *Weeds and Wildings*.

This book has two main sections: "Weeds and Wildings," which has three parts, and "A Rose or Two" with two parts. Part I of "Weeds and Wildings" is entitled "The Year"; it begins with a poem anticipating spring, works through the seasons in order, and ends with two poems celebrating rural Christmas observances. There are seventeen poems in this section. They seem amateurish in many places, either like poems of a beginner or like an experienced writer who is going through a season of drought, forcing himself through subjects that are dutifully considered—desired, even—but finally not deeply felt. The first poem, "The Loiterer," shows some of these difficulties, for example in the amateurish trick of adding an unnecessary pronoun to fill out the meter: "Her pledge it assigns not the day" (l. 2). The colloquialisms seem uncharacteristic of Melville; it is as if he is imagining Bridegroom Dick writing poetry. But one must still admire the potential here. Melville contrasts death and life, age and spring, and man's anxiousness for a dramatic appearance of spring with its own slow way of arriving.

These are not entirely unsuccessful poems, and there is every indication that Melville intended to publish them as they are. They are not in the same vein as "The Berg" or "After the Pleasure-Party," but who is to say that one may not strike out at age seventy with a new poetic voice? One entirely successful poem, quite atypical of Melville's earlier poetry, is "The Dairyman's Child."

> Soft as the morning
>   When South winds blow,
> Sweet as peach-orchards
>   When blossoms are seen,
> Pure as a fresco
>   Of roses and snow,
>   Or an opal serene.

The poem must be read with no preconceptions. There is no wrestling with the angel Art here; things are blended rather than fused. Three qualities are perceived in the rural child: softness, sweetness, purity. The metaphors are absolutely natural, though taken from widely different areas of experience. Colorings from orchard and fresco and opal are brought together to reinforce one another. A poem such as this, a series of similes set up in parallel structure, is difficult to conclude. Melville solves the problem by doubling up on the last simile. Finally part of the vague beauty of the lines comes from the fact that it is really a riddle. The picture is a disembodied construction, beautiful in an abstract way, which suddenly arranges itself as a real child as the title is reread.

Melville's feelings are for the small and impractical things, the weeds and wildflowers which are of no value except to those who notice them. A poem called "When Forth the Shepherd Leads the Flock" combines sensitivity with the whimsical. Little more would need to be said about it were there not the deceptive innocence of one phrase—"since hearsed was Pan"—which is deeply rooted in one of Melville's most important themes. In *Clarel* (I, xxxiii, 64–69) Rolfe compares Jerusalem to a deserted and decaying "house on moor." The presence of the divine, which once gave life, is now lacking: "Well might the priest in temple start, / Hearing the voice—'Woe, we depart!'" Later there is a canto of Rolfe's night thoughts in Bethlehem:

> When rule and era passed away
> With old Sylvanus (stories say),
> The oracles adrift were hurled,
> And ocean moaned about the world,
> And wandering voices without name
> At sea to sailors did proclaim,
> Pan, Pan is dead!
>
> (IV, viii, 1–7)

Rolfe, it has often been noted, is the closest the writer comes in *Clarel* to creating a personal spokesman. The background, for the death of the gods or their flight, is "Ode on the Morning of Christ's Nativity." Melville knew the poem well; in a letter to George Duyckinck, dated November 6, 1858, he refers to "the bankrupt deities in Milton's hymn." Milton enumerates the pagan gods who were driven out by the coming of Christ, beginning in Stanza xx, and he notes the silencing of the oracles in Stanza xix. In the "Ode" there is the easy assumption, common to Renaissance poetry, of Christ as Pan. This clashes sharply with Rolfe's exclamation: "Pan, Pan is dead!"

Melville is able to conceive of the appearance and even the dominance of Good, but only as a temporary phenomenon. Evil reasserted its dominance and Jesus was put to death; the subsequent stories of resurrection and ascension have only the reality of nostalgia and beautiful myth. Christ remains truly dead. This aspect of Melville's thought becomes crucial in *Billy Budd*. Here it may be noted that the apparently innocent poem, "When Forth the Shepherd Leads the Flock," becomes a carrier of this idea with its lighthearted allusion to the hearsing of Pan.

A similar poem is called "A Way-Side Weed." It is also atypical of Melville as one has come to think of him, yet also perfect in its own way—for precise diction, for balance. The insight is presented with economy and clarity. The title was once "Golden-Rod," but that was dropped to allow the poem to work its way toward this ending. Divinity is treated lightly for one who has sounded the depths with the whale, but the universe is different here, and one that has been consciously chosen by the poet.

One other poem must be mentioned in order to appreciate Melville's explorations into a kind of poetry that is entirely new for him. "Field Asters" is another eight-line poem with a perfect division of thought between stanzas. The thematic patterns suggest something like the Great Chain of Being. Stars are above man and their namesakes, the asters, are below, but in this chain of being man is curiously unintegrated. He gazes at the stars above, not comprehending them, while the other stars at his feet gaze at him with a wisdom that is inscrutable to him. There is a kind of platonism also: things are named below as they are above. The poem seems to be a light one, but the two patterns imply that there is an order in the universe which man cannot understand and of which he does not seem to be a part. Man is ambiguously placed in the universe, a puzzle to everything else which fits in so well.

This nature poetry, written under whatever impulse, does come round to an area of interest we associate more easily with Melville. His ambiguities are present in these poems, repressed but not entirely. The poem on robins, "The Little Good-Fellows," re-creates the folk legend that for the children who die in the woods nature at least will perform suitable obsequies. The robins will cover them with leaves and protect them from preying animals. Lines 6–7 make a substitution for the children:

> When some unfriended man we see
> Lifeless under forest-eaves.

Melville had originally written "self-slayer sad" for "unfriended man." The editorial hand is obviously guided by his conscious attempt to avoid unpleasant subjects, but even in its modified form the poem still has a grotesque gaiety about it.

In a "Butterfly Ditty" the Eden theme is picked up again from several other places in Melville's poetry, from "To Ned" and "Syra," for example. The butterfly speaks, sounding very much like Emily Dickinson in line 4. Its rapid movements are imitated by establishing a three-stress line in the first stanza and shortening it to two stresses for the rest of the poem.[2] As in the "Field Asters," the nonhuman looks at the human and finds it out of joint with the universe. "Eden's bad boy" sounds frivolous and banal for the tragedy it implies, but the point of the poem may involve the fact that for butterflies man's tragedy is relatively unimportant. This is one of Melville's Songs of Innocence, with all of the ironies Blake implied in that editorial viewpoint.

Such hints of Melville's darker views are very near the surface, even in the less distinguished poems of this section. One describes the quickness of a chipmunk vanishing. The final stanza of "The Chipmunk" develops this as a metaphor for a child who died in infancy, but it yields no comfort:

> So did Baby [vanish quickly],
> > Crowing mirth
> > E'en as startled
> > By some inkling
> > > Touching Earth,
> > Flit (and whither?)
> > From our hearth!

All the meaning and all the emotional drama are compressed into the short parenthesis. It is a typical Melvillean question, providing no answer. So too does a poem called "Always With Us!" present a jarringly grim theme in a series of poems intended to re-create the Pittsfield idyll. The robin stays only for a short time, says the poem, while the crow, "croaker, foreboder," stays through all the seasons.

In the penultimate poem in the series, "Stockings in the Farm-House Chimney," a wistful glance is cast at the children's belief in Santa Claus. The first two stanzas describe the belief with words like "happy," "hope," "delight," and "blest." The belief in Santa is for the children a key to a larger and richer area of being, since he is "more than mortal, with something of man." But this door is necessarily shut for the adult. "Truth," in the last stanza, inevitably means a smaller and less pleasant version of reality.

For all Melville's attempts to create an idyll from the past here, the darker views are constantly asserting themselves. This is understandable, for these darker views have been the source of his power as a writer from the beginning. Two highly interesting poems from this section of *Weeds and Wildings* remain to be considered.

"The Blue-Bird" may be placed in the tradition illustrated by Ovid's *Metamorphoses*, with explicit Christian elements in the second stanza. Note that every line is rhymed—an unusual practice for Melville. The personified figure of Pity in line 7 unifies the two middle stanzas, perhaps is even the "it" who brings about the resolution in the final stanza (l. 14). Pity tells the lesson of the bird who came too early and was frozen to death, expressing the caution with which Melville has learned to treat the universe; it was "hope" that brought the bird to disaster, "some misgiving had been well." Melville's Gnostic dualism appears here. As matter, the principle of evil, surrounds and limits spirit to form the visible universe, so "His heavenly tint the dust shall tame." Indeed the visible universe was formed in fright, as Captain Ahab had insisted. Christianity surfaces in several ways. Like the word *tares* in "When Forth the Shepherd Leads His Flock," the word *sepulchre* here (l. 7) has been limited almost exclusively to a biblical context to signify the place of Christ's interment. "Garden" in biblical typology stands both for the Garden of Eden and the place where Jesus was buried. In Christian iconography the skull at the foot of the cross of Jesus is Adam's, an illustration of typological continuity: redemption by the second Adam is accomplished in exactly the same place where the first Adam's fall occurred. The Gospel of Saint John is the source; the King James Version reads: "Now in the place where he was crucified there was a garden; and in the garden a new sepulchre, wherein was never man yet laid" (19:41). The association of "Garden" and "sepulchre" shows that the poet is consciously alluding to this passage. Finally the last line of the poem employs another word, "transfigured," also reserved almost exclusively for one of the mysteries in the life of Christ.

Now that we have noted the double level of "The Blue-Bird," the question must be asked concerning the use of this pattern. Richard Chase has commented that this poem celebrates "the transfiguring power of nature in its cycles of death and rebirth."[3] We have seen Melville working through these same themes in *Clarel*. There it became clear that he could genuinely admire the life and works of Jesus, but for him the supernatural aspects of the Christ myth—miracles, resurrection, afterlife—were not historical or believable. He viewed the New Testament with a mixture of nostalgia and regret that such a beautiful story could not actually be true. Here, in "The Blue-Bird," as one reads the poem again, he realizes that the thought is similar. The bird's color may be continued in the June larkspur, but that must be small consolation to the bird. "Pity" may do all it can, myth may attempt some consolation, but in the last analysis individuality is lost in what is a ruthless and impersonal universe. Camus's Caligula may gloss the poem here: "Les hommes meurent et ils ne sont pas heureux."

The final poem to be considered in this series is the one that apparently Melville would have rejected from the printed version of *Weeds and Wildings*, "In the Pauper's Turnip-Field." Obviously its theme of mortality would have clashed noticeably with his conscious theme of the Pittsfield idyll enjoyed many years ago with his wife, but just as obviously it is a fine poem and consideration of it here will shed some light also on Melville's practice of building each collection into a coherent whole.

The crow in this poem is the same one we have already met in "Always With Us!" There he was "croaker, foreboder," calling "from the blasted hemlock's / Whitened spur." Here he is in the same tree, and his foreboding is more explicitly on the theme of death. From the title onward there is nothing to relieve the imagery of crushing poverty, always at the edge of death.

Melville was probably inspired here by Millet's "The Man with the Hoe." The painting, finished in 1862, caused a stir when it was exhibited in the Salon, and it has been reproduced frequently ever since. It was criticized for creating too brutalized a representation of man: poverty and hard labor had blown out the light within his brain, as another poet was to say of the picture. One very concrete connection between Melville's poem and the picture is suggested by the shape of the rude and heavy hoe the man leans against in Millet's picture; it looks very similar to a mattock. The association is one that the speaker in Melville's poem also makes naturally.

The theme of the poem, the imminence of death, was surely too dark for a man in his seventies to allow into a book of happy poems. Perhaps there was an even more persuasive reason for omitting the poem—not that it was untrue, but that it was too true for his present purposes. The poems in "The Year" create an idyll out of the years in Pittsfield, but it was from Pittsfield that Melville wrote his famous "dollars damn me" letter to Hawthorne. And it was for reasons of economic survival that the Melvilles had to abandon their Pittsfield home in 1863. In other words the themes of death and poverty come very naturally to Melville as he is reconstructing this part of his past; the imaginary garden has real snakes in it. Yet the whole truth could not be sustained along with Melville's desire to please his wife with a happy version of their early years of marriage.

Part II of *Weeds and Wildings* is called "This, That and the Other." The title indicates a miscellany. There are eight poems printed under this heading in *Collected Poems*, though Ryan would omit one of them, "Iris (1865)." One fails to find either the same kind of organization that characterized the first section or the tensions still visible in creating that organization. The omitted poem seems to have been left out, at least temporarily, simply because it was not clear. Three of the poems, however, do have either considerable merit or interest and repay study.

"Profundity and Levity" has already been mentioned. In its first stanza Melville changed two words and thus reversed the whole meaning of the stanza. The word "wisdom" in line 2 had originally been "mourners"; the word "progress" in line 4 was "funeral march."[4] Thus the owl had been a cynic, seeing only the death of intellect in the present age of the world and the only progress a funeral march. With the change he becomes an enthusiast à la Longfellow, urging participation in modern progress, but the poem finally discloses its original form in spite of the changes. The owl cannot understand the totally different concept of life enjoyed by the lark; it "blinks at strong light," whereas the lark swims in it rejoicing. The owl's reality is something different: "Life wanders in night like a dream." They are at irreconcilable poles, as if one were predetermined to a particular philosophy by one's given temperament and experience. Literary tradition throws its own weight into the balance, deciding between these two personal views. Owls are birds of wisdom, whereas "skylarking" has never been considered very serious business. The final question of the poem, then, stands as the line of thought to be embraced and pursued. It is a question a sky lark would never consider asking.

"The Cuban Pirate" is another riddle, with the subject mentioned almost casually in the headnote: "Some of the more scintillant West Indian humming-birds are in frame hardly bigger than a beetle or bee." The poem begs for an impossible comparison with Emily Dickinson's riddle on the same subject, "A Route of Evanescence." Her poem had been written in 1879, and several copies were sent in letters to friends. But it was not published until 1891, the month after Melville's death.[5] The short, strongly accented line, the quatrains, the jewelry images are similar in both poems. One finds a vitality in "The Cuban Pirate" not characteristic of Melville. The description is all motion and color, with no philosophy visible even when a sea metaphor is introduced. This is another of his rare poems in which every line is carefully rhymed. A particularly successful experiment is tried in the final stanza, where the rhyme is changed to produce two separate couplets—as if both are necessary to stop the furious motion of the bird. Robert Frost was later to produce the same effect at the end of "Stopping by Woods." Finally the intense unity of the poem is achieved by the multiple developments of the "pirate" suggestion in the title: "buccaneer," "plunder," "sea," "board and ravage."

The last poem to be noticed in this section is "The American Aloe on Exhibition." Another experiment in rhyme appears: the number of rhymes increases in the last two stanzas, intensifying the reader's attention as the poem's point is being made. The poem may be an old one; similar ideas and word combinations appear in a letter to Evert Duyckinck (February 2, 1850). Melville is sending Duyckinck a copy of *Mardi* for his library, a famous one in its day, which he speculates would probably be kept intact even after Duyckinck's death—thus insuring some immortality to the book. "How natural then—tho' vain—in your friend to desire a place in it for a plant, which tho' now unblown (emblematically, the leaves, you perceive, are uncut) may possibly—by some miracle, that is—flower like the aloe, a hundred years hence—or not flower at all, which is more likely by far, for some aloes never flower." [6]

In his poem Melville uses the plant for an allegorical figure of the late bloomer, a variation on the ugly duckling. The allegory is not entirely serious—this would be difficult to achieve without pomposity—yet neither is it entirely playful. The hope that he would finally be read again as the Hawthornes had read him never completely faded. The roses in line 15 stand for a dramatic blossoming that captures attention and then fades quickly and is forgotten, much as did the writings of the man who had written popular sea tales. The aloe has had to wait its time for popularity, yet when it comes this too proves to be disappointing.

Melville has had a long and complicated relationship with his readers. He wanted to be read, but on his own terms—not as "the man who had lived among cannibals" but as the man who had "written a wicked book." He seems to have despaired of finding such a public, yet he never stopped writing and even making the gesture of publishing small editions. When he died, his wife wrote "writer," not "customs inspector," where the death certificate asked for occupation, but his attitude toward his readers was ambiguous. Part of him would have liked to sneer at the Roses that had considered him a weed; still another part of him wanted to treat possible buyers with "strange inert blank unconcern / Of wild things at the Zoo."

These feelings can be pursued through one aspect of their complexity in the first poem of Part II, "Time's Betrayal." According to the poem, it is unhealthy for a young maple tree to be tapped for its syrup. If some culprit does so, the tree declares the crime by turning red earlier in the fall than it ordinarily would. The original title had been "Murder Will Out." Melville allegorizes the story in a final couplet of striking precision and compression:

> So they change who die early, some bards who life render:
> Keats, stabbed by the Muses, his garland's a splendor!

The legend had been that Keats was stabbed by the hostile reviewers. Melville substitutes another word and has the source of inspiration itself as the cause of the writer's premature death. "Render" is also an interesting word. As a term transferred from painting, the poet may be said to "render" life if he captures it perfectly. But scraps of pork also "render" lard when boiled—just as tree and poet, stabbed young, "render" their own lives and die. Thus Melville turns the poem into an investigation of another author-reader relationship. Melville may have wondered what an early romantic death might have done for his own reputation. These two poems announce a theme which will become increasingly important in the later works, as Melville contemplates his own life work and wonders about its future.

The "Weeds and Wildings" section ends with a third part containing just one poem. It is another of those poems introduced by a long prose character analysis, such as one finds in *John Marr* and like the one that developed into *Billy Budd*. "Rip Van Winkle's Lilac" inquires into questions about the character of Rip that Melville seems to think had been left unanswered by Irving. The introduction presents two scenes: Rip's return to his decayed home after the long sleep, and an artist engaged in painting his "picturesque"[7] house. The two strands seem imperfectly woven together. Indeed Melville explicitly states that Rip returned "a few years later," after the painter had already sketched the scene. It is left for the poem itself, and this mostly by implication, to weave the motifs of both strands together.

The Rip section of the introduction is quite faithful to Irving's telling of the story in tone, incident, and characterization. The other section is an addition introduced as a device for exploring the story more deeply. A few years before Rip returns, an artist is painting his decaying house. The willow that had overshadowed it, "lamented over" it, has fallen and is now reduced to a moldering ridge with violets growing from it. In its place is a flourishing pink lilac which attracts the artist; its "picturesque" juxtaposition with the green ruin of the house is what makes the scene worth capturing on canvas. As the artist paints, he is interrupted by a fanatic individual who questions the practicality of such a profession. The painter, twice called a "Bohemian," is challenged in his choice of subject (a freshly painted white church is starkly featured in another direction). When the unpleasant questioner wants to know why someone would paint a rotting house, the painter replies gnomically, "Yes, decay is often a gardener." Melville had once considered using this remark as an epigraph for *Weeds and Wildings;* the fact that he dropped it confirms my earlier speculations concerning his editorial intentions.

As the fanatic leaves, riding his "lank albino," the artist is struck by a verse from the Apocalypse: "And I looked and beheld a pale horse, and his name that sat on him was Death." There is a confrontation between two styles of life, the puritanical with its rigidly moral version of useful and practical work, contrasted with the artistic, its natural enemy, which seems indolent and wayward but which has its own higher purpose and insights. The rotting house and the things that grow from it may be a metaphor for the Calvinist doctrine of total depravity. Man's nature is corrupt and therefore so are all the works that proceed from him. The white church on the hill looks like a New England Congregational church, with its original (Calvinist) coloration recently whitened over by the transcendentalists. This final interpretation is merely suggested by the scene, but the suggestion grows more persuasive as one realizes that it is another form of one of Melville's preoccupations.

With this episode established, Melville is ready to consider Rip and complete his story. The poem tells of the lilac, which Rip had planted many years ago, flourishing now into a sturdy tree of famous color and sweetness. The lilac flourishes because of the decay of the house, which Rip had indolently refused to keep in good repair, and because of the decay of the willow tree which Rip had been too busy to remove. The subsequent history of the lilac is given. Slips of it are tended and transplanted, "neighbor from neighbor begged again":

> On every hand stem shot from slip,
> Til, lo, that region now is dowered
> Like the first Paradise embowered.
> Thanks to the poor good-for-nothing Rip.
> *(ll. 63–66)*

Even the signposts now point to the area as *"Lilac Land."* Melville moralizes his conclusion:

See, where man finds in man no use,
Boon Nature finds one—Heaven be blest!
(ll. 76–77)

The poem may be read as an allegory of Melville's own experience
as a writer who had to trust the future for justification. It was a trust
amply fulfilled for him but only after death. In one phrase Melville
momentarily lets the veil drop to show how closely the issue touched
him personally. He speaks of "Rip's Lilac to its youth still true" (l. 45).
The phrase is close to the saying he kept tacked above his writing desk:
"Keep true to the dreams of thy youth." The tensions of Melville's darker
philosophy also find some resolution here. The poem about the indolent
Rip is far removed from his "Fragments of a Lost Gnostic Poem of the
12th Century," yet it is a successful illustration of the truth of one of its
sayings: "Indolence is heaven's ally here." What seems indolence to
one's neighbors may finally produce a work that later generations will
appreciate. The poem introduces one of Melville's major concerns in
his late poetry: the relation of the artist to posthumous evaluation.

The second major division of *Weeds and Wildings* is called "A Rose
or Two," and it is an impressive exploration of the symbolic meanings
to be discovered in the flower. There are two parts: the first contains
nine poems, the second presents one long poem. The whole is concluded
by another "L'Envoi." The four surviving tables of contents show differ-
ent arrangements. Melville's final order seems to be the following: "The
Ambuscade," "Under the Ground," "Amoroso," "The New Rosicrucians,"
"The Vial of Attar," "Hearth-Roses," "Rose Window," "Rosary Beads,"
and "Devotion of the Flowers to Their Lady." These poems are somber
and solid; there is strength and loveliness in many of them which one
hopes will be noticed. For the most part they show the poet in his most
thoughtful moods.

With "Amoroso" in the first position in *Collected Poems*, a note of the
joyful young lover is struck which seems a false point of entry into the
series. There can be little question why he chose, finally, to begin with
"The Ambuscade," surely one of the finest of his poems, although it has
so far gone almost unnoticed. It is compact and tense; drama is achieved
by directness of address; the perfect couplets and strong rhythm carry
the reader through.

Meek crossing of the bosom's lawn
Averted revery veil-like drawn,
Well beseem thee, nor obtrude
The cloister of thy virginhood.

And yet, white nun, that seemly dress
Of purity pale passionless,
A May-snow is; for fleeting term,
Custodian of love's slumbering germ—
Nay, nurtures it, till time disclose
How frost fed Amor's burning rose.

Four lines compress a not unsympathetic description of the nun, with great understanding for what her habit represents. With dramatic abruptness the tone changes in line 5 to a stern warning for the dangerous position into which she has put herself. The poem comes from the same burst of inspiration that produced "After the Pleasure-Party." The phrase "Amor's burning rose" in the final line combines three words that have powerful erotic content in that poem, and the title corresponds with Urania's recollection of "the glade / Wherein Fate sprung Love's ambuscade" (ll. 19–20). The concept of ambush does not function explicitly in this short poem; the title instead introduces a new metaphor to shed light on the subject, a technique reminiscent of the poems of Herbert and Vaughan.[8] The imagery is complexly wrought. The veil of the nun protects the "slumbering germ" of earthly love within her, but it also calls attention to it, makes her obviously vulnerable. The white veil is like a snow in May which covers seeds in the ground. But the trap here—the ambush which she does not yet suspect—is that this snow, though it retards growth for a time, will actually "nurture" the seeds as it melts. Urania is recalled, in whom conscious repression actually heightened erotic awakening when it happened. Urania and the "white nun" are really the same character. Despite the correspondences between the two poems, and each can well stand separately, "The Ambuscade" must remain itself one of Melville's most intricately worked and strongly felt poems. Part of the tension in the poem is created by the use of the closed tetrameter couplets which show that Melville has totally mastered his four-stress line.

"Under the Ground" is related to "The Ambuscade." One can see in the manuscripts that "Under the Ground" had previously had other titles just as suitable and that "The Ambuscade" originally had a parallel title, "Under the Snow." Obviously Melville had the two linked in his mind for some time.

"Under the Ground" may owe something to Victor Hugo's famous poem, "La tombe et la rose."[9] The juxtaposition of the two objects brings out their symbolic contrast in both poems. While this poem is considerably lighter than its companion piece, its point is also ironic. Cut roses are placed in an old "disused" tomb in order to keep them fresh, and they are later to be brought to adorn a wedding. Practicality seems insensitive to the grisly aspects.

On top of this there is a hint of another level of meaning. Melville capitalizes "Master" in line 10. Though such capitalization is not consistently reserved for the deity in nineteenth-century writing, Melville himself was very much aware of the practice and quite sensitive to it. In an often-quoted letter to Hawthorne, Melville had followed the standard practice himself and then felt the need to comment editorially: "(You perceive I employ a capital initial in the pronoun referring to the Deity; don't you think there is a slight dash of flunkeyism in that usage.)"[10] There is room for an allegorical level of meaning: the Master brings his choice flowers out of the tomb to be a part of the heavenly nuptials. While such an allegorical reading would be uncharacteristic of Melville's poetry, it would furnish a link, in its religious theme, with "The Ambuscade." Melville may be suggesting that hardheaded practicality is a surer way to heaven than the dangerous way of dedication and sensitivity.

"Amoroso" is simply a lyric, a love poem, whose greatest achievement is a subtle interweaving of sounds. The manuscript has a scrap of five lines (14–18) pasted on to the larger sheet containing the rest of the poem.[11] The scrap of paper seems very old, and the ink is considerably more faded than that used in the rest of the poem. It would be irresponsible to attempt any precise dating from this evidence, but the pasted scrap mentions "plighted pair," and the anticipation of "spousal love" appears a few lines later. There is an immediacy here of two young people in love. If one were to conjecture that part of this poem is very old indeed, dating from shortly before Melville's marriage to Elizabeth Shaw, more evidence could be brought to bear. The poems in *Mardi*, published shortly after the marriage, show the same exuberant wordplay. There are also several of the *Mardi* poems in which rose imagery stands out prominently: "Royal is the Rose," "Her Sweet, Sweet Mouth," and "Half-Veiled Above the Hills, Yet Rosy Bright."[12] If this is indeed one of Melville's early love poems to his wife, it is understandable why it would at one time have been considered for first place in this section of the book dedicated to her.[13]

In the next poem Melville returns to one of his favorite targets. "The New Rosicrucians" are the optimists and Emersonian transcendentalists with whom he has argued throughout his career. (Melville may even have Margaret Fuller's poem "Sub Rosa–Crux" in mind.) The author creates another fanatical persona, immediately establishing him as speaker. The rosy cross is the actual symbol used by the Rosicrucians, a mystical order that had been revived in 1866. Whether Melville refers to this group exclusively is questionable, but he is careful to define the kind of people he does have in mind. They are hedonistic: they "have drained the rose's chalice / Never heeding gain or loss." They have taken a negative stand with regard to one of the most troublesome, as well as one of the most traditional, doctrines of Christianity, the idea of a mortal sin. Melville works cleverly with rhetorical structure here: the fanatic reduces himself to absurdity in the second stanza, with a grotesque parody of Emerson's doctrine of "compensation" in the final image that the poem presents.

The theological probing continues in the next poem, "The Vial of Attar," the central issue of which is immortality. The poem is an interior débat; the first stanza depicts one's feeling at the death of a lover, while the second and third stanzas present two sides of an argument about the bereaved's feelings. In pre-Christian times before news of immortality was announced (ll. 3–4), all one had left as a memorial of the departed was an urn containing his ashes and a glass vial filled with the tears of the mourners. The theme of death of the loved one is treated obliquely, under the figure of the dead rose and the vial of its attar which remains. (Attar is a rare and expensive oil pressed laboriously by hand in minute drops from individual rose petals.) The poet, the rose lover, says that the vial he has left provides solace, when the short-lived rose has died. But from a lover complete honesty is demanded; the poet admits, "Rose! I dally," and the last five lines reverse the sentiment. In view of the premises established by the first stanza, one should read the second part more figuratively. Melville's insight recorded here, obliquely and delicately, is that one's knowledge of spirit and the doctrine of immortality does not diminish the sense of pain and loss caused by death. Whatever the attitude is toward the spiritual portion, or attar, "There is nothing like the bloom." One may believe the spirit of the beloved still lives, but physical presence is sorely missed.

In "Rose Window" the exploration of immortality continues, in a dream vision that can bear some modest comparison with Dante's vision of the Rose. Two short stanzas describe the speaker falling asleep during a sermon on "The Rose of Sharon." The sermon is on the Resurrection and the Life and is not an unpleasant one, but the afternoon is "slumberous" and the listener prefers his dream. The two remaining stanzas describe the dream and the waking reality after.

Mrs. Finkelstein's study of Oriental influence on Melville identifies the "Angel with a Rose" (l. 12) as one of the "two angels of Islamic tradition, Munkar and Nakir, who are thought to examine the dead in their tombs." [14] One of them is depicted as a gardener with a spade and a pot of roses; he may also suggest a gravedigger. (If this is so, then the poem has some affinities with "Under the Ground.") The allusion does not exhaust the meaning of the lines; in fact it leaves unexplained the effect of the rose upon the dead. The clue is to be found earlier in the poem where the preacher's theme is announced. The phrase is taken from the Song of Solomon 2:1, which begins a passage of seven verses which has traditionally been interpreted as the mutual love between Christ and the church: "I am the rose of Sharon." In fact, the headnote to the chapter in the King James Version explicitly summarizes the passage as such. To underline the divinity of the speaker, the King James Version prints the passage, "I AM."

Lines 16–19 in this poem thus gain interest as another attempt by Melville to formulate his ideas on life after death and his relationship to Christian doctrine. The dream vision in these four lines goes only a short way along the path indicated by Christian belief: the Rose-Christ *does* shed his light upon the dead, but the image terminates only in an odd visual experience: the robes of the dead are merely brightened "to plaids and chequered tartans." The final stanza (ll. 20–27) concludes the vision with a waking experience. Upon waking, the sleeper's total field of vision is occupied by the Rose-Window. While the mystery remains, some confirmation of the Christian hope seems indicated, since the window is full of light and color and vitality. The dancing motes and rich coloration produce a feeling of resolution and harmony, even if doctrinal certitudes have not completely swayed the pure reason. The dream and the window have spoken a more persuasive sermon than the droning afternoon voice from the pulpit, and Melville has presented an entirely different side of his religious attitudes than the one his readers ordinarily see.

The next-to-last poem in this section, "Rosary Beads," looks similar to the "Pebbles" which conclude *John Marr*. There are three short "beads," illustrating bits of wisdom to be drawn about life from consideration of the rose. The first bead, "The Accepted Time," might have been called "Gather ye Rosebuds," had the title not been already preempted. The message is the same.

> Adore the Roses; nor delay
> Until the rose-fane fall,
> Or ever their censers cease to sway:
> "To-day!" the rose-priests call.

Melville is more religious in his imagery than Parson Herrick. The title alludes to 2 Corinthians 6:2, and the single religious word in each line links them all together. But the religious vocabulary is a mask for a thoroughly secular ethic.

The second bead, "Without Price," seems an overstatement if taken by itself. Too much weight is given to the rose's ability to illuminate one's life, unless the previous poems are taken into account where Melville has already demonstrated the manifold possibilities latent in the rose as symbol. The roses are first defined as something beyond the ordinary garden variety: one can have them without either buying or growing them himself. They are symbolic of some force able to transform the ordinary realities of life. A sacramental transformation is intimated by the final two lines: "Thy meat shall turn to roses red, / Thy bread to roses white." The poem attains a profound theological meaning if the "Rose" is Christ, based on the allusion to the Song of Solomon already established. But it also becomes another poem untypical of Melville.

The final bead, "Grain by Grain," is interesting in light of Melville's feeling for the desert as it developed in *Clarel* and in the two Egyptian poems of "Fruit of Travel Long Ago." The desert is a place of horror where the destructive brilliance of Jahweh was revealed. "Garden" is capitalized in this poem, as if one preserves one's own private Eden only hazardously against the battering presence of a Calvinist God.

> Grain by grain the Desert drifts
> Against the Garden-Land:
> Hedge well thy Roses, head the stealth
> Of ever-creeping Land.[15]

The final poem of Part I is another surprise for the reader, an imitation of the early Provençal poets. Melville has apparently made up his "Clement Drouon," just as he seems to have made up his "Sire de Nesle," since attempts to find historical or fictional characters with these names have so far been fruitless.[16] The poem is divided into two parts, and the two sections are different metrically.

Much is behind this poem: for example, the tradition that derives in part from patristic allegorical interpretations of the Song of Solomon and culminates in the hymns to the Virgin found in the Roman Breviary. The rose here becomes the *rosa mystica*, the Virgin Mother of God. Melville's feeling for history is another remarkable aspect of this poem. His headnote to the poem is quite just: the quondam troubadour, whose devotion had been to the rose as a secular symbol of love, would, as a monk, naturally redirect the energies latent in this symbol to a now more appropriate object, and would find in the tradition a ready-made application to the Virgin.

As the poem develops, the devotees of Mary stand in relation to her as ordinary flowers do to the Queen of the Flowers. The "we" of the first line immediately assumes two levels of meaning: flowers speaking to the rose and monks speaking to the Virgin. The reading of the poem has to be maintained on both levels, though the more interesting is the latter. The monastic life as it developed in the Middle Ages was conceived as an attempt to re-create Eden, insofar as that was possible for fallen human beings, in the harmony, order, and charity that were to prevail under the monastic Rule. Thus the second line of the poem and subsequent references to Eden are entirely correct also. Melville has gone beyond Gibbon's chapter on the development of monasticism for his sympathetic understanding of the movement here. The first section reconstructs with great accuracy a medieval tone such as Henry Adams was shortly to attempt in *Mont-Saint-Michel and Chartres*.

In view of these sensitively realized medieval materials, the reader experiences some shock at coming upon clear echoes of Swinburne in lines 30–31, at the beginning of the second part of the poem: "We the Lilies whose pallor is passion, / We the Pansies that muse nor forget–." We have been prepared for this by the rolling anapests in the first part of the poem, and Swinburne himself was something of a medievalist though of quite a different kind. But a new perspective is demanded. With the light provided by lines 30–31, the reader can now see that the vocabulary of the whole poem is largely Swinburne's: Queen, sad, languish, pale, beguile, weary, wan, decay. Even the roses that dominate this section of *Weeds and Wildings* also dominate the poems of Swinburne.

Melville, then, has thoroughly entered into the poetic universe of Swinburne. The reasons may be set forth tentatively. Melville was by nature a pessimist, but this does not mean that he is automatically to be aligned with any other pessimist. When a correspondent sent him a copy of James Thomson's *City of Dreadful Night*, Melville responded that he "was a sterling poet, if ever one sang. *As to his pessimism, altho' neither pessimist nor optimist myself, nevertheless I relish it in the verse if for nothing else than as a counterpoise to the exorbitant hopefulness, juvenile and shallow, that makes such a bluster in these days— at least in some quarters.*" [17] Melville's pessimism, in other words, is a highly personal view of reality. He strongly resists being categorized with others.

One may infer that his reaction against Swinburne would have been stronger, for the wallowing romantic delight in gloom and the self-conscious naughtiness to be found there. One can be more specific: Swinburne asserts, in his "Hymn to Proserpine" (from *Poems and Ballads*, 1866), "Thou hast conquered, O pale Galilean; the world has grown grey from thy breath." The line is probably Swinburne's most famous; many of the words can be found in Melville's poem. The Virgin Mary, in Swinburne's poem, is pale and passionless when compared with Venus:

> Not as thine, not as thine was our mother, a blossom of flowering
>   seas
> Clothed round with the world's desire as with raiment, and fair
>   as the foam,
> And fleeter than kindled fire, and a goddess, and mother of Rome.
> For thine came pale and a maiden. . . .

In "Delores," from the same volume of poems, Swinburne makes his famous contrast between "the lilies and languors of virtue" and "the raptures and roses of vice." Melville must have such passages in mind as he explicitly asserts the contrary in Swinburne's own language and meter, saying, "We the Lilies whose pallor *is* passion." The poem ends with a confident hope which so very nearly contradicts Melville's ordinary philosophy that one feels he was for the time in the hands of Swinburne and reacting very strongly against him. The multiple possibilities of the rose image, added to the strongly stated premises of Swinburne, furnish him with still another occasion for exploring his own personal feelings. As Merlin Bowen has shown, this philosophy was an evolving one as the complexities of the Self were constantly being explored.[18] This moment of exploration, undertaken in reaction to Swinburne's ideas, results in the most joyful vision his symbol of the rose can grant him, the most Dantesque his rose ever becomes. It is a fit conclusion to this series of rose poems: "Flower, voucher of Paradise, visible pledge, / Rose, attesting in spite of the Worm."

Part II of "A Rose or Two" consists only of a long narrative poem (almost 200 lines) called "The Rose Farmer," to which is appended the "L'Envoi." The poem is an apparently rambling monologue by an old man: he mentions his old age several times in "The Rose Farmer" and admits to being sixty in "L'Envoi" (l. 3). He is able to allude to Carlyle's *Sartor Resartus* (ll. 13–14) and parody Coleridge's "Kubla Khan":

> Which last [river] the pleasure-ground incloses,
> At least winds half-way roundabout—

That garden to caress, no doubt.
But, ah, the stewardship it poses!
(ll. 42–45)

Yet, for all his sophistication, the speaker disarms the reader by a kind of simplistic good fellowship. The issue of the monologue seems trivial after all: whether a man, who late in life has been bequeathed a rose farm by a friend, shall sell the roses for quick profit as they bloom, or go through the laborious process of squeezing out the minute drops of attar—a substance so rare and expensive that it is liable finally to find no buyers. Consulting a more experienced, and wealthy, rose gardener on the question he receives the advice: "I am for roses—sink the Attar!" (l. 171) The real significance is biographical: at least one of its uses is to serve as a convenient model which Melville can use to throw light on his career as a writer. The poem outlines two choices open to a cultivator of roses (or maker of symbols) and the implications of each choice. The early allusions to Carlyle and Coleridge confirm that the theme deals with the career of writing.

It may be possible to date this poem almost precisely. In 1885, still in his sixties like his spokesman here, Melville retired from his job as customs inspector. He must have felt a sense of release: he was now free to devote full time to his writing again. As things turned out, he was to accomplish two volumes of published poetry and one very nearly finished but unpublished volume, as well as *Billy Budd*, in the six years remaining to him. Melville consciously chose the Attar over the Rose— the rare drops laboriously gleaned, rather than the attractive easily plucked blossoms. Since the main speaker in this poem comes to the opposite conclusion, characterization becomes interesting and important. The speaker is portrayed as a naif and a novice in his chosen career —neither of which would apply to Melville except in a whimsical moment of self-portraiture—and the occupation is shifted from writer to gardener. Both of these moves seem to be strategies of distancing, techniques for gaining objectivity as he considers the work that has recently become possible for him again. Melville's disguise at the beginning is transparent: lines 5-6 of this poem,

Nor less upon some roseate way
Emerge the prickly passage may,

can be set next to lines 33–34 of the Epilogue to *Clarel:*

Emerge thou mayest from the last whelming sea,
And prove that death but routs life into victory.

The syntax is similar as well as the doubt-filled subjunctive. Melville is still interested in breaking through to the light, realizing that treading the prickly passage is the only way there, and still acknowledging that one only *may* break through that way. Still the subject is treated lightly in this poem: for example Melville would delight an Ogden Nash with his *Damascus-Alaskus* rhyme in lines 27–29.[19] The character of the man to whom he goes for advice, the experienced rose farmer, is also revealing. This man stands in the midst of his roses, which are personified as awed damsels—his "rose-seraglio." They respond easily to each shift in his thought. There is an ease in his manipulation of his materials. They dance to his tune, and the result is the golden coins of prosperity which he strings conspicuously at his front gate. Here is an almost transparent allegory for the kind of author Melville could never force himself to be, even when he most wanted to: a man led by financial "prudence" rather than the search for a "transcendental essence" (ll. 184–85).

The "L'Envoi" which concludes this section and the collection as a whole continues the materials and the same light treatment of "The Rose Farmer." Melville mimics his own regional pronunciation in rhyming *Noah-score*. The poem seems a summary of the previous long narrative, not a new poem in its own right. Melville says that one should not succumb to the idea that age and arid years "for flowers unfit us." The poem ends with the attitudes he sees himself taking as a writer— wise, sedate, gray-bearded, yet still youthful at the core. One may take these two poems together as a definition of the stance that was to carry Melville through these last productive years.

The rose poems have been neglected by students of Melville, and this has impoverished our idea of his late work. They are remarkable as a series and many of them are remarkable as individual poems. Melville has used the single image of the rose to explore a diversity of areas. His rose is a means of discovery, a key to unlock many doors: immortality, the writer's craft, remembrance of one's first love, the burning destructive force of Eros, the new optimism, and a vision of Paradise. *Weeds and Wildings* was not put together haphazardly.

VII

THE BURGUNDY
CLUB SKETCHES
AND
MISCELLANEOUS
POEMS

And weary days they must have been to this
    friendless custom-house officer, trying to
    kill time in the cabin with a newspaper; and
    rapping on the transom with his knuckles . . .
    he seemed to be a man of fine feelings,
altogether above his situation; a most inglorious
one, indeed; worse than driving geese to water.

Redburn

The more a man belongs to posterity, in other
words to humanity in general, the more of an
alien he is to his contemporaries.

Schopenhauer, The Wisdom of Life
(Marked by Melville in his copy)

THE *Burgundy Club* sketches consist of seven prose pieces of varying length and two long poems. After Melville's death they remained in the possession of his family and were not published until 1924. The most careful analysis of these materials, with regard to their arrangement and date of composition, has been made by Merton M. Sealts, Jr.[1] He has concluded that Melville worked on the materials during 1876–1877, the year after *Clarel* was published, and again during the years of his retirement, constantly trying to find a shape for the public presentation of these sketches. The poems are written in the octosyllabics that Melville had made such a supple form of inquiry in *Clarel.* They seem to be substantially complete as he left them, though there are some places where final editorial work is needed for such details as adding quotation marks to identify speakers more clearly. The prose passages are intended to introduce and support these two poems.

Each poem, "At the Hostelry" and "Naples in the Time of Bomba," has a theme which is developed in detail, and each shows a new area of interest and speculation for Melville which must be considered before this period of his career can be fully evaluated. The first poem is cast as a symposium in which the most popular and most discussed term in esthetic criticism at the time is analyzed by a group of experts. The second poem presents a monologue by a man of unimpeachably democratic credentials discussing his recollections of life in a city ruled over by fear and tyranny.

The dominating personality in the sketches is the Marquis de Grandvin. He is an embodiment of Melville's own need for genial conviviality, of a kind expressed elsewhere in such diverse places as his letters to Hawthorne, the Duyckincks, and his brother Tom, in the long conversations of *Mardi,* and in his Christmas poems in *Weeds and Wildings.*[2] The other side of the coin is the enervating loneliness experienced by those characters described by Melville whose one transcending deed sets them outside the ordinary processes of human life, isolating them from this kind of conviviality. *Pierre,* "Timoleon," and *John Marr* describe the phenomenon, as do a group of poems to be discussed later in this chapter. The marquis himself is a figure for the wine, *pas ordinaire,* which stimulates the flow of genial conversation. Under his inspiring influence the *Burgundy Club* sketches were probably conceived of as finally being a series of literate conversations and monologues on a variety of subjects beyond the two poems that Melville actually finished.

The first, "At the Hostelry," is presided over by the guiding genius of the marquis. In an opening section and a closing one he comments on

recent events in the city of Naples; these sections can best be discussed
in connection with the next poem. His main concern, in the long middle
section of the poem (Cantos II–VIII) is with the meaning of the term
"picturesque." To appreciate the weight of this word as Melville ap-
prehended it, one must totally dissociate oneself from present meanings
of the word, where it connotes, perhaps, the quaint, the provincial, a
kind of art that is skillful but by no means of the highest esthetic order.
As Melville inherited the word, however, it was the most laudatory
term that could be applied to the visual arts of painting, architecture,
and landscape gardening.

We are here in one theater of the more general war between clas-
sicism and romanticism, and a series of manifestos had been drawn up
on each side to state the issues of the debate. The main voice for the
older classical thought had been Edmund Burke's, in *A Philosophical
Enquiry into the Origin of Our Ideas of the Sublime and Beautiful*
(1757), a work which Melville owned (Sealts #97). Coming after him,
arguing on the terms he set down but opposing him, were such British
writers as Archibald Alison, the Reverend William Gilpin, Richard
Payne Knight, and Uvedale Price. Knight spanned the fields of poetry,
landscape, and painting by writing an *Analytical Inquiry into the Prin-
ciples of Taste* (1805) as well as a long didactic poem called *The Land-
scape*, all illustrating the superiority of the picturesque. Gilpin was
early in the battle against Burke. He attempted descriptions of the
picturesque at length in his multivolumed tours of English scenery.[3]
In the second edition of his *Three Essays: On Picturesque Beauty; On
Picturesque Travel; and On Sketching Landscape* (1794) he believed he
had found a distinction that would allow him to move beyond Burke's
definition. Gilpin found beauty in the objects he had described, whether
they were rustic scenes, shaggy animals, withered or decayed trees,
broken columns or mountain crags. On the basis of these broken textures
he proposed "roughness" as the characteristic of the picturesque, in
opposition to the "smoothness" which Burke had considered essential
to beauty in his *Enquiry* (III, xiv). Arguing to the contrary, Richard
Payne Knight found the quality of fusion to be characteristic of the
picturesque, and the term is interesting when compared to the "esem-
plastic" power attributed to the imagination by Coleridge and, more
especially, when one comes upon the word "fuse" in Melville's poem
"Art."[4]

In Melville's immediate background American writers were also
using the word to characterize particularly modern apprehensions of
beauty. Emerson, for example, used the word technically, precisely

placing it in an important position within his philosophy. He is speaking of "Language" in Chapter 4 of his book *Nature*. A distinction is made between levels of language based on an ethical norm. Those who have lost a "simplicity of character" and succumb to "duplicity and falsehood" speak a perverted language with no fresh imagery in it, since they have cut off their contact with Nature. Emerson continues: "But wise men pierce this rotten diction and fasten words again to visible things; so that picturesque language is at once a commanding certificate that he who employs it is a man in alliance with truth and God." The usage of "picturesque" here is Emerson's deft weaving of a current esthetic term into his moral and mystical philosophy. The best men use this highest kind of language, the picturesque, because they alone are able to see that "the world is emblematic."

In another book that Melville knew well, Thoreau spoke more in the tradition of the debate being carried on in England. In the first chapter of *Walden* he described the "unpretending, humble log huts and cottages of the poor" as being more "picturesque" to the painter's eye than meaningless architectural ornamentation. And coming closer, to one of Melville's enduring sources of inspiration, Hawthorne used the term in his preface to *The House of the Seven Gables*, among other places. He identifies the peculiar effect that legendary materials add to the story as "picturesque." This is the preface in which Hawthorne continued his definition of the romance, as distinguished from the novel. Melville also links the two concepts in his line, "The *Picturesque* and *Old Romance!*" ("At the Hostelry," II, 2) In 1878, while Melville was writing the early stages of this poem, Henry James testified to the currency of the word in his *Daisy Miller*. Innumerable examples of this now obsolete, technical use of the word could be chosen, but these are particularly close to Melville either psychologically or chronologically.

Melville's setting and topic also owe something to Thomas Love Peacock's novel, *Headlong Hall*, a book already mentioned as a source for the characterization of Derwent in *Clarel*. The novel is a developed form of the symposium: an odd mixture of characters is assembled for a long Christmas holiday at the estate of the culture-seeking Squire Headlong. Melville's interest would have been engaged by the first debate, humorously treated, between Mr. Foster the perfectibilian and Mr. Escot the deteriorationist. The second major discussion has Mr. Milestone, the "picturesque landscape gardener," at its center. Peacock's book, which was first published in 1816, is a fairly early entry into the discussion of the picturesque. His sympathies are clearly with an older Burkean esthetic, and he satirizes Knight and others of the new persuasion. His Mr. Milestone is a ridiculous figure who would raze the natural landscape and replace it with artificial lakes and grottoes and odd statues, in the name of the picturesque. Throughout the book the various discussions are helped along by the squire's liberal decanting of burgundy—a lubricating principle which Melville easily appropriated for his own discussion in the *Burgundy Club* sketches.

"At the Hostelry" is also a symposium, in Plato's sense of the word, carried on by many of the painters mentioned in the sources above. The discussion proceeds in two phases. Phase 1 (Canto II) opens the discussion with a small group composed of Jan Steen, Fra Lippo Lippi, Spagnoletto, Swanevelt, and Claude. After a canto (III) intended to suspend the reader's disbelief that such a gathering of immortals could take place, the curtain is fully opened on an upper room at Delmonico's where the group is seen to include Frans Hals, Vandyck, Tintoretto, Brouwer, Carlo Dolce, Rembrandt, Salvator Rosa,[5] Michelangelo, Leonardo da Vinci, Veronese, and about a dozen more of the world's most famous painters.

As an opener Jan Steen, a utilitarian painter "bustl[ing] along in Bentham's shoes," dismisses the importance of any theory: "For the Picturesque—suffice, suffice / The picture that fetches the picturesque price!" (II, 18, 19–20) When asked for an example, Spagnoletto (Jose Ribera) offers his own pictures of the "Flaying of St. Bartholomew" and "Lawrence on the gridiron lean." Characterization of the painters is important: Spagnoletto has "a brow by no blest angel sealed, / And mouth at corners droopt and drawn" (II, 39–40). In other words there is a connection between the character of the painter, his works, and his theories as well. It also becomes obvious quite early in the conversation that, if it is left up to the artists, their own best paintings will be the examples meriting this term of highest praise. But the point is made too obviously by Spagnoletto, and a howl of jeering laughter rises from the rest of the painters. Melville picks a Dutchman to bridge this disharmony gracefully and give a more profound direction to the discussion. Swanevelt states that "Like beauty strange with horror allied / . . . so as well / Grace and the Picturesque may dwell / With Terror. Vain here to divide" (II, 64, 66–68). Melville here gives his own version of romantic art as beauty wedded with strangeness. Though he is a man of wide tolerance, Swanevelt's own preference is for any natural scene "set off serene / With any tranquil thing you please— / A crumbling tower, a shepherd piping" (II, 71–73). He receives a friendly nod of assent from Claude, who prefers himself not to enter into "theory's wildering maze" (II, 83).

Having set the scene and briefly opened some of its possibilities, the marquis tries to disarm the incredulity of his hearers: such things can happen "in wine's meridian" (III, 22). The subject is then pursued with a larger cast. After some sparring Tintoretto ventures a statement about the picturesque: "Some decay must lurk" (IV, 42). From his comments Adrian Brouwer picks out the words "*grime* mark and *slime!*" and hopes to jostle the fastidious Carlo Dolce with them. Continuing, he develops a current theory of idealization in art: in painting the ugly can be beautiful precisely because the offensive aspects are not present. The comment recalls the discussions of Rembrandt's "Slaughtered Ox" carried on in the manifestos of the picturesque mentioned above. Brouwer says, "In Art the style / Is quite inodorous" (IV, 55–56). He goes on to analyze Tenier's "L'heure du repos" (which Melville had described with feeling in his poem "The Bench of Boors"). Art can use even the ugly and the unpleasant:

> "Under rafters foul with fume that blinks
> From logs too soggy much to blaze
> Which yet diffuse an umberish haze
> That beautifies the grime, methinks."
> *(IV, 63–66)*

With these words Brouwer makes a sudden comparison between Tenier's technique and Rembrandt's. But Rembrandt is too olympian to notice the slighting comparison and maintains his silence.

The mention of Rembrandt, however, creates a link with the next canto (V), where the Dutch painters are mainly in the spotlight. Melville had a particular feeling for one of them, Adrian Van der Velde, a painter of seascapes and naval engagements who had once himself been a sailor. His idea of the picturesque is also highly personal:

> "On Zealand's strand
> I saw morn's rays slant 'twixt the bones
> Of the oaken *Dunderberg* broken up;
> Saw her ribbed shadow on the sand.
> Ay—picturesque!"
> *(V, 19–23)*

His "earnest tone" distresses the company for a moment, until another Dutchman, Gerard Douw, promotes his own version of the picturesque: a still life of gleaming kitchenware and food, especially if a pleasant wench is put into the picture. The dispute degenerates again with each individual pushing forward his own pictures or his own national school as best embodying the picturesque. Rubens ("Sir Peter Paul," l. 61) would change the peasant girl for Venus and her pheasant for a swan: "Then in suffused warm rosy weather / Sublime them in sun-cloud together" (V, 59–60). As Watteau describes how he would achieve the picturesque in a Venetian setting, the churlish Spagnoletto breaks in again, suggesting a cynical treatment of Watteau's subject.[6]

As the sixth canto begins, "the superb gentleman from Verona" (Veronese) smooths over these ruffled waters and goes on to describe one of *his* pictures, a sensuous and sentimental one of cavaliers and ladies at play. Jan Steen argues this is good, but he would not limit the picturesque to scenes from the higher ranks of society:

> "Be it cloth of frieze or cloth of gold,
> All's picturesque beneath the sun;
> I mean, all's picture.
>
> *(VI, 27–29)*

Watteau attempts to take up the conversation from here, but Veronese feels he has been attacked by a "realist" and interrupts to rebut Steen:

> "This cabbage *Utility, parbleu!*
> What shall insure the Carnival—
> The gondola—the Grand Canal?
> That palaced duct they'll yet deplete,
> *Improve* it to a huckster's street.
> And why? Forsooth, *malarial!*"
>
> *(VI, 70–75)*

The outburst draws a snort of glee from Brouwer, who thinks his own kind of painting is vindicated (VII, 5–6). The other painters remain silently communing with their own thoughts and their own paintings. Poussin, for example,

> with antique air
> Complexioned like a marble old,
> Unconscious kept in merit there
> Art's pure Acropolis in hold.
>
> *(VII, 17–20)*

In a short by-scene Fra Angelico commiserates with Dürer, who remains a "seraph" in spite of his shrewish wife. But Leonardo, like Poussin,

> lost in dream,
> His eye absorbed the effect of light
> Rayed thro' red wine in glass—a gleam
> Pink on the polished table bright;
> The subtle brain, convolved in snare,
> Inferring and over-refining there.
> *(VII, 33–38)*

Michelangelo also remains aloof and withdrawn from the discussion. "Irreverent Brouwer" notices this and remarks to Lippi about "yon broken-nosed old monolith / Kin to the battered colossi-brood" (VII, 44–45). A superb characterization of Michelangelo concludes this section:

> Challenged by rays of sunny wine
> Not Memnon's stone in olden years
> Ere magic fled, had grudged a sign!
> Water he drinks, he munches bread.
> And on pale lymph of fame may dine.
> Cheaply is this Archangel fed!
> *(VII, 46–51)*

The final section, Canto VIII, quickly sketches the remaining topics of conversation: the romanesque, character painting, costume. But the voice of the Marquis de Grandvin comes up again as stage manager, dissolving this scene of the immortals in "the Inn of Inns," and introducing the next poem and its speaker, Jack Gentian.

It has seemed necessary to give a detailed description of the poem because none has yet been attempted, and there are several points where problems of identifying the speaker require some study. In an overview of the poem, one can see that Melville, while surveying the complexities of the current discussions of the picturesque, believes that discussions of art are never pure and nonpartisan. In fact the main interest of the poem comes to be the characterization of each painter and the matching of his verbal style (or his silence) to his paintings. Each puts forth as candidate for the picturesque what he likes best; and, in the case of the ordinary artists, each prefers what he himself has done. The exception is to be noted here, and it is an interesting one to the reader of Melville. Three artists, whom Melville seems to consider beyond the rest, in an olympian category by themselves, remain aloof from the dispute: Poussin, Leonardo da Vinci, and Michelangelo. The lesser members of the profession are piqued by their superiority and at the same time acknowledge it.

A final theme emerges from the dramatic movement of the cantos. Melville assembles his symposium guests with gusto and begins to develop the conversation with wit and brilliance. In the long middle section the conversation tends to stray, egotisms are pushed forward, and rough edges of contrasting personalities abrade. In its last stages the conviviality has dissipated and the pace grown sleepy. Snatches of small talk pass here and there, but the greatest minds have withdrawn totally within themselves, unable to commune even with fellow geniuses. F. O. Matthiessen has suggested that Melville might have found at least one kindred spirit in New York during these lonely years, the elder Henry James whose studies of Swedenborg had taken him into the broadest questions of ethics and society,[7] but Melville's poem seems to indicate that the deepest divers work alone.

This first poem, "At the Hostelry," has an introductory canto and "A Sequel" at the end, both of which set the scene for the other poem, called "Naples in the Time of Bomba." The introduction, Canto I of "At the Hostelry," opens with a gracious appeal to the reader by the genial marquis:

> Not wanting in the traditional suavity of his countrymen, the Marquis makes his salutation. Thereafter, with an ulterior design, entering upon a running retrospect touching Italian affairs.
>
> > Candid eyes in open faces
> > Clear, not keen, no harrowing line:
> > Hither turn your favoring graces
> > Now the cloth is drawn for wine.

Melville's feeling for Italy has yet to be fully appreciated by his readers. That he attentively studied Italian painters is obvious, and in this first canto Italy is "Art's Holy Land" (l. 70). The names of her cities and districts are savored on the marquis's tongue. The historical moment is also important for this poem; it takes place during the complicated wars of Italian independence and unification. Melville's focus is on the city of Naples and the figure of Garibaldi, which helps simplify matters considerably. Garibaldi was a major folk hero in the popular imagination, and he seems to have had some special attractiveness for Melville. In one of his periods of exile, in the early 1850s, Garibaldi lived in Melville's own city, New York. Earlier he had been an enthusiastic member of Mazzini's *Giovine Italia*—a name paralleled in New York by the group calling themselves "Young America" to which Melville belonged. It must be admitted that the American group was considerably smaller and less warlike, yet there is a similarity in the intensity of the nationalism characterizing each group and in their intellectual aspirations.

Melville concentrates a large amount of this recent history into this stanza from "At the Hostelry."

> Then Fancy flies. Nor less the trite
> Matter-of-fact transcends the flight:
> A rail-way train took Naples' town;
> But Garibaldi sped thereon:
> This movement's rush sufficing there
> To rout King Fanny, Bomba's heir,
> Already stuffing trunks and hampers,
> At news that from Sicilia passed—
> The banished Bullock from the Pampas
> Trampling the royal levies massed.
>
> *(I, 15–24)*

"Bomba," King Ferdinand II, controlling Naples and Sicily, has been seen before, in Melville's poem "Pausilippo," a poem originally written for this sequence and later printed as part of "Fruit of Travel Long Ago." His repressive government was one of the worst in recent history, with thousands of respectable Neapolitans incarcerated for mere suspicion of unorthodox opinion and fifty thousand more on police lists which rendered them liable to imprisonment without trial. The major governments of the world all protested this regime, but Ferdinand resisted their efforts and was successful in putting down insurrections when they occurred. When he died in 1859, his son Francis II, whom Melville calls "King Fanny," succeeded and continued his policies, in spite of solicitations from Victor Emmanuel, king of Sardinia, whose minister, the political genius Cavour, was in the process of liberating Italy from the Austrians and who would finally achieve the unification of Italy almost single-handedly. "The banished Bullock from the Pampas" in the lines above is Garibaldi, so called because of his dozen years of exile in South America for revolutionary activities. By now he was a popular hero for his part in the revolutions that had been breaking out all over Italy during the past decades. He had first liberated Sicily from King Francis's rule and then proceeded to the mainland. This is the moment focused on in the stanza above, when "King Fanny" and his wife and ministers are "stuffing trunks and hampers" preparatory to their flight to Gaeta, where the regime fell in a decisive battle and Naples was absorbed into the united Italian kingdom under Victor Emmanuel.

For Melville, Garibaldi is glorious and heroic, a man worthy to be memorialized by a modern Plutarch (1. 43), only less great than Cavour himself who directed these wars of liberation.

> But he [Garibaldi] the hero was a sword
> Whereto at whiles Cavour was guard.
> The point described a fiery arc,
> A swerve of wrist ordained the mark.
> Wise statemanship, a ruling star
> Made peace itself subserve the war.
>
> *(I, 45–50)*

The canto goes on to memorialize the falling of town after lovely town, once "locked as in Chancery's numbing hand" (1. 58),[8] and their confederation into a united Italy. The last stanza of the canto presents this not as a final stage but as a beginning. New projects can now be launched. Among other signs of the new peace and prosperity, "Swart Tiber, dredged, may rich repay" (1. 94)—a project actually overseen by Garibaldi himself.

It will be seen immediately that this introductory canto has little to do with the rest of "At the Hostelry," the discussion among the great artists meeting in the upper room at New York's Delmonico's restaurant. But the final section of that poem picks up the Naples materials again, and extends the theme of Garibaldi as a modern version of the legendary "knight-errant" ("A Sequel," 1. 21). The question is asked: what is left for a Saint George when all the dragons are dead (11. 39–40)? A debate ensues between two voices, one of them very close to Melville's own and the other that of the nineteenth-century optimist. The first voice replies that the aging warrior

> Perchance, would fag in trade at desk,
> Or, slopped in slimy slippery sludge,
> Lifelong on Staten Island drudge,
> Melting his tallow.
>
> *(ll. 57–60)*

The work is perilously close to Melville's own during these years. The other voice opposes:

> "Pardon," here purled a cultured wight
> Lucid with transcendental light;
> "Pardon, but tallow none nor trade
> When, thro' this Iron Age's reign

The Golden one comes in again;
That's on the card."

(ll. 62–67)

There can be no doubt about Melville's attitudes in the second line here. He has met these fellows before and finds anyone shallow who merely *believes* that the best is yet to be. "A Sequel" ends with a beautiful quatrain, showing Melville in one of his mellowest moods:

Angel o' the Age! advance, God speed.
Harvest us all good grain in seed;
But sprinkle, do, some drops of grace
Nor polish us into commonplace.

Naples, then, is the focus of Melville's attention at the beginning and at the end of the first poem, Naples and the whole of Italy as they had become after liberation by Garibaldi. All this is to set off, by contrast, the historical time at which the next poem takes place—"Naples in the Time of Bomba." Melville developed several pages of prose about the character who narrates the poem, Major Jack Gentian. Some of it he seems finally to have jettisoned, but the remaining prose passages add considerably to one's knowledge of the speaker.[9]

The major is one of the most genial members of the Burgundy Club. A disciple of the marquis, he can often be seen flushed and exhilarated from a meeting with him. He is urbane, gallant, witty, a great conversationalist and storyteller. But there are credentials even more important. The major appears before the public with two symbols which he wears with pride: an empty sleeve and a badge of the Cincinnati. The first is a personal achievement, recalling his participation in the Civil War. The arm had been "lost in the Wilderness under Grant." The Badge of the Cincinnati indicates even deeper and more historic roots of patriotism. The Cincinnati is "a venerable order whereof he who still reigns 'first in the hearts of his countrymen' was the original head. This decoration descended to the Major from his great-grandfather, a South Carolinian, a white-haired captain of infantry at the battle of Saratoga Springs, who therefore, being eligible as a Revolutionary officer, was enrolled in the order upon its formation just after the Peace."[10]

As the poem opens, then, we are in the presence of a man of genial charm, who is known to be a fascinating raconteur, and who is thoroughly devoted to democratic principles—though with a touch of something very much like personal aristocracy.

The title, "Naples in the Time of Bomba," gives the reader an important chronological orientation. This is Naples before Garibaldi liberated it, even before "King Fanny" took over from his father—Naples, in other words, at the worst moment of repression by its harsh King Ferdinand. In the first canto the major describes driving through the city in a rented "nondescript holiday hack" festooned with ribbons. The atmosphere is festive, "in the season when the vineyards mellow" (I, 6). Crowds fill the street, laughing and innocent. Eventually his carriage is blocked by an acrobat performing in the middle of the street. Jack is momentarily non-plused, but the tumbler, seeing his situation, "brisk somersetted back, and stood / Urbanely bowing, then gave place" (I, 35–36). Not to be outdone, the major stands in his carriage and doffs his hat to the man as the carriage drives on. The crowd responds with applause to a gallant gesture from a stranger "from o'er the Alps, and so polite!" (I, 48) The canto ends with the major's feeling of rapport with the city and its people, and his frank pleasure from their flattery.

> —I aver
> No viceroy, king, nor emperor,
> Panjandrum Grand, conquistador—
> Not Caesar's self in car aloft
> Triumphal on the Sacred Way,
> No, nor young Bacchus through glad Asia borne,
> Pelted with grapes, exulted so
> As I in hackney-landeau here
> Jolting and jouncing thro' the waves
> Of confluent commoners who in glee
> Good natured past before my prow.
>
> *(I, 58–68)*

The last word in these lines should raise some suspicions about the speaker: is he a mask for Melville himself, one aspect of Melville's thought and personality?

In the second canto the major drives off musing that the stories he had heard about tyranny in Naples must be untrue since the people seem so happy: "True freedom is to be care-free!" (II, 7) Immediately, however, he comes upon another scene which must also be taken into account:

> But, look: what mean yon surly walls?
> A fortress? and in heart of town?
> Even so. And rapt I stare thereon.
> The battlements black-beetling hang
> Over the embrasures' tiers of throats
> Whose enfilading tongues seem trained

Less to beat alien foemen off
Than awe the town. "Rabble!" they said,
Or in dumb threatening seemed to say,
"Revolt, and we will rake your lanes!"
(II, 11–20)

The sight abashes even a tourist and the major wonders what would happen if he went up and knocked on the gate. As if his mind were being read, the gates immediately clash open and a thousand infantry with fixed bayonets march out. These are mercenary Sicilians and their main purpose is to march once a day from one fort to another, through the most crowded part of the town, merely "to threaten, intimidate, and cow" (II, 53).

Jack sees the faces of the people and is educated to the realization of another level of life here, of both fear and hatred, beneath the festive appearances. He is confused by the contradictions: the beautiful city and the menacing fort, the carefree mood of the people and the brutal soldiers—"Ah, could one but realities rout / A holiday-world it were, no doubt" (II, 94–95). As an observer striving for objectivity in a strange town, the major is still unwilling to believe that Naples in the time of Bomba is as bad as has been rumored, and it takes the remainder of the action to complete the education. One of the unifying principles employed for the rest of the poem is a rose which a pretty street vendor, jumping on the step of his carriage, pins on the major. The flower opens gradually throughout the day, in correspondence with the growing awareness of the major, and finally lies shattered in petals on his coat "and its soul / Of musk dissolved in empty air!" (IX, 37–38)

The development proceeds by juxtaposition of contraries. In Canto III a battered derelict sings a lushly sensuous song, one which might be "questionable to a Hyperborean professor of Agnostic Moral philosophy" as the headnote states. In the next canto the beautiful girl alights like a hummingbird to pin the rose on his lapel, just after he has seen a nervous captain drilling his soldiers in full view of the public. Canto V contrasts the legend that the bones of Vergil rest somewhere in the area, with the stark reality of Mt. Vesuvius suddenly seen in the distance, still active, still menacing like a "Mohawk" with "scalp-lock of Tartarian smoke" (V, 24–25). The major muses on the appropriateness of the place for tourists, with Vesuvius still threatening on one side and the guns of Bomba on the other. As his carriage continues along the seacoast he comes upon a group of young men and women enjoying themselves on the beach, being entertained by a juggler and a tumbler. But the scene suddenly recalls an old story that took place in view of the

same sea. The story concerns Joanna I, queen of Naples in the time of
Boccaccio and Petrarch, an often married lady who seems to have con-
spired in the assassination of her first husband Andrea, prince of Hun-
gary. Melville re-creates the story in tones of an old folktale:

> And Queen Joanna, queen and bride,
> Sat in her casement by the sea,
> Twining three strands of silk and gold
> Into a cord how softly strung.
> "For what this dainty rope, sweet wife?"
> It was the bridegroom who had stolen
> Behind her chair, and now first spoke.
> "To hang you with, Andrea," she said
> Smiling. He shrugged his shoulders; "Nay,
> What need? I'll hang but on your neck."
> And straight caressed her; and when she
> Sat mutely passive, smiling still.
> For jest he took it? But that night
> A rope of twisted silk and gold
> Droopt from a balcony where vines
> In flower showed violently torn;
> And, starlit, thence what tassel swung!
>
> (VI, 74–90)

Still another contrast is immediately recorded as a tragic scene of an-
other kind comes to mind: Agrippina, the noble widow of Germanicus,
exiled to an island off these shores as the innocent victim of court in-
trigues in ancient Rome. Suddenly the major's rose catches his attention,
trying to win him from such morose thought. A fruit seller momentarily
attracts him also with her beautiful song "Love Apples." But "the dun
annals would not down" (VI, 137). The story of an earlier Garibaldi is
recalled who, in 1647, also led a revolt against an oppressive Neapolitan
government when the city was under Spanish rule. Melville tells the
whole narrative in a few quick strokes:

> And, see, dark eyes and sunny locks
> Of Masaniello, bridegroom young,
> Tanned marigold-cheek and tasselled cap;
> The darling of the mob; nine days
> Their great Apollo; then, in pomp
> Of Pandemonium's red parade,
> His curled head Gorgoned on the pike,
> And jerked aloft for God to see.
>
> (VI, 156–63)

The major finds the betrayal a "type" of the kind of terror that is to prevail from that era, through the French Revolution, to the present: "Hell's cornucopia crammed with crime!" (VI, 171) As the canto ends, the rose no longer even tries to intervene.

Melville has found his way deep into the levels of history again. It is difficult to believe that the genial Major Jack was originally intended for this purpose; he is a spokesman who, like Ishmael, develops and finally transcends himself in the course of his experiences. As the major exposes himself to the rich sources of history available in the city of Naples and its environs, he becomes an ever more lucid intelligence, a tool for inquiry into the meaning of these aspects of life. He becomes Melville's own intelligence, depressed anew by what his investigations uncover.

Melville's own days in Naples had been in February of 1857, probably two decades before this poem was begun. That the impressions here developed are at least partly Melville's own experience is evident from the journal entries he made during his trip. The journal is a rich source for the student of Melville's poetry, as it was for the poet himself. One realizes gradually how important a source of inspiration this pilgrimage of 1856–1857 was for the second part of Melville's career as a writer. He spent February 18–24, 1857, in Naples, cramming his journal with details, some of which found their way into this poem:

> Dim mass of Vesuvius. . . . Great crowds, noble streets, lofty houses. . . . Sallied out for a walk by myself. Strada de Toledo. Noble street. Broadway. Vast crowds. Splendor of city. Palace— soldiers—music—clang of arms all over city. Burst of troops from archway. Cannon posted inwards. . . . Vesuvius in sight from square. Smoking. . . . Posilipo—beautiful promontory of villas— along the sea. . . . (At Posilipo found not the cessation which the name expresses.) . . . Visited Virgil's tomb—mere ruin—high up. . . . Long narrow lanes. Arches, crowds.—*Tumblers in narrow street.* Blocked way. Balconies with women. Cloth on ground. They gave way, after natural reluctance. Merriment. Turned around & gave the most grateful & graceful bow I could. Hand[kerchie]fs waved from balconies, and good humored cries &c.—felt prouder than an emperor. Shabby old hack but good fellow, driver. . . . The beauty of the place, in connection with perilousness.—Skaters on ice.[11]

The mask vanishes slowly as "Naples in the Time of Bomba" progresses. Melville may have appeared disillusioned with the American theory of government in *Battle-Pieces* and even in *Clarel*, in the criticisms voiced by Ungar. But here he shows himself a man intensely democratic in principle nevertheless; this is the rule by which he judges Naples and reacts with distress to what he sees.

In Cantos VII and VIII a precocious little boy entertains the crowd with some songs that can be taken as critical of the government. The mood of the crowd changes in an instant as Bomba's soldiers march into view. In the final canto (IX), a small procession enters the scene, attending a priest who carries the Eucharist to a dying man. The entrance transforms the crowd in yet another way. All movement is arrested as idlers, mountebanks, and ordinary folk all bow reverently. All noise stops, except for the small tinkling of bells on the canopy held over the priest. Melville executes a dramatic maneuver to conclude his poem:

> And here this draught at hazard drawn,
> Like squares of fresco newly dashed,
> Cools, hardens, nor will more receive,
> Scarce even the touch that mends a slip:
> The plaster sets; quietus—bide.
>
> *(IX, 39–43)*

The scene is frozen; all the fluid variety of Naples which the poem has accomplished to this point is immobilized by his art: "Like to Pompeiian masquers caught / With fluttering garb in act of flight, / For ages glued in deadly drift" (ll. 33–35). The figure is a grim one, applied to the worshipers, and the act a kind of artistic murder-to-preserve.

Melville no longer pretends that his spokesman is Jack Gentian, entertaining fellow club members with his flowing conversation. The sudden freezing of the scene has its purpose. This is a moment in history, before events that are now known to have happened. Garibaldi was about to enter the scene to depose King Fanny, Bomba's son:

> And presently freedom's thunder clapt,
> And lo, he fell from toppling throne—
> Fell down, like Dagon on his face.
>
> *(IX, 53–55)*

"Dagon" is the idol of the Philistines which appears also in "Gettysburg" in *Battle-Pieces*. In one of the few places where Melville is able to divide his universe clearly into absolute right and absolute wrong, Dagon appears as symbolic of the totally evil, the satanic. The reference has the same weight in the present poem. As Melville backs away for perspective, he is unmistakably clear in his judgment of oppressive government.

The poem ends with a reference that indicates that Melville was still working on the poem at least as late as 1882, the year that Garibaldi died.

> But Garibaldi—Naples' host
> Uncovers to her deliverer's ghost,
> While down time's aisle, mid clarions clear
> Pale glory walks by valor's bier.
>
> *(IX, 57–60)*

The lines introduce the subject of fame and immortality which exercised Melville's mind frequently during these years. The subject is a hero's immortality, and it must be seen that the last line contains some major contradictions for the thoughful man: glory and pale, valor yet death.

In a curious "After-Piece," a quatrain to match the one which ends "At the Hostelry" (giving the two poems a visual resemblance), the last line is extrapolated thus:

> Pale "Glory-walks-by-Valor's-bier."
> Now why a catafalque in close?
> No relish I that stupid cheer
> Ringing down the curtain on the Rose.

About forty more poems remain that were not prepared for publication during Melville's lifetime. (A selection was published by Raymond Weaver in the Constable Edition of Melville's works, and the rest were added in Vincent's *Collected Poems*.) Many of these poems are remarkably homogeneous. They project the interior world of a writer growing old, feeling his age, wondering about the shape of his life, comparing his own with the finished and whole lives of other writers, discovering analogues for his feelings in literary authors and characters. Thus Montaigne in his retirement, two phases in the life of Camoens, the deserted Falstaff, the aging Quixote, the enduring reality of Shakespeare—these are the figures that loom meaningfully before him.

One should proceed with care here, but some conjectures are possible. If "The Rose Farmer" does indeed document the new surge of energy and purpose which carried Melville through the highly productive six years of retirement, these poems may represent his moods toward the end of his nineteen-year stint as a customs inspector, when a definite end seemed to be nearing and his career as a writer seemed over. The poems carry a few hints of internal evidence that this may be the case, but in the absence of firmer data the theory must remain only that. But if this is true, it would explain why these poems, some of them very fine ones, were left out of collections that were being prepared for the printer, and why the poems themselves, with the homogeneity they display, were never considered for publication as a separate group. The subject was simply too personally felt and too depressing to return to for very long.

"My Jacket Old" refers to Melville's years as customs inspector. The contrasts developed in the poem line up neatly one against the other: old, narrow, dull, dust; versus Asia, dream, free, Edenic. "Jacket" is not a usual word in Melville, occurring only when it seems to carry the connotations of a uniform or a costume which sets one apart—for difficulty and even for ridicule in the case of the protagonist in *White-Jacket.* It is also the garb which characterizes one whose life is singled out for special horrors. In *Clarel* (I, xxxvii), a sea captain's ship founders on a hidden rock. He takes to a lifeboat with several other survivors. He is the only one remaining alive when the boat is sighted many weeks later —"him they picked up, where, cuddled down, / They saw the jacketed skeleton" (ll. 68–69). The phrase recalls as well the canvas shrouded skeleton at the figurehead of Benito Cereno's ship.

In this poem the jacket is the coat Melville wore while carrying out his duties as customs inspector, soiled after a day's work by the dust of cargoes from all over the world. The work he complains about is what used to be called "servile," a concept derived from Genesis 3, as is clear from the final line of the poem. Melville seems always to have exempted his work of writing from this category. What is finally interesting about this poem is the word "edenic" and the connections it causes in the reader's mind with other passages that describe what might be called a countercenter of power in his system of symbols. The word recalls oriental memories: the "glenned isles" of the Pacific in "To Ned," for example, and the legendary stories of Jesus in *Clarel.* The idea is handled again in these miscellaneous poems in "Time's Long Ago." There the poet considers the past that is long dead and finds it as bright and serene as the lagoon of a coral isle. The short poem ends:

> There, Fates and Furies change their mien.
> Though strewn with wreckage be the shore
> The halcyon haunts it; all is green
> And wins the heart that hope can lure no more.

Here, then, is another Eden, but one that exists only in memory and one that can exist there only by sacrificing part of the remembered past as it really was. The last line and a half, which considerably deepen the impact of this short poem by returning to the despair of the present, were penciled in almost, it seems, as an afterthought.[12]

Serving as a corollary to these poems is an idea that Melville has pursued throughout his career. Contrary to those who read in the data of evolution signs of a constant rise in the level of man's civilization, Melville's reason and his instincts produced exactly the opposite conviction. One poem, "In the Hall of Marbles," shows that the beauty of ancient Greek statuary, and the ideals there embodied, are no longer the "aims" of modern man: "waxes the world so rich and old? / Richer and narrower, age's way?" It ends with a significant parallel:

> This plaint the sibyls unconsoled renew:
> Man fell from Eden, fall from Athens, too.

The lines stand out as a rare and successful attempt, on Melville's part, of the closed couplet. Other endings, not quite so striking and in Melville's usual four-stress line, are crossed out in the manuscript. Melville has stated, with the controlled beauty of the classic English line, that this classic kind of control is no longer sought or appreciated.

Two playful poems also lament the decline of grandeur and of the gods. One, "The Dust-Layers," left out of the travel series "Fruit of Travel Long Ago," describes carriers with water skins moving through the streets of an Egyptian town, squirting water as they go to keep the dust down. "Osiris! what indignity," the observer exclaims, "Offered the arch majesty / Of Thotmes passed away; / The atoms of his pomp no prouder / Than to be blown about in powder, / Or made a muddy clay!" Thotmes is another name for Tethmosis. Probably the third bearer of this name is referred to. He reigned during the eighteenth dynasty and is considered to have been the greatest of the Egyptian rulers. He controlled an immense empire and yet managed to rule it with order and justice while also encouraging the development of Egyptian art and architecture. Beneath the playful exaggeration of the poem can be glimpsed the themes of fame and the glorious past and what they have been reduced to in the present.

The other poem, "A Rail Road Cutting Near Alexandria in 1855," also from among Melville's gleanings of his Mediterranean trip, concerns the intrusion of the railroad upon the ancient land of the pyramids:

> Plump thro' tomb and catacomb
> Rolls the Engine ripping;
>   Egypt's ancient dust
>   This before the gust,
> The Pyramid is slipping!

Too long inurned, Sesostre's spurned,
What glory left to Isis
Mid loud acclaim to Watts his name
Alack for Miriam's spices.

Modern improvements show no respect for ancient "glory." In this poem the emphasis seems to be not so much on political history as on cultural. "Sesostre" is a legendary Egyptian king and empire builder; Isis and Miriam (Moses' sister) cover two different religious traditions rooted in Egypt. Yet it remains quite possible that the main point is the magnificent pun in the penultimate line.[13]

The roots of this decline from ancient levels of civilization are pursued through several other poems. "A Reasonable Constitution" recalls the concepts of "The House-Top: A Night Piece" in *Battle-Pieces*. The poems are so close in thought that they would seem to derive from the same period in Melville's life, from the same moment of insight.

What though Reason forged your scheme?
'Twas Reason dreamed the Utopia's dream:
'Tis dream to think that Reason can
Govern the reasoning creature, man.

The chiasmus between reason-dream and dream-reason in the middle lines gives the poem a logician's kind of drama in contrast to the visual drama of "The House-Top." The repetition of the word "reason" in each line adds to the tight unity in the poem, and ironically contrasts with the thematic proposition of the impossibility of reasonableness. Vincent was the first scholar to publish the note on Melville's manuscript version of this poem: "Observable in Sir Thomas More's 'Utopia' are First Its almost entire reasonableness. Second Its almost entire impracticability. The remark applies to the Utopia's prototype 'Plato's Republic.' "[14]

Finally, at the root of decline, "The Ditty of Aristippus" suggests that man's troubles may not be all man's fault. The "noble gods" have been relaxing and carousing these long eons since they ended their "labor divine" of creation. The poem ends:

Ever blandly adore them;
But spare to implore them;
They rest, they discharge them from time;
Yet believe, light believe
They would succor, reprieve—
Nay, retrieve—
Might but revellers pause in the prime.[15]
(ll. 15–21)

One may consider all these poems as introductory to the major poem concerned with decline and disintegration, the justly famous "Pontoosuce." This lake in the Berkshires was a favorite place for the Melvilles. The descriptive parts of the poem seem to have an immediacy which would argue for the poem being written during the Pittsfield years, though it seems impossible to date it with any certainty.

One can see from the shape of the poem that it has been carefully planned. Structurally it divides into two parts at line 60. The first part has two sections (ll. 1–35, 36–50), each developed in the same way: a descriptive treatment of the setting, philosophical musings, then the dramatically brief "all dies!" All this is preparation for the vision which occupies the second major part of the poem. The issue is between the two contrary facts of existence: the death of all things in nature and the ongoing thrust of life. The achievement of the poem is the momentary stasis that is accomplished, in which these two contraries exist side by side, at least for the moment, and actually seem to form a compatible whole. The catalyst for this achievement is a female spirit who visits the poet with the gift of perception. She is interesting because of her ethereal quality and also because Melville was rarely visited by the totally feminine view of reality. She is more real than Fayaway in *Typee*, and she performs an integrating and harmonizing function that was never to be achieved by Clarel's Ruth. Perhaps she is closest to the Yillah of *Mardi*; but here the girl, though described in erotic terms, does not stimulate the same kind of passion that adds a note of the frantic to the pursuit of Yillah. And finally Yillah is never obtained at all. In other words the poem records a moment unique in the poet's experience.

In a sense this poem is Melville's "Tintern Abbey." Melville's "indistinct abodes / And faery-peopled neighborhoods" sound like the landscape as Wordsworth also perceived it. For Wordsworth there is a clear distinction between the vital principle which harmonizes the contrary propositions one must read from nature, and the feminine principle, in the person of his sister for whom he must articulate the lessons he has learned. For Melville nature and the feminine merge into one as the source and inspiration of this kind of wisdom, and the reader fulfills the function of the confidant to whom this vision of reality is to be communicated.

The most concentrated description of Melville's female spirit is to be found in lines 61–70, at the beginning of the second part of the poem. She embodies the two contrasting aspects of reality from the beginning. She comes "vocal," singing, with the colors of the dawn, "pure, rose-clear, and fresh." She "floats" (like Venus when Aeneas met her in the woods) as she sings her song. Contrasting with these aspects of life, she is also presented as embodying the "chill" of the early morning air. She has bound her hair with ground-pine sprigs, as a goddess may, but it seems that by some deliberate oversight she has also left their tangled roots attached, with earth still clinging to them. In other words the lady embodies the two contrary facts of life that nature proposes, and she combines them in a harmonious whole. The description is bracketed at each end by lines that insist on this. She is first seen in the glade "where light and shadow sport at will": she is perfectly a part of both aspects. And toward the end of this passage the idea is repeated, with the added notion that she in some way mediates between the two contrary facts and harmonizes them:

> Over tufts of moss which *dead* things made,
> Under *vital* twigs which danced or swayed.

The concluding lines of the poem recapitulate the substance in a more intensely personal situation: where the poet is present merely as an observer in the section just mentioned, at the end of the poem the lady communicates her sense of meaning with a kiss.

The poem is the record of an early experience in which the wholeness of life is deeply felt, such as Jonathan Edwards recorded in his *Personal Narrative*, where the horrifying aspects of his inherited Calvinist theology actually came to seem "sweet," or such as Whitman tried to describe in "Death's outlet song of life" under the catalytic inspiration of the thrush's song. Melville also has achieved a harmonization of these opposing realities, but the stasis is uneasy. The kiss from her warm lips may thrill, but in the very kiss he is also aware of the "cold" wreath she wears "with all their humid clinging mould" actually brushing him at the same time. The lady is Death trying to seduce him into complacency with her ways. But the wedding, spoken of in the last lines, of such contrary bedfellows as "warmth and chill," of "life and death," only sets out the terms more clearly on which the battle will continue. In their final conversation on the dunes near Liverpool, Hawthorne believed that Melville had "pretty much made up his mind to be annihilated." But the judgment was premature. Annihilation and eternal vitality were to be the issues as late as the final chapter of *Billy Budd*. The solicitation in this poem to complacency with some sort of mysterious harmony, never very clearly or persuasively defined, was to be resisted until the end. Had the female spirit been allowed to dominate his thinking in any final sense here, she would have grown old in the way that Bridegroom Dick's wife had, preventing any further deep diving on the grounds that it would be a challenge to her adequacy as a wife.

"Pontoosuce" displays other interesting facets. The second stanza has some echoes from "After the Pleasure-Party"—indeed line 7 is another version of the first line of that poem. One wonders if the setting for Urania's fall had not originally been a picnic by a lake in the Berkshires, until another lady intruded, settings separated, and two different poems developed. The interest in geology and its meaning, shown in lines 56–67, also forge a link between this poem and the other works of Melville from *Mardi* through *Moby-Dick*, *Pierre*, and *Clarel*, to "The Great Pyramid" where Melville's interest in geology also appears.[16] A closer link between this poem and *Moby-Dick* can be found in the endings of both pieces. The lady tries to represent a complacency with death in life for the poet, whereas the struggling survivor Ishmael snatches life from death at the last moment as the "coffin life-buoy" rises to the surface. Finally part of the distress caused in the first part of the poem, by thoughts of mutability and death, involve Melville's own work as an artist: "The poet's forms of beauty pass, / And noblest deeds they are undone" (ll. 46–47). The idea is touched on only briefly here, but it forms the major theme of another large group of these miscellaneous poems which Melville left unpublished.

Similar to his evocation of the great artists and his placing himself in their presence in the *Burgundy Club* sketches, Melville in several of his unpublished poems communes on more or less familiar terms with several of the world's great authors and literary figures. They form some kind of fellowship: "all / Dexterous tumblers eluding the Fall," he says of Hafiz and Horace and Beranger in "Hearts-of-Gold." The best point of entry into these poems is one in which Melville clearly sets out the terms of the problem:

> Thy aim, thy aim?
> 'Mid the dust dearth and din,
> An exception wouldst win
> By some deed shall ignite the acclaim?
> Then beware, and prepare thee
> Lest Envy ensnare thee,
> And yearning be sequelled by shame.
> But strive bravely on, yet on and yet on,
> Let the goal be won;
> Then if, living, you kindle a flame,
> Your guerdon will be but a flower,

Only a flower,
The flower of repute,
A flower cut down in an hour. . . .

"Thy Aim, Thy Aim" may seem to move with too galloping a meter, but the repetitions and the urgency of the rhythms arrest the reader's attention. In the first four lines Melville concerns himself again with "the one transcendent deed" that had been so thoroughly analyzed in "Timoleon," a deed belonging to the same category as Pierre's mad and pure decision to save the honor of his father and of Isabel in one self-destructive movement. Such an act puts one beyond the understanding of ordinary people and is thus worthy to be called "transcendent." It leaves one open to the larger powers of the universe which single out the person who lifts his head above the masses; here, envy and the possibility of shame (l. 7) are waiting. It is fairly easy to recognize such a gesture in an external action such as Pierre's or Timoleon's. By comparison the matter becomes much more difficult where the action is interior and some drama within the private mind is being analyzed, as must be the case here. The importance of this poem, then, is that it interiorizes the same pattern found in the two other poems by Melville. The issue is the tension between fame and keeping true to the dreams of one's youth. The word "fame" is emphasized by reserving it for the final word in this poem; it is prepared for by six separate line-endings rhyming with it throughout the poem. Two separate kinds or phases of fame are analyzed here. The first seems to be the kind he felt he had achieved in the popular mind as the man who had lived with cannibals. As the popular tastes shift, this kind can be "cut down in an hour." But the second kind of fame, where "you truly ennoble a name," has an outcome hardly more satisfying: a flower for one's coffin.

The poem *as* poem presents a generalized model for whatever specific action a reader can fit to its dimensions, but as a statement by Melville, it must surely refer to his unwillingness to meet popular demands in his writings. Like any man of talent he was thirsty for a reputation and, if not fortune, at least fame. The decision was to write as he wanted to or not write at all. Even when bowing to public taste, as in *Pierre*, he so manipulated and offended his readers that they went away confused and vaguely insulted. A momentary personal victory, but where does that leave the writer who would have a readership like Shakespeare or Cervantes had? Perhaps with the hope that such a readership would develop late. The poem pursues this thought to the end. Supposing one can achieve that lasting kind of fame, what does it signify? "Again but a flower! / Only a flower, / A funeral flower."

Such a personal, or biographical, interpretation of these poems requires more data. Melville furnishes the personal links in poems inspired by Cervantes and Camoens. Both poems explore areas set out in the model above. In the first the subtitle establishes a relation between subject and the author himself.

THE RUSTY MAN
(*By a Soured One*)

In La Moncha he mopeth,
    With beard thin and dusty;
He doteth and mopeth
    In library fusty—
'Mong his old folios gropeth:
    Cites obsolete saws
    Of chivalry's laws—
    Be the wronged one's knight:
    Die but do right.
So he rusts and musts,
    While each grocer green
Thriveth apace with the fulsome face
    Of a fool serene.

Melville picks up Don Quixote here at the beginning of his story, before the curate and the barber have burned his library, but also before the chivalric materials he has been reading form themselves in his mind into an imperative which must be translated into action. The poem develops a contrast between the high ideals of the man who will shortly commit the transcendent deed of estrangement and the kind of practical activity which the world rewards. A further set of contrasts is developed by the subtitle: if the author of the poem is soured, he must have been through such a process and, though still able to understand Don Quixote's position sympathetically, he knows what the residue of such an experience will be.

The next poem in this series explores in more concrete and personal terms the model developed in "Thy Aim, Thy Aim!" It is ostensibly concerned with Camoens, Portugal's most famous writer and author of its national epic, who died in a hospital without even enough money to furnish a sheet for his deathbed. The poem contains one of Melville's most magnificent metaphors: "Then hunt the flying herds of themes."

Once again the manuscript throws interesting light on the nature of this document, showing that the title was added later to an already finished poem. "Thou dost" in line 21 was at one time "I do." These changes indicate that Melville may have been trying to prepare some of these very personal poems for publication, perhaps as a series on the relationship between the writer's ideals in relation to his public reputation. As it stands, the poem can be taken as an exercise in empathy for Camoens, who steadfastly worked at his epic through the most distracting of travels and adventures—but the poem was not originally so. Two voices of the poet can be distinguished in the first section of the poem. The questioning "I" of line 2 is answered by another part of his self beginning with line 4. The first section portrays a writer who is mastering the difficulties of his trade, wrestling with the angel Art and winning. By contrast the speaker in the second section is another "soured" man. The earlier dream of a transcending action in one's life looks different when viewed from the other end of the process. Whereas the adversary in the previous poem had been merely the prosperous "fool," here the whole practical world is now mounted in conspiracy against the writer. Its wile and guile are but "ill understood" by the innocent writer. While the new poem runs neatly in the channels of the actual life of Camoens, the older and more personal one beneath it records a moment very close to paranoia. But it is a work of art still, and there are signs of intense control in the superior first part. The traditional fire imagery is developed with freshness and power. The God of the fourth line is a personal one, felt to be acting directly on the individual. These two points are used in a contrasting way in the second part, "Camoens in the Hospital." There the fire is "vain," damped down to a fever-producing "delirium mere." And the God is reduced to a vague entity whom prudent folk "claim" they serve.

Still another stance possible for the misunderstood writer is found in "Montaigne and His Kitten." Again the genius finds himself alone in a world of "fools," but the great French essayist maintains himself with aloofness from the world, trifling with the honors that have been granted him by the king, far more content to spend an evening playing with his cat than living up to the expectations of high seriousness from his public. This, however, is a rarely achieved immunity. In another mood Melville would perhaps give up his genius and its demands, as in "A Spirit Appeared to Me."

On the other hand there can be a fellowship among the lonely geniuses, an infinite fraternity of feeling; geniuses may touch hands and feel the shock of recognition run the whole circle round. The manuscript shows that at one stage of "In the Old Farm-House" Melville had tried out "my brother" for "good fellow." But the claim may have seemed immodest and the original phrase was restored—though the poem still records a moment of intense communion that Melville experienced with Shakespeare.

Another set of these miscellaneous poems can be grouped on the subject of death and old age. One short poem presents a light view of the subject. Old age usually looks at youth with raillery and scorn, according to "Old Age in His Ailing," but with a clever turn the author wishes to be saved "from waxing so grave / As, reduced to skim milk, to slander the cream." Yet this is the unique poem with such a light and easy touch. Two companion poems, "Madam Mirror" and "The Wise Virgins to Madam Mirror," contrast the solitude of old age, alone with its decrepitude and memories, with the insensitivity of the "wise" young.

These two poems take their inspiration from a sketch by Hawthorne in *Mosses from an Old Manse* called "Monsieur du Miroir." The title may be translated "the man in the mirror," and the piece is what used to be classified as the informal or imaginative essay—a rambling discourse, with observations more or less profound, on the subject of contemplating one's image in a mirror. In Hawthorne's essay the image flatters one's youth or derides his old age with the truth. It can appear unexpectedly, at the theater, in a woodland pool, or grotesquely mocking in one's own polished andirons. The mirror image comes to be regarded as an uncanny intruder upon one's loneliness, always present, but only potentially, anywhere—demanding by its personal ties a frightening responsibility. Finally the image is the other part of one's self, with whom there is no communion: "Oh friend, canst thou not hear and answer me? Break down the barrier between us! Grasp my hand! Speak! Listen!" One is freed from this projection only at death. It is too horrible to contemplate the prospects of such an image continuing, even perhaps to "sit down in the domestic circle where our faces are most familiar and beloved." The mirror image will finally vanish, says Hawthorne: "He will pass into the dark realm of nothingness, but will not find me there."

In "Madam Mirror" Melville takes up the contrary option: the image remains embodied, long after the person has vanished and the mirror has been relegated to a garret. Hawthorne's last line was: "Of you, perhaps, as of many men, it may be doubted whether you are the wiser, though your whole business is REFLECTION." Melville's poem begins with the same pun. Alone now Madam Mirror takes "to reflections the deeper / On memories far to retrace." Melville's speaker, however, is not the image sent back by a mirror but the mirror itself, capturing the impressions of all that come before it and retaining them for the kind of "reflection" Hawthorne punned on. Melville's speaker is the observer of life, taking in all images and reacting with whatever emotion is appropriate, but unable to praise or blame or in any way touch the life that goes on outside of it. The poem is brutally applicable to the author unable to write, stranded in the traditional garret of the artist. One hardly believes Madam Mirror to be capable of the resignation and self-effacement she claims in her last two lines: "Content I escape from the anguish / Of the Real and the Seeming in life."

The painful isolation of those who have remained alive beyond their prime is increased by the taunting voices of a younger generation in "The Wise Virgins to Madam Mirror." "Wise" is bitterly ironic. The phrase is a deliberate one, heightening the irony merely touched on by an earlier title: "Madam Mirror Condoled with by Damsels." The damsels ingenuously deride the old lady for her age and protest that they will never be caught in the same situation: "Youth is immortal; / 'Tis the elderly only grow old!" They end their gratuitous taunt with Hawthorne's pun again: "Oh yes, we are giddy, we whirl in youth's waltz, / But a fig for *Reflections* when crookedly false."

A mellower view of old age is presented in "The Old Shipmaster and His Crazy Barn." The speaker is an individualistic and cantankerous old man, though by no means an Ahab, who describes his old barn as "bewrinkled in shingle and lichened in board" in the first ten lines. The poem continues:

> Pull it down, says a neighbor.
> Never mind be that labor!
> For a Spirit inhabits, a fellowly one,
> The like of which never responded to me
> From the long hills and hollows that make up the sea,
> Hills and hollows where Echo is none.
>
> The site should I clear and rebuild,
> Would that Voice reinhabit?—Self-willed,
> Says each pleasing thing
> Never Dives can buy,
> Let me keep where I cling!
> I am touchy as tinder
> Yea, quick to take wing,
> Nor return if I fly.

If the old man is unlike Captain Ahab, he is also unlike John Marr, who found no "fellowly" spirit in his landlocked old age. This shipmaster has gladly given up life at sea for the security of solid land under him. Melville crossed out "on Cape Cod" from the end of the title in his manuscript, perhaps because his character would prefer to live removed from even the sight and sound of the sea. The man is also content with what looks like eccentricity to others. He has found his "Voice," his "Spirit," in the life he has finally settled down to and will not do anything to break the spell. This is not to be read as Melville settling down to bland domesticity; instead he is borrowing a fleeting hint from Joan of Arc and keeping true to his own voices, finding a tranquillity in this pursuit that cannot be bought in any other way. In some minor way the old shipmaster is another Timoleon, finding that the price of dignity and self-respect is isolation. Refusing to raze one's dilapidated barn is, once again in a very minor way, his transcendent act.

Two very interesting poems remain, not easily categorizable with the rest. "The New Ancient of Days" is Melville's response to a particular discovery by geologists, recorded by Sir Charles Lyell in a very popular book. The first stanza reads:

> The man of bone confirms his throne
> In cave where fossils be;
> Outdating every mummy known,
> Not older Cuvier's mastodon,
>   Nor older much the sea:
>   Old as the Glacial Period, he;
> And claims he calls to mind the day
> When Thule's king, by reindeer drawn,
> His sleigh-bells jingling in icy morn,
> Slid clean from the Pole to the Wetterhorn
> Over frozen waters in May!
>   Oh, man of the cave of Engihoul,
>   With Eld doth he dote and drule?

Melville wrote on his manuscript, "See Lyell's Antiquities of Man and Darwin's Descent of the Species." The full title of the first book is *The Geological Evidence of the Antiquity of Man*. It was published in 1863 and went through three revised editions in that same year. It is in this book, Chapter 4, that Lyell describes the finding of three fragments of a very old skull, analyzed unfortunately as not capable of enclosing a very intelligent brain, among the debris at the bottom of a cave at Engihoul.

The other book does not add any factual information necessary to the poem, but is still relevant. The full title of Darwin's book is *The Descent of Man and Selection in Relation to Sex* (1871). What it also adds to the poem is some evidence, at least a *terminus a quo*, for dating the poem. Melville's note, then, has the added value of calling attention to two key books in the argument for evolution, showing that Melville could have been using them during the years immediately before *Clarel* was published.

The meter of the poem is rollicking and irreverent: "Yea, the man of the cave of Engihoul / From Moses knocks under the stool." Melville has great fun rhyming the recherché categories of the scientists:

> In *bas-relief* he late has shown
> A horrible show, agree—
> Megalosaurus, iguanodon,
> Palæotherium Glypthæcon,
> A Barnum-show raree.
>
> (*ll. 27–31*)

The man in the cave is coeval with the antique monsters who shared the world with him: "The cubs of Chaos, with eyes askance, / Preposterous griffins that squint at Chance / And Anarch's cracked decree!" (ll. 35–37) The poem grows serious here: "Anarch" is Melville's version of the purblind Doomsters who are responsible for man's loneliness and incompleteness in "After the Pleasure-Party." But the poet is soon back to punning. Against all comers the cave man "flings his fossilifer's stone" (l. 55). The poem, a taunt from man's deep past, ends quite seriously, with the major issue presented to the nineteenth century by the new science; and in the final line the word "Gorgon" connects these data from the deep past with other data from the depths of the sea, to further identify the monstrous power which rules the universe.

> But the ogre of bone he snickers alone,
> He grins for his godless glee:
> "I have flung my stone, my fossil stone,
> And your gods, how they scamper," saith he.
> Imp! imp of the cave of Engihoul,
> Shall he grin like the Gorgon and rule?
>
> (*ll. 71–76*)

"Shadow at the Feast" re-creates one of Melville's favorite situations: wine and a luxurious setting, genial good fellowship and good conversation, against the background of what Yeats would call "ceremony." It is the setting Melville strove for again in his *Burgundy Club* sketches and to which he alluded in hoping to share a hamper of champagne with Hawthorne in some nontemperance Paradise.[17] In contrast is the "shadow" flitting in the background. The poem has its origins in family life: the female is "kinswoman." The title in the manuscript is in Mrs. Melville's hand and may be a deliberate attempt to disguise the real person intended. Lines 27–28 originally read "But Lonie, but Lonie / Thy story we know." And the final stanza was:

> Come, coz, the decanter!
> Our hearts let us cheer,
> Yea, chirp *Merry Christmas*—
> So Lonie not hear!

Ryan's studies of the tables of contents for *Weeds and Wildings* indicate that at one time a poem entitled "Lonie" was included with the Christmas poems at the end of the first section. But, as we have seen, *Weeds and Wildings* came to be a re-creation of Pittsfield as an idyll. The poem would have clashed so with this overall theme that it had to be dropped finally from this gift dedicated to Melville's wife.

The subtitle ("Mrs. B———, 1847") dates the reminiscence from the year of the Melvilles' marriage, which means that the numerous relatives of two large families must be considered for the mysterious identity of the lady. Whoever the actual person may have been, the poem retains a poignant charm for the reader, in the contrast between family celebration and the one who is present but not a part of it. And the characterization is interesting; she has her own kind of character and stability in the experience she has suffered: an early marriage and early widowhood, a reception back into the family when she has scarcely left it, and an added mystery because of her youthful innocence and experience. Melville underlines this by "elf-sorrow" and "elf-child." One can trace the word with growing interest through the writings of Melville, and yet find in the end that all its meanings seem to derive finally from Hawthorne's frequent use of the word "elf" for the mysterious Pearl in *The Scarlet Letter*.

VIII

THE ART OF POETRY
AND BILLY BUDD

All these I set
For emblems of the day against the tower
Emblematical of the night.

W. B. Yeats

Yea, and shall he also at last vanish, sailing
into the boundless Nil, leaving no phosphorescent
wake or magic moon-glades behind?

Burgundy Club

But no one, in any case, measuring the long
anguish that runs through his life and work,
will fail to acknowledge the greatness, all the
more anguished in being the fruit of self-conquest.

Albert Camus, "Herman Melville"

I TAKE "the art of poetry" to mean the techniques of literary construction, much in the sense that Aristotle used the term "poetics." Any generalizations that can validly be made will have an obvious bearing on Melville's final literary work. Melville approaches *Billy Budd* with a complex technique worked out—one that is not obvious, however, to the reader who knows only the great fiction written more than three decades earlier. If we are fully to know this last work, it must be as the final flowering of a long and cumulative effort. The great mind of the man is totally present here.

One of Melville's most direct comments on the nature and function of art occurs in the middle of *Clarel* (II, xxxv, 1–37). In this passage Melville consciously aligns himself with the most profound insights achieved by the romantic theorists. He is discussing the architectural etchings of Giovanni Battista Piranesi. While acknowledging that they are fantasies, he insists at the same time that they give one access to the deepest levels of truth. These are the resources within man, his power of expressing the mysterious truth in symbolic form. Much of his own nature is ordinarily hidden to man, constituting the "penetralia" of his heart. But one can dwell at length on the simple "fables" of the race that are always and everywhere believed, and his "Imagination" can express in visual brilliance and in symbolic manner the dark truth that they contain:

> Thy wings, Imagination, span
> Ideal truth in fable's seat;
> The thing implied is one with man,
> His penetralia of retreat—
> The heart, with labyrinths replete:
> In freaks of intimation see
> Paul's "mystery of iniquity." . . .
> *(ll. 18–24)*

The concluding phrase, one of Melville's favorites, will function again when he himself goes over another old story in search of its symbolic truth—in *Billy Budd*. The passage continues, developing Melville's idea of the artist's quest. The work is not only difficult but in some way forbidden, "interdicted." And finally the result is to be published prudently. Such knowledge is esoteric; it must be obscured in haze, though enough is given for the careful observer to catch one's meaning, to follow the artist's track through the maze.

The inventor miraged all the maze
Obscured it with prudential haze;
Nor less, if subject unto question,
The egg left, egg of the suggestion.
(ll. 29–32)

Melville devotes himself to an expansion and commentary on this theory of art in several shorter poems. One of them has become a classic:

ART

In placid hours well-pleased we dream
Of many a brave unbodied scheme.
But form to lend, pulsed life create,
What unlike things must meet and mate:
A flame to melt—a wind to freeze;
Sad patience—joyous energies;
Humility—yet pride and scorn;
Instinct and study; love and hate,
Audacity—reverence. These must mate,
And fuse with Jacob's mystic heart,
To wrestle with the angel—Art.

The first two lines seem to echo Wordsworth, as if they would lead the reader into a theory of the origin of poetry from "emotion recollected in tranquility." The impression is erased at the beginning of line 3. Behind the poem lies also the Shakespeare who played such a dramatic role in Melville's mind in 1850, the year he was writing the essay on Hawthorne and also *Moby-Dick*, trying to establish a new Shakespeare in the first instance and to create a modern American equivalent for Shakespeare's language in the second. The opinion of Theseus in *A Midsummer Night's Dream* is directly relevant to "Art." Theseus requires poetry to furnish airy nothing with a local habitation and a name; Melville criticizes both Shakespeare and Wordsworth according to the same canon: such dreams are too "*un*bodied." Theseus speaks of what Coleridge would call the "esemplastic" function of imagination, which unites diversities and contraries into one construction which seems to have a life of its own. Melville has his own wording for the kind of life which results: "pulsed life create." What Coleridge called the "organic unity" of the poem is achieved in similar terms here, with two metaphors. The first is "mate" in line 4, which is repeated in line 9 and reinforced by two rhymes. The second is "flame" in line 5, which is more subtly developed into "fuse" in line 10, as if the metaphor were concerned with a kind of welding. But it is Melville's theory, as well as Coleridge's, that the elements must not be allowed to fuse into a static union—hence the word "wrestle" in the final line.

The greatness of this short poem lies in the compressed achievement of the last two lines. Here the figure of the poet himself is introduced, finally, as the place where these contraries meet and are still to be shaped into a work of art. The use of "Jacob" as a figure for the poet sets up a rich system of allusions. His story has three phases: first the dream of an active communion between heaven and earth, with angels ascending and descending between the two spheres of being; then the desire to set up a monument to memorialize this vision; and finally the wrestling with an angel who, it turns out, may be God himself. Melville has already, in the first lines of his poem, said that "dream" is not enough. (One must note here that the use of Jacob in the last line creates a new and more specific meaning for "dream" in the first line.) From what Wordsworth had called tranquillity, and what Melville calls "placid hours" of dream, the artist proceeds, through conflicts and contradictions presented by one's existence, to the terrifying contest with ultimates. This is not in any sense of the word a gentlemanly belletristic theory of what the poet does. Melville touches the subject perfectly with the word "mystic." The poem rises beyond the narrow area of technique to define the driven, probing kind of personality whom Melville had once called the "deeply thinking mind."

The work of the poetic intelligence is illustrated by another famous poem.

IN A GARRET

> Gems and jewels let them heap—
> Wax sumptuous as the Sophi:
> For me to grapple from Art's deep
> One dripping trophy!

"Grapple" here is not the same as "wrestle" in the previous poem, though one may be tempted to make a connection. The figure is different and, though innocent enough in appearance, one needs to pause at this word to consider the usual function of grappling hooks and dragging operations. The figure has much in common with Melville's consistent diving imagery and his feeling for the kind of reality one encounters in the depths. A kind of curious tension is set up between the poem and its title: the poem is clearly not about rescuing ancient works of art from the bed of ocean—as it had been, for example, in the "Disinterment of Hermes." It is instead about the work of solitary and poverty-stricken seekers, artists, who dwell in the conventional garret. The poem is one of Melville's many statements against commercial man, but it also fits into another context of his polemic against Thoreau and Transcendentalism. When Thoreau had probed the depths of Walden Pond in the icy dead of winter, he was reassured of the continuing vitality of Nature by pulling up a green weed on his anchor. Melville opposes this as a theory of life in his poem "The Tuft of Kelp" and as a theory of art in the present poem. One who has dived with Melville before has no such optimistic prospects. Death and evil are at the center of his universe; one's grappling hooks are likely to bring up some ultimate horror.

The artist is also one who plays with his reader or viewer. The wisdom he has achieved is by nature esoteric. Though all may be allowed to look, not all may understand. Art may become a private dialogue between the artist and a very narrow privileged audience, no matter how large and public the setting. Melville experienced this phenomenon himself while studying a painting, and wrote about the experience in "The Marchioness of Brinvilliers" while retaining the secret.

> He toned the sprightly beam of morning
>   With twilight meek of tender eve,
> Brightness interfused with softness,
>   Light and shade did weave:
> And gave to candor equal place
> With mystery starred in open skies;
> And, floating all in sweetness, made
>   Her fathomless mild eyes.

Born of a wealthy family in Paris, this woman married the Marquis de Brinvilliers, a man attached to the French army in Normandy. He seems to have been a naive and unsuspicious husband with regard to a wife who was famous for her beauty. One of the men he introduced to her was Godin de Saint-Croix, a dashing cavalry officer, the illegitimate and unacknowledged son of an illustrious and wealthy family. She quickly became his mistress and the marquis, harassed by financial worries, allowed the scandal to continue and grow. Finally her father put a stop to the affair and had Saint-Croix imprisoned in the Bastille for a year, where he met an Italian expert in poisons named Exili. After her lover was released, the marquise experimented with his poisons on poor people and on the sick she charitably visited in hospitals. When

Saint-Croix and his mistress felt that they had perfected the poisons, they began to destroy the whole of her family and gain the inheritance. After several deaths—the father took several months to die because they were uncertain at first of the dosage—the plan was exposed by the accidental death of Saint-Croix. The marquise herself was captured after a chase through several countries and after several suicide attempts. She was beheaded and her body burned in 1676. She had confessed and gone to her death with such piety (harmonizing so well with her famous petite beauty) that many in the crowd thought her a saint. Madame de Sévigné witnessed the execution and described it with irony in her *Lettres*. The painting Melville has in mind is by Charles le Brun (1619–1690), court painter for Louis XIV and one of the designers of Versailles.[1]

Melville's poem, then, becomes a complex statement about the art of poetry as well as the art of painting, since he has duplicated Le Brun's approach to the subject in his own poem. The beautiful surfaces are not to be trusted. The picture itself is a pasteboard mask and so is the poem. It appears to be a slight development of the contraries mentioned in "Art" (it is printed in the same section of *Timoleon* as that poem); here the contraries are morning and evening, light and shade, candor and mystery. They converge in a portrait of exquisite beauty, but the real contrast is within the experience of the poem itself: what it means to the naive reader and what it means to one who will look beneath the surface. Only the latter will see that with the word "fathomless" in the last line we are again diving with Melville into the mystery of iniquity. Lawrance Thompson has documented this technique of withheld meaning in *Moby-Dick*, where writing yields its true meaning only to the ideal reader for whom Melville was constantly searching.[2] Writing here becomes a technique of concealment as much as communication and revelation, and the work produced is a quasi-gnostic document whose meaning is revealed only to the initiated. Perhaps the reader is given a clue by the fact that "The Marchioness of Brinvilliers" immediately follows "Fragments of a Lost Gnostic Poem of the 12th Century" in *Timoleon*.

Still another sidelight is cast upon the poet's work by a poem called "The Weaver." This too is from the first section of *Timoleon*. The manuscript shows some significant developments in the evolution of the poem. In line 2 the word "Arva's" first read "Mecca's," then "Marva's." In line 8 the word was first "Allah's," then "Marva's," and finally "Arva's." Thus the poem was originally a study of religious devotion. In the second stage it was also a religious study, but perhaps focused on religious fanaticism concerning meaningless ritual. Among the many rituals that must have seemed strange to the American Protestant, a pilgrim to Mecca was expected to run seven times between the two hills of Safa and Merwa (also called "Marva," the tradition which Melville follows). But in its final stage the poem seems to be a study of the kind of devotion demanded by art; in the evolution the word undergoes in the poem, "Arva's" is developing by natural stages toward "*ars.*" The word "wight" in line 3 is also interesting. Melville uses the word rarely. The most prominent use is in the poem "The Conflict of Convictions" in *Battle-Pieces.* There man the searcher is seen as a feeble groper in the dark: "His forehead bears a taper dim" like a miner; as prober for truth he is, in Melville's final version of the poem, "a meagre wight." Finally the poem recalls another aspect which Melville had always felt characterized the true artist— his constant impecuniousness.

These are the major poetic statements Melville cares to make about his poetics, but much more can be inferred from his practice.

Melville consistently used poetry as an instrument of criticism, in the philosophical sense of that word. The poems are conscious uses of the inquiring intelligence to determine the possibilities and limits of knowledge and the kinds of reality discernible. As such his poetry shows the kind of thought that begins with epistemology and finally yields at least fragments for a metaphysics. This is not to deny his positive qualities as a poet in the more general sense. The list of genres he attempted, from ballad to masque, is a long one, as is the list of nonce forms he devised for the individualizing of particular poems. His fidelity to the four-stress line and his experimentation with its uses are as impressive as the fidelity of earlier poets to the more supple pentameter. His use of the formula or the *Stichwort* as a structural principle, as in "The Berg" and "The Scout Toward Aldie," must be noted, as must be his idiosyncratic preference for rhymes based on regional pronunciation. But I have in mind something at a more profound level, the unique *use* to which each author finally puts his work. In the last analysis, I believe, the distinguishing characteristic is Melville's use of poetry as *Kritik.*

One can see this element, for example, in the rose poems which come at the end of *Weeds and Wildings* or in the sea poems which were collected for *John Marr.* In both cases there is the conscious use of one item for its symbolic potential. "Rose Window" from *Weeds and Wildings* may serve as a quick example of this use of poetry. The middle section is clearly a dream vision or fantasy, mysterious even to the dreamer. But this central material clearly is connected with other kinds of reality: with the strongly physical reality of the rose window which dominates his field of vision as he awakens and which leaves him with a curiously dynamic kind of joy. It ties in also with the traditional narrative materials announced as the title of the sermon early in the poem: "I am the rose of Sharon." The line has had an ancient and rich place in Christian exegesis, and since the preacher was uninspired, the dreamer himself worked out the text and finally brought up the materials latent in it for a real waking experience.

Clarel contains even more interesting and enlightening uses of poetry for this epistemological purpose. In his sustained inquiry into the Christ story Melville has affinities with the nineteenth-century higher criticism. But his sources are impossible to determine, unless they are merely familiar journalistic accounts. Melville's habit of haunting bookstores and reading rooms allows us to assume a reader's knowledge far beyond those books for which an actual record of ownership can be found. And it must also be emphasized that his meditations in this poem are so clearly connected with his actual experience in the Holy Land as well as with his own enduring symbols that they stand with a distinct clarity of their own in the more general stream of nineteenth-century thought.

Melville's problem was to reconcile the apparent contradictions in his actual experience. The Holy Land should have been holy, a theater fit for the divine actions that had reputedly taken place there; yet it was a wasteland worse than any he had yet experienced. Melville's earliest literary impulse had been to believe in a world of simplicity and innocence; he seems to have conceived of himself as being its champion and apologete for a moment in writing *Typee*, and it was to remain an area of his mind that would never entirely disappear. So also the stories about Jesus illustrated an ideal of freedom and pure joy that was belied in the very lives of those who claimed to follow him most devotedly. And the physical experience showed that the stories about Jesus and the land that was their setting were utterly incompatible. No such narratives of pure innocence could be staged in such a menacing landscape. Yet all these elements impinge upon consciousness in some way and so are "real." The problem of the poem, as it operates at this critical level, is to discern the quality of each reality and the level to which each is to be assigned. Melville had done this before; *Mardi* contains two major leaps from one kind of reality to another, and the third section of that novel contains further attempts at this kind of categorization. *Clarel* is a more carefully planned and mature work.

Here he is not selling satire for its entertainment value, but recording a private quest for the very few he believed would be interested.

Upon rereading *Billy Budd* at this point, one can quickly become aware of the importance of the poetry as immediate background for this masterpiece. Verbal similarities abound, some of which have already been pointed out by earlier critics, and many of these parallels add to the richness of texture of the story. When Melville speaks of Billy's "*barbaric* good humor" in the first chapter,[3] one recalls that he had already identified this characteristic with the two innocent wanderers in a marquesan Eden, in the poem "To Ned." In the third chapter, where Melville develops the historical setting for his story, the flag of the French Directory is described as "the enemy's red *meteor* of unbridled and unbounded revolt." The most striking use of this image is of course in the introductory poem to *Battle-Pieces*, where the hanged John Brown's beard streams from his cap as "the meteor of war." The allusion can summon up recollections of a civil war and Melville's strong suggestion throughout that the American war is a dim parallel with the cosmic war of Good and Evil described by Milton. This early clue will prove correct as the theological materials in the story continue to accumulate.

Melville still has his own *Battle-Pieces* in the back of his mind in the next chapter of *Billy Budd*. In a digression on Nelson and the "picturesqueness" of older sea warfare he considers the prosaic criticism of later "martial utilitarians" and "the Benthamites of war" who would go about the business more practically with their clumsy and efficient *Monitors*. This recalls his "A Utilitarian View of the Monitor's Fight." Melville retains a strong and precise recollection of the Civil War poems he wrote more than two decades earlier; we will shortly come to see the larger thematic patterns from *Battle-Pieces* functioning strongly and intelligently in *Billy Budd*.

Other allusions to the poetry function more incidentally. For example, Billy's protestation of innocence, "I have eaten the King's bread and I am true to the King," has, for many commentators, fit into the recognizable pattern of religious imagery and theme. The interpretation becomes even more probable when one recalls Melville's less equivocal allusion to the sacrament at the end of "The Margrave's Birthnight": "Into wine is turned the water, / Black bread into white." So also, and more obviously, the comparison of Claggart's eyes to those of a "torpedo fish" or to "the alien eyes of certain uncataloged creatures of the deep," in Chapter 19, must be read in the context of the other sharks and monstrous sea creatures in Melville's poetry. In Chapter 24, when the gunbays where Billy spends the night between the trial and his death are compared to "confessionals," one recalls Melville's use of the confessional in "In a Church of Padua" and remembers that it is a "dread diving bell" in which the depths of the mystery of evil are explored. Melville is again probing for the heart of the evil mystery. A few pages later the imagery is confirmed. At the beginning of Chapter 25, the deck where Billy is incarcerated is compared to one of the levels "so like the tiered galleries in a coal mine." The words recall the strata imagery in *Clarel* as well as the comparison of man groping for meaning to a coal miner with only a "taper dim" to light his way, in the poem "The Conflict of Convictions."

At the end of this same chapter a very precise correction visible in the manuscript gains all its meaning from one of his recent poems. As Billy is hauled up to the yardarm the sun comes out transforming the clouds "with a soft glory as of the fleece of the Lamb of God. . . . Billy ascended; and, ascending, took the full *rose* of the dawn." Until very late in the composition of the story the word "shekinah" had stood in the place of "rose." The full meaning of "shekinah," as the visible manifestation of God's presence, is a powerful center in Melville's imagination. One may recall his poem "In the Desert" where "shekinah" is defined and its origin in the intolerable brightness of the Egyptian desert is conjectured. The use of the word here would be too powerful, would state explicitly the apparition here of the God who is defined in biblical terms. Melville was never able to accept those terms; in fact the redefining of the final powers that rule the universe is obvious from *Moby-Dick* through the poetry. As a last and precise stroke in the composition of *Billy Budd*, the word is removed and the more probing image from his rose poems is substituted.

Two other explicit echoes from the poems may be mentioned. When Billy's body is committed to the sea, in Chapter 27, "certain large seafowl . . . flew screaming to the spot. So near the hull did they come, that the stridor or bony creak of their gaunt double-jointed pinions was audible. As the ship under light airs passed on, leaving the burial spot astern, they still kept circling it low down with the moving shadow of their outstretched wings and the croaked requiem of their cries." These birds are not neutral or innocuous. They are agents as much as the demonic birds of fate that preside over the destruction of the admiral's ship in "The Haglets." Indeed the two scenes resemble one another in many details. As a final poetic echo one may notice the name of the ship which is responsible for the fatal wounding of Captain Vere in Chapter

28, the *Atheist*. Melville's other prominent use of the term is in *Battle-Pieces*, in the poem called "The House-Top: A Night Piece." This is the poem describing the draft riots of 1863 as another outbreaking of irrational and uncontrolled evil—"the Atheist roar of riot."

What is finally to be noted about these echoes is the fact that they each tie down a separate place in the story to one or other of Melville's poems where a particularly dark and terrifying view of the universe is proposed. The dispute continues between those who would consider *Billy Budd* to be Melville's Testament of Acceptance and those who would consider it the final confirmation of his view of a universe totally dominated by evil. The final term of each allusion heavily tips the balance in favor of the latter view.

Interesting as these verbal parallels are between the poetry and *Billy Budd*, they do not exhaust the matter, nor do they take us as deeply into the story as we might go. For this we must now turn to some larger patterns of thought that have developed with unique clarity in Melville's poetry. These patterns are part of the essential fabric of *Billy Budd*. They emerge gradually but surely in the poems.

The first major development of Melville's mind which is recorded in the poetry is in *Battle-Pieces*, where the discrimination of the two cycles of Law and Evil and the final dominance of the second over the first are worked out in careful detail. We have already noted how clearly present some of the phrases and images from *Battle-Pieces* were in Melville's mind as he wrote *Billy Budd;* the way is paved for our finding the *whole* of the earlier book, its shaping thought, present somewhere in the later book. The distinction is operative in the characterization of Captain Vere, and once this is noted, a great amount of controversy over Melville's exact feeling toward this character can be dismissed. The most direct allusion to the earlier work is to be found in the words of Vere himself, in Chapter 27, cited after the major action of the book has been completed and cited as a characteristic sentiment which he often uttered: " 'With mankind,' he would say, 'forms, measured forms, are everything.' " The words are a precise echo of the central poem in the Cycle of Law in *Battle-Pieces*, "Dupont's Round Fight." The Cycle of Law is superseded in *Battle-Pieces;* a truer and more menacing version of reality dominates in the Cycle of Evil. Vere, then, cannot be Melville's truth-teller; he is a man who sees only partially, at a lower level than the real. Like Amasa Delano and the other Bachelors of Melville's fiction, he is unable, with his limited experience and vision, to comprehend the true evil of the universe.

Vere, like Delano, is a man who has tried to dive. He has read much and thought deeply. He has reflected on men he has known and experiences he has had, not content merely to have lived but demanding an account of that life. Yet this study and seriousness have resulted, in both cases, in a complacency that actually hinders profound understanding. Vere's reading, carefully reported by the author, is a search for models of behavior, not for the knowledge of how one ought to behave based on principles and ideas: "books treating of actual men and events no matter of what era—history, biography. . . ." Vere also reads Montaigne, whom critics have long seen to have been one of Melville's own favorite authors, especially for his satire and devious subtleties. Vere sees him quite differently; the quotation above continues: "and unconventional writers like Montaigne, who, free from cant and convention, honestly and in the spirit of common sense philosophize upon realities" (Chapter 7). Both Vere and Delano are proud of the knowledge they have painstakenly gathered, and this pride prevents any true wisdom from developing. Unlike Timoleon, for example, they would be unable to stand far enough away from conventional behavior to perform the truly transcendent act. Furthermore their superficial knowledge has a social dimension; not only are they stunted, but they can be a positive menace to others whose lives they touch. Both have studied hard to discover formulas that pass as wisdom, that hold for 90 percent of human life, but which do not at all hold for the crises at the outer edge of experience.

Vere's typical saying, that "forms, measured forms, are everything," furnishes the point of view from which his trial remarks are to be read. This is surely one of the centers of the story, the major locus for the intellectualizing that is carried on in it; yet Melville has been misread or only partially understood many times here. First it must be noted that the trial is not a fair one. Melville insists twice that the judge has already made up his mind. Just after Billy has killed Claggart, Vere exclaims, "Struck dead by an angel of God! Yet the angel must hang!" Vere sees the irony of hanging an angel, but not the irony of prejudging the outcome of the inquiry that must follow. Again, in Chapter 21, the narrator exclaims that Vere, a prudent man, needs to gain some time for reflection, "until he can decide upon his course, and in each detail." At this point the goal or final outcome is not in doubt, but only the means of getting to it, the "course" which the nautical man should take.

With regard to the purely intellectual center of the story, Vere's charge to the board in the middle of Chapter 31, it must be one of the most wicked uses to which rhetoric has ever been put. Yet one finds in a typical class of students, for example, that readers are able to race across its surface with ease, straining for the end of a story that is now finally in view; nor has Vere's speech functioned as strongly as it might in analyses of the narrative that have so far been published. But so far, one of the major keys to the story, furnished by the poetry, has been lacking.

There is only one argument in Vere's charge, followed by answers to three objections (two of which Vere phrases himself), and concluding with the dismissal of a compromise suggested by one of the jury. The question, as Vere puts it, is, "How can we adjudge to summary and shameful death a fellow creature innocent before God, and whom we feel to be so?" This he dismisses as the appeal of "Nature" acting upon mere "sailors," whereas their duty is to "the King . . . as the King's officers." This is a strange chopping up of men for a dedicated humanist like Vere. Yet the dilemma mirrors the distinction he had already established between "military duty" and "scruple vitalized by compassion." The argument, as he phrases it, is that because of their oath of allegiance they are not free to choose the latter side of the distinction: "in receiving our commissions we in the most important regards ceased to be free agents." Then in a parody of the insight in "Dupont's Round Fight," Vere argues: "Would it be so much we ourselves that would condemn as it would be martial *law operating through us?*" Vere counsels abandonment of ethical responsibility: "For that law and the rigor of it, we are not responsible." This verges on a parody of the legalistic mind which abdicates its humanity and its personal accountability; it is the perennial defense of those who plead innocence on the basis of acting upon orders from above.

Vere confirms this analysis in the answers he gives to the objections. In the first one, which he phrases himself, he ridicules the opposing view as proceeding merely from "the heart." Melville's lifelong sympathies have been with the heart; Vere's contrasting view should be noted. In the second objection, also phrased by Vere, he puts the "private conscience" secondary to "the rule under which we alone officially proceed." The officer of marines proposes the third objection: that Billy's intention was innocent. This door had already been closed in Vere's main argument. With a parallel that is not really to the point—that war often kills the good and the innocent in battle—Vere concludes: "Budd's intent or non-intent is nothing to the purpose."

Vere, then, remains capable only of thought patterns at the level of the Cycle of Law. He is unable to penetrate more deeply into the nature of the universe. Indeed he actually resists the invitation to do so when earlier he acknowledges: "Ay, there is a mystery; but, to use a scriptural phrase, it is 'a mystery of iniquity,' a matter for psychologic theologians to discuss. But what has a military court to do with it?"

The inadequacy of Law as a rule of life involves the inadequacy of human reason to construct generalizations that cover every particular. In this view the character of Claggart also takes on new meaning and coherence—and, as a corollary, gives the precise reason why Vere cannot comprehend the depths of evil in him. The references are numerous, but let the following one stand as typical. Melville, in Chapter 11, is analyzing "so exceptional a nature" as Claggart's: "Though the man's even temper and discreet bearing would seem to intimate a mind peculiarly subject to the law of reason, not the less in heart would he seem to riot in complete exemption from that law, having apparently little to do with reason further than to employ it as an ambidexter implement for effecting the irrational." Melville's perennial distinction between the head and the heart indicates that we are at one of the thematic centers of his interest. Law is mentioned twice here—and the possibility that some events can take place totally beyond the limited patterns of law and rationality. The concepts at work are the same as those operating in the two cycles of *Battle-Pieces*. They serve here both to categorize Claggart's evil nature precisely, and also to furnish the basis for understanding Vere's inadequacy to deal with such phenomena. Vere's ability to comprehend is limited to the operations of the head, and to events that follow rational pattern or law. Claggart's evil goes far beyond these patterns.

Another major achievement of Melville's poetry is the identification and analysis of the "transcendent act." Melville's use is personal, and not to be identified with Emerson's and Poe's attempts to shake loose from Kantian categories, to soar "out of space, out of time." In Melville's sense the phrase receives its fullest definition in "Timoleon." Timoleon's action—to kill the tyrant, though he be one's brother—springs from an impulse of sheer goodness and altruism, of the kind that considers only the act to be done and not the personal consequences to be suffered. Pierre's act was similar and so was Billy's. We have seen that toward the end of his life Melville was pondering the nature of this act in such poems as "Thy Aim, Thy Aim?" and "The Rusty Man" as well as in his poetic treatment of Garibaldi in the *Burgundy Club* sketches. Connected with the theme is an analysis of the problem of fame: what will survive as the popular estimate of this kind of action;

and what, finally, does fame of any kind have to do with a man once he is dead anyway?

These patterns illuminate the story of Billy Budd. His attack on Claggart springs from his own personal sense of innocence, his outrage at betrayal and guile, his desire to "strike through the mask" as the evil thing momentarily discloses itself fully. Unfortunately for Billy his immediate environment is controlled by a clearly defined web of rules and procedures which were created for ordinary contingencies and were not conceived with extraordinary situations in mind. The act is transcendent because it removes Billy from the ordinary pieties which give clarity and order to 90 percent of life. Vere recognizes this when he rules out the element of the mysterious in the trial. As in the cases of Timoleon and Pierre the hero becomes an outsider, prey to the forces of violence in the universe.

The complexity of a transcendent act also integrates into the story the Admiral Nelson passages which have hitherto proved not completely tractable. Nelson is a man of flair and dash, and his battles "stand unmatched in human annals." He himself stands, in Melville's mind, above and beyond ordinary human beings. In fact ordinary human beings cannot altogether condone his disdain for "forms, measured forms." As Melville puts it, "these martial utilitarians may suggest considerations implying that Nelson's ornate publication of his person in battle was not only unnecesary, but not military, nay, savored of foolhardiness and vanity." The two chapters on Nelson (4 and 5) appear between the lengthy characterizations of Vere and Billy and shed light in both directions. Billy, it will turn out, is also capable of rising above ordinary behavior; Vere, though jestingly compared to Nelson as a seaman and fighter (in Chapter 7), will nevertheless be incapable of rising above the view of "these martial utilitarians" who were unable to condone the actions of Nelson. As in the case of Timoleon the prevailing evil is "legalized by lawyers"; in Billy's case too, "no sanction Virtue knew / For deeds that on prescriptive morals jar" ("Timoleon," ll. 5, 123–24).

In a late development of the transcendent act we have seen that Melville began to consider the problem of fame or popular regard granted to such a figure. Timoleon was finally vindicated in the popular judgment, for example, as Pierre was not, and Melville gave quite a bit of thought to his feelings on the subject of his own immortality in a series of poems already considered. This development plays a crucial part in one's final reading of *Billy Budd*, but it can best be handled in connection with the next point to be taken up. Let us here conclude by emphasizing what must already be clear, that the notion of the two cycles of Law and Evil dovetails nicely with the concept of the transcendent act. It is obvious that *Billy Budd* is a complex synthesis of much of Melville's later thought.

The final major set of materials from the poems which finds its way into *Billy Budd* may be called the christological. The strands here are tightly interwoven but in no way overly complicated or confused. A convenient point of entrance is with one of Melville's earliest attempts to find a controlling theme for *Billy Budd*. "Gnosticism" in Melville's specialized sense of the term was one of the schools of thought that attracted him quite early[4] because it explained the absolute dominance of evil in the material universe, while still acknowledging the conviction, so deeply rooted in western civilization, of the absolute goodness of God himself. We have already seen that a medieval version of Gnosticism, taught and practiced by the Albigensians, was the subject of "Fragments of a Lost Gnostic Poem of the 12th Century." There one of the key phrases was "the Good Man." In the Albigensian doctrine the Good Man is primarily Christ, secondarily the devotee who has arrived at the inner circle of perfection. Signs that this material was on Melville's mind can be found in the earliest version of "Billy in the Darbies" with which the story concludes. The poem opened, as it still does, with praise for the chaplain for coming to pray for Billy before his execution. It continued, "Nor bad his story, / The Good Being hung and gone to glory."[5] Melville seems to mean that the chaplain had, for Billy's comfort, told him the story of Christ. Billy's words here make it clear that he has not identified himself as Christ but has grasped the implications of the story for himself. Of all the words tradition offers for the death of Christ, Billy chooses the one identical with his own situation, "hung"; and of all the terms applicable to Christ, "the Good Being" is the one found here. The point here to be made is small but important. At the first conception of his story, Melville had in mind the gnostic patterns which played a large part in the thematic universe of *Moby-Dick* and which were given expression again in "Fragments from a Lost Gnostic Poem of the 12th Century." The issues in that poem were the identification of matter with evil, the dominance of evil, and the inability of even "the Good Man" to escape from or counteract this "ancient brutal claim" of evil.

Commentators have noticed for decades that there are several unmistakable comparisons of Billy with Christ. Billy is not to be identified with Christ, because there are too many other things he is also compared with: an angel, for example, or a barbarian in Melville's best sense of the word, or Adam before the Fall. But Melville's parallels between Christ and Billy are too numerous and too clear to be dismissed as only minimally relevant. Some of the most obvious may be cited. In the first chapter, Billy's first captain describes him in terms used to describe Christ in Mark 5:30—"a virtue went out of him." To reinforce the idea that he is working with biblical allusions, the captain concludes by calling Billy "my peacemaker." The lieutenant confirms this cynically: "Well, blessed are the peacemakers." Billy has a "crucifixion" in Chapter 19; "Billy's agony" the night before he dies is mentioned in Chapter 24; he is kissed on the cheek by a man who professes to be a Christian minister yet who serves the god of war; finally "Billy ascended." The force of these examples is constantly to underscore the similarities between Billy and Christ by using for the former words which piety has traditionally reserved for denoting the mysteries in the life of the latter. These references come to a climax in Chapter 30, in the remark concerning the sailors and the spar from which Billy was hanged: "To them a chip of it was a piece of the Cross."

Still another set of references link Billy and Christ by an almost unique kind of similarity. Billy's total innocence is stressed, but this innocence has a theological root which is mentioned no less than four times in the course of the story. After hinting in the first chapter at the totality of this innocence ("to deal in double meanings and insinuations of any sort was quite *foreign to his nature*"), Melville goes on to develop the theme. In the second chapter Billy's unknown parentage is conjectured. There was, in him, "something suggestive of a mother eminently favored by Love and the Graces." In the same passage Billy answers the question concerning the identity of his father with the enigmatic "God knows, sir." Implied is the notion of the Virgin Birth, with its attendant doctrine in the Christian tradition that Mary herself was conceived without the hereditary guilt for original sin. (Wordsworth calls her "our tainted nature's solitary boast" in this connection.) That she was eminently favored by Love and the Graces is indicated in the angel's address to her, "Hail, full of grace," in Luke 1:28. The matter comes fully to the surface a few lines later: "For the rest, with little or no sharpness of faculty or any trace of the wisdom of the serpent, nor yet quite a dove, he possessed that kind and degree of intelligence going along with the unconventional rectitude of a sound human creature, one to whom not yet has been proffered the questionable apple of knowledge." The root of Billy's innocence, then, is his freedom from the universally inherited effects of the sin of Adam. Only

Christ and, according to an ancient Christian tradition, the Virgin Mary were similarly exempted. The point is confirmed: "Billy in many respects was little more than a sort of upright barbarian, much such perhaps as Adam presumably might have been ere the urbane Serpent wriggled himself into his company." As the theological issues grow thicker in the story, this theme comes to a climax in Billy's encounter with Claggart: "If askance he eyed the good looks, cheery health, and frank enjoyment of young life in Billy Budd, it was because these went along with a nature that, as Claggart magnetically felt, had in its simplicity never willed malice or experienced the reactionary bite of that serpent."

Melville takes us a step deeper into the kind of identification he makes between Billy and Christ. At several points he mentions Adam; in Chapter 18 he mentions Jacob and Joseph; and during the private interview, in Chapter 22, where Vere communicates the sentence to Billy, the two are likened to Abraham and Isaac. Melville is working with biblical types here and the peculiar nature of typology must be noted. Unlike metaphor or simile, or other figures of speech which are used more conventionally, the type works progressively and cumulatively. In a platonic sense there is an identity between each of the types, since each represents an embodiment of the same pattern or experience, the same (religious) configuration of meaning. In the mystical interpretation of the New Testament the types are seen to culminate in Christ and reveal their latent meaning to the fullest degree in him. Melville, by citing the other biblical types, tells the reader what kind of similarity is to be seen in Christ and Billy. In them both the same kind of universal meaning or reality is exemplified.

A major step in interpreting *Billy Budd* must now be taken. The question that has hitherto been asked on this point is what is to be made of Melville's comparison between Christ and Billy, as if Melville had an orthodox idea of Christ, common to anyone in his Christian society, and that this is not the term of the comparison that needs clarification. But the opposite is true. If Melville compares Billy to Christ, it becomes immediately relevant to the meaning of the story to recall that Melville's idea of Christ was not sanctioned by orthodoxy.

Melville's formal break with orthodoxy is announced as early as the end of *Mardi*, which has yet to be appreciated fully for its importance in Melville's theological thought. There are really two endings to the book, one for the four subordinate characters and a different one for the main character. The speech of the old man concerning the quality of life in Serenia (in Chapter 187) is what a later theologian would call religionless Christianity. The universal and voluntary acceptance of an altruistic style of life, without the offensive domination by an organized institution, appeals deeply to Babbalanja, Mohi, Yoomi, and King Media. The chapter is followed by the account of Babbalanja's subsequent vision of eternal wisdom. The vision has confirmed Babbalanja's conversion and his narration of it confirms the other three. A methodological supposition is enlightening: suppose the book to have ended here, in the midst of Chaper 189. Surely we would now esteem *Mardi* differently. It would rank with the remarkable works of religious literature and be one of the rare successful examples of the genre to be found in American literature, so powerfully beautiful is Babbalanja's vision. *Mardi* would then be compared to Sylvester Judd's *Margaret*, for example—a novel which works its way toward a similar revelation of ideal religious life, and which was enjoying such a brisk sale during the months that *Mardi* was being written that a second edition would shortly be demanded. In such a comparison *Mardi* would surely emerge the better by far of the two. The fact remains that Melville did not end his novel here, but the speculation is useful: Melville could have found a willing public for such a novel, and it is interesting to reflect on the churlish reception given to the same novel with only a few more chapters added.

In Chapter 65 the novel takes one of its many new starts; here it is the final allegorical journey through different value systems. Up to this point the narrator's view has been sufficient, but now Melville splits the one voice into five. To the already established figure of King Media he adds the philosopher Babbalanja, the poet Yoomi, and the historian Mohi. Their distinctive functions and areas of expertise are quite clear: man's intelligence, memory, imagination, and ability for practical management will all be useful for such a journey. In addition to them there is still the semidivine Ego, Taji, who continues to narrate in the first person. For all four characters the green world of Serenia is ending enough and more. It is fulfillment of all of their deepest needs and they gladly capitulate, submitting themselves totally to this ideal. Media even renounces his claims to semidivinity at this point. But it is not so for the more basic Ego in man, Taji. He continues to grasp his individuality and his total independence, even though it almost surely leads to "perdition" and is clearly self-destructive. Melville has created a hitherto unrecognized successor in the line of Blake's Satan and Shelley's Prometheus. But it is important for the present study to note that in addition to creating a Romantic Hero in Taji, Melville is also announcing his departure from orthodox Christianity.

To come back, then, to Melville's understanding of Christ and its bearing on *Billy Budd*, we must go on to a development in the author's theological thought, to the critical or epistemological issue that he pursues in *Clarel*. The Christ story was a reality for Melville, as it is for any individual in western culture, in the sense that some version of the story impinges upon his awareness, usually from a very early age, and makes deeply felt demands upon the individual which must be responded to. For Melville this story is a complex bundle of materials, including the realistic narrative of Christ's life and teaching, the miracles also included in that narrative, and the supernatural events and significances represented by the mysteries of his divine origin, his resurrection, the descent of the Holy Ghost, and so on. But during the confrontation of this story *in situ*, during his pilgrimage in the Holy Land, it is the landscape that impinges on his consciousness with the strongest insistence, contradicting the materials, forcing him to sort them out into different kinds of "reality." He admires the sweetness and purity in the figure of Christ, for his role as peacemaker and teacher of goodness. He communicates a sense of reverent nostalgia for the idyll of that life—more precisely for the Eden that he re-created and caused to spread by his presence, but in *Clarel* the achievement was only momentary. The Christ was destroyed and the sects that undertook to perpetuate his name were guilty of greater cruelty, greed, and corruption than had been known in the world before him. In other words the "ancient brutal claim" of evil was reasserted with an even greater force after this momentary interruption of goodness. Goodness can appear and it is real; but it is only temporary when seen against the permanent reality of evil. The supernatural aspects of the Christ story are unreal; they give no valid idea of the nature of transcendent reality. Goodness is powerful and Melville's evocation of it in *Clarel* demonstrates that power, but it is finally less powerful than matter.

Billy Budd is, then, a retelling of that story. The strong comparisons between Christ and Billy indicate that Melville saw both stories in the same way. His use of typology confirms this; Billy is another instance of the general pattern. We must have Melville's version of the Christ story in mind when reading this final work. In Melville's version the subsequent history of Christ, the supernatural events, are merely stories without substance. Evil renews its onslaught more vigorously afterward. Such a momentary appearance of truth and goodness can exert no power on people or events that follow.

Billy's subsequent history follows the same pattern. The two officers who discuss his death, in Chapter 26, quibble about an irrelevant detail—whether the fact that his body did not convulse after the hanging has any significance or not. The "authorized" version of Billy's career, in an official naval magazine, garbles the details and reverses the good and evil characteristics of Billy and Claggart. A small remnant of the sailors keep track of the spar from which he was hanged with a kind of blind instinct that tells them Billy was an extraordinary being. But even the rude ballad written by one of Billy's own watch shows an extraordinary perversion of his true character.

The ballad of Billy in the Darbies has always proved mysterious and fascinating. I believe that it fits the story perfectly, but only if seen as capping the story as we have read it so far. It also integrates the theme of fame and posthumous reputation, from Melville's late poetry, into the final synthesis of *Billy Budd*. The manuscript remnants show that Melville first wrote a version of the poem; then he worked on an introductory headnote, after the manner of the first four poems in *John Marr*, which developed in complexity and length to the present form of *Billy Budd*; he also revised the ballad to fit the story which had now become primary.

The ballad, to begin with, contains no sign of the drama Billy has just participated in. There is no sign of his innocence or of Claggart's malice, no understanding of his story as the tale of goodness betrayed by evil once again. Instead the rude poet makes the easy assumption, along with the naval chronicle, that Billy was indeed guilty of some conspiracy. He has Billy admit, in line 11, "Ay, ay, all is up." So little does the balladmaker, "one of his own watch," know of Billy that he explicitly contradicts Melville's characterization of him in at least two places. Melville insists on Billy's total innocence throughout the story; the balladmaker assumes at least a sexual noninnocence in line 9, where he has Billy recall a gift he gave to a young lady who sounds very much like a prostitute. Second, Melville has insisted, as part of Billy's innocence, that he was incapable even of such deviousness as would be necessary for punning: "Billy, though happily endowed with the gaiety of high health, youth, and a free heart, was yet by no means of a satirical turn. The will to it and the sinister dexterity [Melville himself puns here] were alike wanting. To deal in double meanings and insinuations of any sort was quite foreign to his nature" (Chapter 1). Yet the ballad writer has Billy pun twice in his monologue: "'tis me, not the sentence they'll suspend" (l. 10); and "Ay, ay, all is up; and I must up too" (l. 11). The ballad sounds very little like Billy Budd's. Perhaps the writer had forgotten his man partly and confused him with another. There is a recollection of this other—perhaps the real Billy Budd—in lines 25–26: "I remember Taff the Welshman when he sank. / And his cheek it was like the budding pink." If punning is one of the keys to Melville's ironic intention in this poem, then the pun here indicates that the real Billy *Budd* has even lost his name among the sailors and had a garbled version of his story transferred to someone else. Melville makes his peace here with the questions of fame and oblivion. Billy's last perception is that "the oozy weeds about me twist"—at, of course, the bottom of the sea.

Billy Budd contains most of the major thematic patterns developed by Melville during his career as poet. The story also synthesizes these themes into a coherent philosophy. The issues of law and evil developed in detail in *Battle-Pieces* are used to discriminate those who are capable of a transcendent act (developed in "Timoleon" and related poems) from those who cannot deal with it justly—Billy and Vere in the story. The various levels of reality and truth which are discerned in the Christ story throughout *Clarel* here come into play as a means of understanding the conflict between good and evil wherever it is enacted. Only the secular, nonsupernatural aspects of the story can have had any historical reality. Finally the question of one's posthumous state of being can now be settled. One's story is likely to be garbled, if he is remembered at all.

Billy Budd is not only the confirmation but the synthesis of the life's work that preceded it. With the last stroke of his pen Herman Melville accepts annihilation and, with an irony that would have delighted him, joins the immortals.

NOTES

INTRODUCTION

1. See John Bernstein, *Pacifism and Rebellion in the Writings of Herman Melville* (The Hague, 1964), p. 180.

2. The two letters are quoted from Eleanor Melville Metcalf, *Herman Melville: Cycle and Epicycle* (Cambridge, Mass., 1953), pp. 230–31, 237.

3. The physical record of Melville's ownership of books is recorded by Merton M. Sealts, Jr., in *Melville's Reading: A Check-List of Books Owned and Borrowed* (Madison, Wis., 1966). See p. 6.

I

1. The poems and their dates of publication were "The March to the Sea," February 1866; "The Cumberland," March 1866; "Sheridan at Cedar Creek" (published with the title "Philip"), April 1866; "Chattanooga," June 1866; and "Gettysburg: July, 1863," published in July 1866. No explanation has been discovered for the omission of a poem in the May issue.

2. Gene B. Montague, "Melville's *Battle-Pieces*," *University of Texas Studies in English* 35 (1956): 106–15.

3. Ronald Mason, *The Spirit above the Dust: A Study of Herman Melville* (London, 1951).

4. Stein's comments on this point can be found in his article in the *Emerson Society Quarterly* No. 27 (1966): 10–13, "Melville's Poetry: Two Rising Notes." F. O. Matthiessen dealt briefly with the subject in his introduction to *Herman Melville: Selected Poems* (Norfolk, Conn., 1944). The quotation is from Warren, "Melville's Poems," *Southern Review* 3, n.s. (1967): 804–5; this essay has recently been revised for an introduction to his *Selected Poems of Herman Melville: A Reader's Edition* (New York, 1970).

5. The quotation is from Pommer's *Milton and Melville* (Pittsburgh, Pa., 1950), p. 77.

6. Frank L. Day has written the most complete study of Melville's use of *The Rebellion Record*. See his unpublished thesis (University of Tennessee, 1959), "Herman Melville's Use of *The Rebellion Record* in His Poetry." I have taken the above quotation from Hennig Cohen's annotations to the poem in his edition of *The Battle-Pieces of Herman Melville* (p. 217), where one may also find the map of the battle reproduced.

7. Even more should be claimed for Melville here. The poets of the nineteenth century are noted for resurrecting obscure verse forms and for inventing new ones. Longfellow is an obvious example, as is Tennyson. Melville too tried his hand with considerable success at various forms, from the drinking songs in *Mardi* to the powerful Masque of the Wandering Jew in *Clarel*. But mostly Melville's stanzas are nonce forms, created to embody the specific patterns of each individual poem.

8. Cohen notes several parallels in Shakespeare, which Melville would have known, where "crown" is used as a "head-king" pun. See his edition of *Battle-Pieces*, pp. 204–5.

9. Melville's enthusiasm for Shakespeare is well documented. For example, he described his late discovery of Shakespeare in a letter to Evert Duyckinck (February 24, 1849), and commented, "I fancy that this moment Shakespeare in heaven ranks with Gabriel Raphael and Michael." The essay on Hawthorne contains an extended comparison of the New Englander with the Old. For Shakespeare holdings in Melville's library see Merton M. Sealts, Jr., *Melville's Reading* (Madison, Wis., 1966), #209, and 460–65 (hereafter cited as Sealts).

10. The Dome of the Capitol Building has its own drama in *Battle-Pieces*. Early in the book, one finds that the Iron Dome, still in the process of construction, is already showing signs of rust. This is in "The Conflict of Convictions" (l. 44). In the same poem, lines 74ff., one of the voices predicts that the authority symbolized by the Dome will endure, stronger for the ordeal through which it has passed. The present poem, "The Victor of Antietam," is the next in the series to use the image of the dome. McClellan's loyalty and military abilities help keep it "propped." In the poem printed separately at the end of the collection, "The Scout Toward Aldie," Melville attempts to capture the sense of immediate danger which could pounce and destroy unexpectedly, because of Mosby's Confederate guerrillas who dared "to prowl where the Dome was seen," in the northeastern corner of Virginia. After the war Robert E. Lee mused on the Dome which he had once threatened, but which now looms as victor over the demolished landscape ("Lee in the Capitol," ll. 28–39). Finally, in the dream-allegory "America," the dome becomes, probably, the dome of the firmament embracing the whole sunny universe where the figure of America stands fertile and exultant.

11. There are several reasons for considering "The Portent" as prefatory to the collection: it was printed by itself on a separate page; it is the only poem printed entirely in italics; and its title does not appear on the original table of contents. This would give more authority to the poem as setting the tone for the whole collection.

12. Richard Chase was probably mistaken in saying that these dates in the subtitles of many of the poems are the dates of composition. See his headnote to *Battle-Pieces* in Perry Miller, ed., *Major Writers of America* (New York, 1962), 1:920–21. The dates are part of the titles and furnish the reader with chronological perspective.

13. *The American Adam: Innocence, Tragedy, and Tradition in the Nineteenth Century* (Chicago, 1955).

14. "A Meditation" (l. 49).

15. Several critics have attempted to read the poem as a clear debate between optimist and pessimist. See, for example, William B. Dillingham's "'Neither Believer nor Infidel': Themes of Melville's Poetry," *Personalist* 46 (1965): 501–16. But Melville's technique is more complex here.

16. Henry F. Pommer has shown the pervasive influence of Milton on Melville's prose and poetry in *Milton and Melville*. Melville relies on Miltonic allusions to help establish a cosmic significance for the events of the Civil War; but Milton's world view was not Melville's: here, for example, Milton's splendid heavenly warrior becomes merely "a white enthusiast."

17. For Saint Paul on slavery see Ephesians 6:5, Colossians 5:22, and Titus 2:9.

18. The most accessible source of Blake's thought at the time was Gilchrist's *Life* (1863). Melville probably purchased his copy in 1870 (Sealts, #224).

19. In Vincent's edition, as well as in Jarrard's, a new verse paragraph seems to begin at line 12, but in the original edition of 1866 the lines follow immediately with no spacing, indicating close connections in thought between the two sections. The word "shame," in line 35, appears in the printed edition of *Battle-Pieces*. In Melville's personal copy the word is changed to "some," in Mrs. Melville's hand. Whether this is Melville's correction of an actual misprint or his later attempt to tone down the ending cannot now be determined.

20. Hayford and Sealts explain their reason for dropping this paragraph in *Billy Budd, Sailor (An Inside Narrative)* (Chicago, 1962), p. 19.

21. Cohen's note to the poem in his edition of *Battle-Pieces* contains the following interesting paragraph: "From his acquaintance with Renaissance painting, Melville may have known that the swallow appears as a symbol of the Incarnation in Annunciation and Nativity scenes. But more pertinent is the association with the Resurrection because of the belief that the swallow hibernated in the mud, from which it was reborn each spring" (p. 229).

22. Walter Harding records Thoreau's comments on these three symbols in his *Variorum Walden* (New York, 1963), p. 259.

23. Mrs. Metcalf quotes the letter in her *Herman Melville: Cycle and Epicycle* (Cambridge, Mass., 1953), p. 119.

24. Once again one is tempted to speculate on a much earlier date for one of the "later" poems. To judge by the immediate power of "The Maldive Shark," so similar to the power of the image generated in these two *Battle-Pieces* poems, one is tempted to date "The Maldive Shark" quite early. The only other alternative, by no means impossible, is that the shark retains its symbolic power in Melville's mind for several years. It is true that precisely this same shark appears throughout Melville's novels. Hennig Cohen's edition of *Battle-Pieces* lists them on page 286, but these are all published earlier than the poems under discussion. The interesting aspect is that the passage closest in feeling to "The Maldive Shark" occurs in *Mardi*, Chapter 19. See also Merrell R. Davis, *Melville's Mardi: A Chartless Voyage* (New Haven, Conn., 1952), pp. 112ff.

25. "In a Church of Padua," though printed in the 1891 *Timoleon* volume, contains recollections of Melville's Mediterranean trip of 1856–1857. Hence it is quite possible that it was also among the poems Melville had prepared for the volume he had tried to publish in 1860.

26. The emphasis on *"dive"* is Melville's. I cite the version of the letter as it appears in Metcalf, *Herman Melville*, p. 58. For other diving references see, for example, Cohen's note to the poem in his edition of *Battle-Pieces*, p. 223.

27. Cohen reproduces the picture and gives some details of its history on pp. 267–68.

28. Hell is really "a half-extinct volcano" according to Mr. Smooth-it-away in Hawthorne's "The Celestial Railroad." The point may seem minute here, but it will be interesting to note the continuing and increasing signs of Hawthorne's presence in Melville's mind during this second part of his writing career.

II

1. *Journal of a Visit to Europe and the Levant, October 11, 1856–May 6, 1857*, ed. Howard C. Horsford (Princeton, N.J., 1955).

2. See the reviews cited in Jay Leyda, *The Melville Log* (New York, 1951), 2: 750–55.

3. Walter E. Bezanson, ed., *Clarel: A Poem and Pilgrimage in the Holy Land* (New York, 1960). A summary of criticism appears on pp. xliii–xlix.

4. *The Long Encounter: Self and Experience in the Writings of Herman Melville* (Chicago, 1960), p. 253.

5. *Herman Melville* (New Haven, Conn., 1963), p. 127.

6. "Melville the Poet," *Kenyon Review* 8 (1946): 208, 219.

7. "Melville's Poems," *Southern Review* 3, n.s. (1967): 826–31 passim.

8. Boston, 1968, pp. 227–33 passim. It is also curious that Roy Harvey Pearce gives only the briefest mention of Melville as a poet in his monumental book, *The Continuity of American Poetry* (Princeton, N.J., 1961).

9. "Melville's *Clarel*: Doubt and Belief," *Tulane Studies in English* 10 (1960): 116.

10. Robert Joslin Packard in his dissertation (Columbia University, 1963) studied the geography of *Clarel* in detail, relating the sites closely to the phases of the poem's faith-doubt problem. He concluded that Melville did not solve his central question of metaphysical doubt ("A Study of Herman Melville's *Clarel*").

11. The numbers respectively refer to part, canto, and line numbers in Bezanson's edition.

12. No one has been able to conjecture a source or meaning for this unusual name. John Howard Payne, popular as the author of "Home, Sweet Home," en-

closed that song in a drama called *Clari: or, The Maid of Milan* (1823). Melville may have been struck by the possibilities of the name, though the melodramatic seduction-restoration plot could have offered little inspiration for his own narrative. Melville may also have known that de Tocqueville's full name was Alexis Charles Henri *Clerel* de Tocqueville. (Melville and de Tocqueville were roughly contemporaries). Sealts has no record of Melville's having owned or borrowed his *Democracy in America*, but editions of the Reeve translation had been available since 1835. By the time *Clarel* was published there had been eight British and thirty-four American editions. It is pure conjecture, but not impossible, that Melville may have seen some similarity between de Tocqueville's encyclopedic attempt to portray the civilization of America in all its complexity and his own attempt to portray the complex life of the mind in the nineteenth-century.

13. For the death of the pagan gods, and the Miltonic overtones of this passage, see the discussion of "When Forth the Shepherd Leads the Flock" in Chapter VI.

14. *The Vision; or Hell, Purgatory, and Paradise* by Dante Alighieri, trans. Henry Francis Cary (London, 1864). This is a reprinting of the 1844 edition; Melville owned either the 1845 or the 1847 reprinting of the 1844 edition. The quoted lines are from "Hell," viii, 66–76 passim, p. 41.

15. Ecclesiastes 12:5–8 (King James Version).

16. See Jay Leyda, *The Melville Log*, 2:521, 525.

17. Bezanson, in his note to this Vergilian reference, says that this is "the first of several references equating the Siddim Plain [the region into which the pilgrimage is now entering] with the underworld" (p. 594). Quite possibly this is an attempt to find some of the structural principles of the epic in Melville's long poem, an attempt at genre criticism which does help here to comprehend parts of the large masses of material Melville has laid down in these 18,000 lines. An awareness of Vergil enriches one's reading of *Clarel*, as it does one's reading of *The Divine Comedy*, but finally Melville's long poem, like Dante's, must be considered unique in its genre.

18. Bezanson (p. 596) comments on these lines that in Chapter 8 of *Journal . . . of* H.M.S. *Beagle* (Sealts, #175) Darwin quotes from Shelley's "Mont Blanc":

> None can reply—all seems eternal now.
> The wilderness has a mysterious tongue,
> Which teaches awful doubt.

19. "The Encantadas or Enchanted Isles," *Piazza Tales*, ed. Egbert S. Oliver (New York, 1962), pp. 149–50. I have italicized the biblical allusions in these citations.

20. Most of the elements in the ship-monastery comparison above had been used earlier in the opening pages of *Benito Cereno*. The effect is the same. Melville used the comparison to emphasize the forbidding strangeness of Cereno's ship, the fleeting sense of danger that Amasa Delano experienced—and naively dismissed—as he drew closer to the ship.

III

1. New York, 1844.

2. *The Melville Log: A Documentary Life of Herman Melville, 1819–1891* (New York, 1951), 2:708. Bezanson believes that it was begun a bit earlier, but that by 1870 Melville had finished only "a quarter or a third of his poem." See the Introduction to his edition of *Clarel: A Poem and Pilgrimage in the Holy Land* (New York, 1960), p. xxxiii.

3. Quotations from *The Innocents Abroad* are from Charles Neider's edition of *The Complete Travel Books of Mark Twain* (Garden City, N.Y., 1966).

4. Derwent, the bland and smiling ecclesiastic, is one of Melville's more fascinating characterizations in *Clarel*. He solves every problem with a platitude and ends every argument by forcing a change in the focus of attention, thus serving as

one of the major irritants creating the intellectual tension of the poem. His theology makes up in latitude for what it lacks in depth. He is ready to embrace all truths. The new science and the new theology—which so agitate others of the party—will eventually be seen to flow into the same broad stream of traditional orthodoxy, he is sure. In many ways he is the happiest and best adjusted of the pilgrims; his way appeals intermittently to Clarel, but the shallowness of his participation in life makes the sacrifice seem too great. Derwent's curious name seems to come from Wordsworth's beloved river in the Lake Country. Coleridge was also enamored of "the Derwent waters" and named one of his sons after them. The boy went on to become a mild and well-liked, ultraconservative Anglican clergyman. He was nineteen years Melville's senior and was prominent enough in his own right to have come to Melville's attention. But Melville has also developed this characterization with hints from the Reverend Doctor Gaster in Thomas Love Peacock's *Headlong Hall* (1816). Melville would use this book again, both for setting and theme, when he finished *Clarel* and began his work on the *Burgundy Club* sketches. Peacock's Gaster also has a way of blocking the smooth flow of conversation with such comments as "It requires no proof . . . it is a point of doctrine. It is written, therefore it is so." He stops another line of inquiry before it is fairly started with, "It is a mystery." It is quite possible that Melville found this kind of character useful for terminating conversation on a subject when he himself came to the end of his thoughts on a particularly knotty problem and wanted to evade personal responsibility for leaving the question unanswered.

5. The image occurs with surprising frequency in the poem. It seems certainly to come from Matthew Arnold's "Dover Beach." Melville read and annotated Arnold's 1867 volume of poems. Arnold's extensive influence on Melville has been analyzed by Walter Bezanson in "Melville's Reading of Arnold's Poetry," *PMLA* 69 (1954): 365–91.

6. *Collected Poems of Herman Melville*, ed. Howard P. Vincent (Chicago, 1947), pp. 226–27.

7. *Horace*, trans. Philip Francis (New York, 1856). These two volumes are Numbers 18 and 19 of the Harper's Family Classical Library, all thirty–seven volumes of which Melville purchased in 1849 (Sealts, #147). The citations which follow in the text are from 2:159–61.

8. Selections from these "Invenzioni" are frequently reprinted, for example in Luzius Keller's recent *Piranèse et les Romantiques Français* (Paris, 1966), pp. 255ff. Melville was an avid print collector but unfortunately we do not know exactly what prints were in his collection, nor does Sealts have any entry under Piranesi. Melville may have become interested in Piranesi from any of several sources available to him; he is mentioned in Walpole's *Castle of Otranto*, Beckford's *Vathek*, and de Quincey's *Confessions of an English Opium Eater*.

9. *Billy Budd, Sailor (An Inside Narrative)*, ed. Harrison Hayford and Merton M. Sealts, Jr. (Chicago, 1962), p. 108.

10. See *Melville's Reading: A Check-List of Books Owned and Borrowed* (Madison, Wis., 1966), p. 6, and "Calvinism and Cosmic Evil in *Moby-Dick*" by T. Walter Herbert, Jr., *PMLA* 84 (October 1969): 1613–19 for Melville's library of theology and for speculations about some of Melville's Calvinist sources.

11. Hyatt H. Waggoner, *American Poets: From the Puritans to the Present* (Boston, 1968), pp. 230–31. Robert Penn Warren's earlier article, "Melville the Poet," also cited these lines and called them "the affirmation at the end of *Clarel*." See *Kenyon Review* 8 (1946): 221.

IV

1. Charles R. Anderson sees the poem as preparatory for *Billy Budd* in "The Genesis of *Billy Budd*," *American Literature* 12 (November 1940): 338, as also does Leon Howard in his biography *Herman Melville* (Berkeley, Calif., 1951), p. 324.

Howard P. Vincent, in a note to "Bridegroom Dick" in Collected Poems, sees it as "in a sense, a companion piece to Melville's novel White Jacket (1850)," closing the link to connect the poem with Melville's past as well as his future work.

2. Journal of a Visit to Europe and the Levant, ed. Howard C. Horsford (Princeton, N.J., 1955), p. 72.

3. The text of "The Admiral of the White" can be found in Collected Poems, pp. 404ff. Melville seems to have been predisposed to the implications of the story he heard on his pilgrimage; Ahab, in Chapter 124 of Moby-Dick, manufactured a new compass needle when a storm had reversed the ones already in place. Ahab is demonically above this sort of trap, declaring himself "lord of the level loadstone."

4. Jarrard records Melville's comments to his printer (p. 355). Hennig Cohen, in Selected Poems of Herman Melville (Garden City, N.Y., 1964), p. 215, was the first to notice a similarity between Spenser and Melville here.

5. A reproduction of this painting can be found in Charles H. Chaffin, Study of American Painting (1907).

6. I quote from Arthur Hugh Clough's edition of the "Dryden" Plutarch (1864).

7. For a complete study of Emerson's debt to Plutarch see Edmund G. Berry, Emerson's Plutarch (Cambridge, Mass., 1961).

8. See Jay Leyda, The Melville Log (New York, 1951), 2: 790, 804, 808, 815. The locale gains in interest from the fact that Margaret Fuller's ship had been wrecked off Fire Island in 1850.

9. The Anatomy of Melancholy . . . by Democritus Junior, 5th ed. (Philadelphia, 1852), p. 242.

10. Jarrard records the differences in the various versions of "The Berg" in his edition, pp. 220–21 and pp. 363–64. Cohen (Selected Poems, p. 220) notes that Melville's change from "dead indifference" to "dense stolidity" in the last line "echo[es] the initial description of the iceberg in the fourth line and underscore[s] its essential unconcern." Vincent (Collected Poems, p. 203) prints the poem without a break between lines 15 and 16. Such a break is clearly indicated in the manuscript; the fact was obscured in the first printing of John Marr, where line 16 began a new page.

11. The 1866 volume, Battle-Pieces, in "The Battle for the Bay," contains the line "Before their eyes the turreted ship goes down!" I believe, on the basis of evidence to be discussed shortly, that "The Berg" was written first. It was probably in the volume Poems that Melville had tried to have published in 1860. Melville here salvages a good line from a poem he had been unable to publish earlier.

12. Lubbard, a clumsy stupid person, possibly derives from lob, "hanging flesh," suggesting sexual impotence. If Melville were aware of this conjectural origin of the word, he may have chosen it for the added overtones of psychological horror it would have contributed to the poem.

13. Perry Miller, in The Raven and the Whale (New York, 1956), describes the literary circle which had formed around the Duyckincks.

14. The word "turreted" also appears in this section of the article, forging another link between the poem and "The Battle for the Bay," mentioned in note 11 above.

15. Another John Marr poem in this section influenced by the Literary World is "Crossing the Tropics." Its subtitle, "From 'The Saya-y-Manto,'" seems to indicate that it is from a larger sequence. (See the treatment of "The Enviable Isles: From 'Rammon'" later in this chapter. In the case of "Crossing the Tropics" there is nothing left in manuscript to indicate the nature of the larger sequence.) Vincent in Collected Poems (p. 472) reprints a section from a book published in 1835 which describes the saya (skirt) and manto (veil), a walking dress of the ladies of Lima. But in the Literary World for February 27, 1847, at the time when Melville was writing for the periodical, there is another description of the costume, underlining the fact that the heavy veil was useful for anonymity and amorous intrigue. Some

of the wording here could have led to Melville's poem. The issues of the *Literary World* published during this month of February 1847 are especially interesting as sources for several of Melville's pieces. We shall see, in the next chapter, how "After the Pleasure-Party"—several of the manuscript leaves of which are considerably older than others—begins from different items in the February issues of the *Literary World*. So also, in this issue of February 27, Melville read the following: "The grand theological question of the freedom of the will, the most natural and obvious subject of inquiry to all who ever think, and one environed with numberless subtleties, while we attempt to evolve its difficulties in language, although its practical solution of their life, furnishes the subject for a very able essay on the 'Consistency of the Eternal Purpose of God with the Free Agency of Men,' by the Rev. J. W. Ward." Melville retained the pith of this ungainly sentence, and much of the first twenty-five words as well, for his "Hawthorne and His Mosses." Finally the next issue (March 6, 1847) contains Melville's own review of J. Ross Brown's *Etchings of a Whaling Cruise* . . . , the book which played a large part in the formation of *Moby-Dick*.

16. The best edition is by Eleanor M. Tilton, "Melville's 'Rammon': A Text and Commentary," *Harvard Library Bulletin* 13 (1959): 50–91. I am not aware of any speculation concerning the name "Rammon," but given the kind of complex inquiry that characterizes the prose section, there is quite likely a process of association at work here linking the central figure with the fact that one of Montaigne's ancestors was named Ramon. The name also sounds close to the French pronunciation of the surname in Montaigne's *Apology for Ramond Sebond*. For Melville's interest in the ironies of style in this essay, and for his actual quotation from it in *Moby-Dick*, see Lawrance Thompson, *Melville's Quarrel with God* (Princeton, N. J., 1952), pp. 21, 187.

17. The passage is from the *Mahā-Parinibbāna-Sutta*, ed. R. C. Childers (London, 1878). More conveniently it can be found reprinted in *Buddhism in Translation* by Henry Clarke Warren (New York, 1963), pp. 109–10.

18. There seems to be no connection between this poem and the "Daniel Orme" sketch, even though in his manuscript Melville experiments with "Orm" as a possible spelling for the old sailor's last name. That prose sketch, unpublished during Melville's lifetime, depicts a stern withdrawn old sailor who has a mysterious air about him, but who dies with the mystery uncommunicated to anyone. It is likely that Daniel Orme was a man engaged in pursuing his own lines of thought, communing with the deeper aspects of his consciousness. But nothing in the sketch allows any interpretation of the word "schools" (from the poem) to function meaningfully in his characterization.

<h1 style="text-align:center">V</h1>

1. Eleanor Melville Metcalf, *Herman Melville: Cycle and Epicycle* (Cambridge, Mass., 1953), p. 294.

2. In the folder marked "Egypt and Greek Pieces" are "The Continents" and "The Dust-Layers." These can be found in Vincent, *Collected Poems*, pp. 409–10. The "Greece" folder contains "Suggested by the Ruins . . ." and "Puzzlement" reprinted in Vincent, pp. 407–8.

3. Vedder says, for example, "the knowledge that my art has gained me so many friends—even if unknown to me—makes ample amends." The letter is dated April 19, 1896, and can be found in Metcalf, *Herman Melville*, p. 288.

4. Sealts, #392.

5. For Melville's interest in Plutarch see the discussion of "The Æolian Harp at the *Surf Inn*" in the previous chapter. For Melville's purchase of Bayle's *Dictionary* (Sealts, #51) see his letter to Evert Duyckinck, April 5, 1849. Bayle's influence on Melville has been studied by Lawrance Thompson, *Melville's Quarrel with God*

(Princeton, N. J., 1952), and by Millicent Bell, "Pierre Bayle and *Moby-Dick*," *PMLA* 66 (September 1951): 622–48. Jay Leyda has pointed out that the psychological aspects of the clash between brothers in this poem also owes something to Balzac's *The Two Brothers*. See *Log* 2: 829. According to Sealts (#37) Melville owned the 1887 translation of this novel. The source, then, shows the late date which must be given to Melville's poem.

6. Later in *Timoleon* "The Garden of Metrodorus" picks up this theme again. Metrodorus is given a few lines in Plutarch's biography of Lucullus. As counsellor of King Mithridates, Metrodorus is sent as an ambassador to his rival Tigranes to ask his help against the invading Romans. When Tigranes asks him for advice, Metrodorus replies that "as ambassador he counselled him to it, but as a friend dissuaded him from it." Tigranes immediately betrayed this friendship to Mithridates. Metrodorus is made scapegoat for the ills that separated the two tyrants and is executed. Here again the single-minded good man is crushed by less naive forces and cast out. In Melville's poem the sense of awesome emptiness surrounding the garden of Metrodorus can only be explained by the fact that its inhabitant is dead; another act of transcendent goodness has led to the destruction of an individual.

7. Melville's manuscript is a late, relatively clean copy. The lines in question are written in the margins of two pages and careted in.

8. Vincent (*Collected Poems*, p. 474) has suggested a connection between Melville and Tennyson's *The Princess* here. It is true that the general outlines of the two female characters bear some surface resemblance. But Melville is terse and ironic where Tennyson is diffuse and romantic. Melville presents the conflict as internal; in Tennyson it is carried out at the level of melodramatic action.

9. Jarrard restores the quotation marks from the hints given in Melville's manuscript in his edition of the poems, pp. 236ff. (See also pp. 376ff. for his notes on these quotation marks.)

10. See Sealts (#443–48) and Thompson, *Melville's Quarrel with God*, pp. 350–51. See also Olive Fite, "Billy Budd, Claggart, and Schopenhauer," *Nineteenth-Century Fiction* 23 (December 1968): 336–43.

11. Melville owned and marked the translation of *The World as Will and Idea* by R. B. Haldane and J. Kemp, 2d ed., 1888 (Sealts, #448). The quotations are from this translation.

12. The quotations cited here are from pp. 56, 58, and 59 of the *Literary World* 1 (February 1847).

13. See his article in *Papers of the Bibliographical Society of America* 61:266–67. At this point the reader may turn ahead to our discussion of "Pontoosuce" where the theory is proposed that both poems are closely connected in origin.

14. Metcalf, *Herman Melville*, p. 284. The exhortation is Schiller's, quoted by Margaret Fuller in her essay on Goethe.

15. *Collected Poems*, p. 475.

16. Thomas Vargish has traced one of the sources of Melville's knowledge of Gnosticism to a very popular book, Andrews Norton's *The Evidences of the Genuineness of the Gospels*, to which Melville would have had easy access. See Vargish's "Gnostic *Mythos* in *Moby-Dick*," *PMLA* 81 (June 1966): 272–77.

17. Sealts, #224. The quotations below are from Gilchrist's *Life*, 1:79–80.

18. See, for example, Bezanson's treatment of the Hawthorne-Melville relationship and his identification of the character of Vine with Hawthorne: Introduction to *Clarel: A Poem and Pilgrimage in the Holy Land* (New York, 1960), Section vii. Bezanson discusses "Monody" on p. xcviii.

19. Ibid., p. xcix.

20. See *Journal up the Straits*, ed. Raymond Weaver (1935), and *Melville's Journal of a Visit to Europe and the Levant, October 11, 1856–May 6, 1857*, ed. Howard C. Horsford (Princeton, N.J., 1955).

21. The *Encyclopedia Britannica*, 11th ed. (1910), contains a lengthy article,

"Divers and Diving Apparatus," with a history of the development of the diving bell and illustrations that shed light on the poem.

22. See note 2 above.

23. The Melville manuscript quoted here is in the Houghton Library coded MsAm 188 (386.c.2). See also Hennig Cohen, *Selected Poems*, p. 248.

24. See F. Barron Freeman, *Melville's Billy Budd* (Cambridge, Mass., 1948), p. 7.

VI

1. Robert C. Ryan, "*Weeds and Wildings Chiefly: With a Rose or Two*, by Herman Melville; Reading Text and Genetic Text, Edited from the Manuscripts, with Introduction and Notes" (Ph.D. diss., Northwestern University, 1967). Ryan's dissertation has been helpful throughout this chapter.

2. Ryan's edition omits Vincent's spacing between lines 8 and 9. Confirmation that this was probably Melville's intention can be found in the effect of this omission of spacing: the stanzas with two-stress lines are now printed together and more effectively set off from the stanza of three-stress lines.

3. Introduction to "Herman Melville" in *Major Writers of America*, ed. Perry Miller (New York, 1962), 1: 889.

4. The handwriting for these changes is Mrs. Melville's. In view of the other editorial corrections in the manuscripts, and also because they seem always to have worked together in preparation of manuscript for the printer and in reading of proofs, there is no reason to believe that she was not making revisions at Melville's direction.

5. In the *Atlantic Monthly* for October 1891 Thomas Wentworth Higginson wrote an article introducing several of Emily Dickinson's poems to the public; among them was "A Route of Evanescence." Actually Melville had the title of his own hummingbird poem in mind several years earlier. Writing to James Billson on January 22, 1885, in acknowledgment of a book entitled *Sunday up the River*, Melville called it "a Cuban hummingbird, beautiful in fairy tints, flying against the tropic thundercloud." Quoted in Eleanor Melville Metcalf, *Herman Melville: Cycle and Epicycle* (Cambridge, Mass., 1953), p. 268.

6. Metcalf, *Herman Melville*, p. 75.

7. Melville will investigate this word as a formal esthetic term at length in "Marquis de Grandvin." See Chapter VII.

8. Herbert's "Jordan" poems may be mentioned as examples of this type as well as his famous "The Collar" and "The Pulley." All are collected in *The Temple*, a copy of which Melville owned (Sealts, #270).

9. See Sealts, #290, for an 1883 edition of Hugo owned by Melville.

10. Metcalf, *Herman Melville*, p. 109.

11. Ryan reads "Frost" for "First" in line 17, a definite improvement.

12. The poems can be found in Vincent, *Collected Poems*, pp. 425, 433, and 436. For more roses in the *Mardi* poems see "The Song" and "Hail! Voyagers Hail" (*Collected Poems*, pp. 426, 439).

13. Melville reveals another of his sources in "Moss-Rose" in the last line of this poem. According to the nineteenth-century floral dictionaries the moss rose was the most beautiful of them all.

14. Dorothee Metlitsky Finkelstein, *Melville's Orienda* (New Haven, Conn., 1961), p. 111. Ryan reads "dawn" for "down" in line 17, a change which adds brilliance to the image here.

15. Ryan reads "Sand" for the final word "Land," a reading which strengthens the unity of the imagery considerably. The two initial capital letters are almost identical in Melville's hand; early students of his manuscripts often confused the two.

16. The search should go on, though, since all studies of Melville's use of sources show him to have been a relentless gatherer of little-known facts from odd and

out-of-the-way places. See, for example, the meticulous and illuminating source study conducted by Merrell R. Davis: *Melville's Mardi: A Chartless Voyage* (New Haven, Conn., 1952).

17. Metcalf, *Herman Melville*, p. 268; Melville seems to have underlined the long sentence here.

18. *The Long Encounter: Self and Experience in the Writings of Herman Melville* (Chicago, 1960).

19. The Damascus setting allows one of Melville's sources to appear here, *The Cyclopedia of Biblical Literature*, ed. John Kitto, 2 vols. (New York, 1852). The entry under "Rodon" (2: 638–39) contains the following sentences, for example: "That the rose was cultivated in Damascus is well known. Indeed one species is named *Rosa Damascena* from being supposed to be indigenous there."

VII

1. "Melville's Burgundy Club Sketches," *Harvard Library Bulletin* 12: 253–67.

2. Sealts has also written an interesting article on this aspect of Melville's personality throughout his life, "Melville's 'Geniality,'" in *Essays in American and English Literature Presented to Bruce McElderry, Jr.* (Athens, Ohio, 1968) pp. 3–26.

3. William Gilpin, *Observations Relative Chiefly to Picturesque Beauty in Several Parts of Great Britain*, 8 vols. (London, 1782–1809).

4. The battle has recently been fought anew. See Walter John Hipple, Jr., *The Beautiful, the Sublime, and the Picturesque in Eighteenth-Century British Aesthetic Theory* (Carbondale, Ill., 1957). See also J. T. Boulton's introduction to his edition of Burke's *A Philosophical Enquiry into the Origin of Our Ideas of the Sublime and Beautiful* (New York, 1958).

5. Melville's interest in Salvator Rosa presents a puzzle that may have no solution. When *The Encantadas* were first serialized in *Putnam's* (in March, April, and May of 1854), they were signed pseudonymously "Salvator R. Tarnmore."

6. Quotation marks need to be supplied, in *Collected Poems*, at line 94, "If by a sketch . . ." to indicate Watteau's comment, and at line 103, "I'll lead you . . ." to indicate the continuation of Spagnoletto's words.

7. *The James Family* (New York, 1947), p. 7.

8. Melville is certainly recalling Dickens's *Bleak House* (1853).

9. The prose passages were edited and published by Raymond Weaver in the Constable Edition of *The Works of Herman Melville* (London, 1924) 13: 346–81. The reader is once again referred to Sealts's analysis of the development of this work.

10. Ibid., pp. 358, 356–57.

11. *Journal of a Visit to Europe and the Levant: October 11, 1856–May 6, 1857*, ed. Howard C. Horsford (Princeton, N.J., 1955), pp. 176–88 passim. The italicized section was later underlined by Melville himself.

12. Melville's manuscripts quoted in this chapter are in the Houghton Library, coded MsAm 188 (369).

13. The pun is clearly indicated by hyphens in "Watts-his-name" in the manuscript.

14. *Collected Poems*, p. 487.

15. "The Ditty of Aristippus" is actually a part of *Clarel* (III, iv, 313ff.). However, it justifies separate study since it survives as a poem by itself on a single manuscript sheet. Melville also wrote it out and sent it to Edmund C. Stedman when he asked for a handwritten "specimen" in 1885.

16. An exchange of articles in one of the scholarly journals several years ago surveyed the popular interest in and knowledge of geology at the time Melville was writing his novels. Several possible sources for his detailed knowledge of the science were suggested. See Elizabeth Foster, "Melville and Geology," *American Literature*

17 (1945): 50–65, and "Another Note on Melville and Geology," *American Literature* 22 (1951): 479–87; see also Tyrus Hillway, "Melville's Geological Knowledge," *American Literature* 21 (1949): 232–37.

17. Letter of June 1851, reproduced in *Herman Melville: Cycle and Epicycle* by Eleanor Melville Metcalf (Cambridge, Mass., 1953), p. 108.

VIII

1. Melville owned a copy of *The Letters of Madame de Sévigné* (Sealts, #459). The biography of the Marchioness of Brinvilliers can be found in the *Nouvelle Biographie Générale* (Paris, 1855) 7: 422–26.

2. *Melville's Quarrel with God* (Princeton, N.J., 1952).

3. Chapter references are to the authoritative text: *Billy Budd Sailor (An Inside Narrative)*, ed. Harrison Hayford and Merton M. Sealts, Jr. (Chicago, 1962). Italics in the cited passages are mine.

4. Thomas Vargish's article on Melville's use of gnosticism in *Moby-Dick* has been cited earlier in these notes.

5. The opening lines of the original version of this ballad can be found in the Hayford and Sealts edition of the story (p. 4).

BIBLIOGRAPHY

In the following list I have tried to include everything of any significance written on Melville's poetry. Some of the items are totally concerned with the poetry; others are longer studies of Melville which include sections on the poems. Still others, for example the works by Wilson and Woodward, are books on other subjects which contain remarks on Melville's poetry of some depth and interest. Where I am either in basic agreement or disagreement with the authors I have generally preferred to let the matter go unmentioned; but where I have particularly profited from certain insights or factual materials I have acknowledged this fully in the text and notes above.

Abel, Darrell. "'Laurel Twined with Thorn': The Theme of Melville's *Timoleon*." *Personalist* 41 (1960): 330–40.

Arvin, Newton. *Herman Melville: A Critical Biography*. New York: William Sloan Associates, 1950.

————. "Melville's *Clarel*." *Hudson Review* 14 (1961): 298–300.

————. "Melville's Shorter Poems." *Partisan Review* 16 (1949): 1034–46.

Ault, N. A. "The Sea Imagery in Melville's *Clarel*." *Research Studies of the State College of Washington* 27 (1959): 72–84.

Baird, James A. *Ishmael*. Baltimore: Johns Hopkins Press, 1956; reprinted, New York: Harper & Brothers, 1960.

Barrett, Laurence. "Fiery Hunt: A Study of Melville's Theories of the Artist." Ph.D. dissertation, Princeton University, 1949.

————. "The Differences in Melville's Poetry." *PMLA* 70 (1955): 606–23.

Benet, William Rose. "Poet in Prose." *Saturday Review of Literature* 30 (August 2, 1947): 17.

Berlind, Bruce. "Notes on Melville's Shorter Poems." *Hopkins Review* 3 (1950): 24–35.

Bernstein, John. *Pacifism and Rebellion in the Writings of Herman Melville*. The Hague: Mouton, 1964.

Bezanson, Walter E., ed. *Clarel: A Poem and Pilgrimage in the Holy Land*. New York: Hendricks House, 1960.

————. "Melville's Reading of Arnold's Poetry." *PMLA* 69 (1954): 365–91.

Bowen, Merlin. *The Long Encounter: Self and Experience in the Writings of Herman Melville*. Chicago: University of Chicago Press, 1960.

Braswell, William. *Melville's Religious Thought: An Essay in Interpretation*. Durham, N.C.: Duke University Press, 1943.

Bridgeman, Richard. "Melville's Roses." *Texas Studies in Literature and Language* 8 (1966): 235–44.

Cambon, Glauco. *The Inclusive Flame: Studies in Modern American Poetry*. Bloomington: Indiana University Press, 1963.

Camp, James Edwin. "An Unfulfilled Romance: Image, Symbol, and Allegory in Herman Melville's *Clarel.*" Ph.D. dissertation, University of Michigan, 1965.

Cannon, Agnes D. "Melville's Concept of the Poet and Poetry." Ph.D. dissertation, University of Pennsylvania, 1967.

———. "Melville's Use of Sea Ballads and Songs." *Western Folklore* 23 (1964): 1–16.

Chapin, Henry, ed. *John Marr and Other Poems.* Princeton, N.J.: Princeton University Press, 1922.

Chase, Richard. *Herman Melville: A Critical Study.* New York: Macmillan, 1949.

———, ed. *Selected Tales and Poems of Herman Melville.* New York: Holt, Rinehart, and Winston, 1950.

Cohen, Hennig, ed. *The Battle-Pieces of Herman Melville.* New York: Thomas Yoseloff, 1964.

———. "Melville's Copy of Broughton's *Popular Poetry of the Hindoos.*" *Papers of the Bibliographical Society of America* 61: 266–67.

———, ed. *Selected Poems of Herman Melville.* New York: Anchor Books, 1964; Carbondale: Southern Illinois University Press, 1964.

Day, Frank L. "Herman Melville's Use of *The Rebellion Record* in His Poetry." Thesis, University of Tennessee, 1959.

———. "Melville and Sherman March to the Sea." *American Notes and Queries* 2 (1964): 134–36.

Dillingham, William B. " 'Neither Believer Nor Infidel': Themes of Melville's Poetry." *Personalist* 46 (1965): 501–16.

Donahue, Jane. "Melville's Classicism: Law and Order in His Poetry." *Papers on Language and Literature* 5 (1969): 63–72.

Donoghue, Denis. *Connoisseurs of Chaos: Ideas of Order in Modern American Poetry.* New York: Macmillan, 1965.

Finkelstein, Dorothee Metlitsky. *Melville's Orienda.* New Haven, Conn.: Yale University Press, 1961.

Fite, Olive L. "Billy Budd, Claggart, and Schopenhauer." *Nineteenth-Century Fiction* 23 (1968): 336–43.

Fogle, Richard H. "Melville and the Civil War." *Tulane Studies in English* 9 (1959): 61–89.

———. "Melville's *Clarel:* Doubt and Belief." *Tulane Studies in English* 10 (1960): 101–16.

———. "Melville's Poetry." *Tulane Studies in English* 12 (1962): 81–86.

———. "The Themes of Melville's Later Poetry." *Tulane Studies in English* 11 (1961): 65–86.

Freeman, F. Barron, ed. *Melville's Billy Budd.* Cambridge, Mass.: Harvard University Press, 1948.

Goforth, David S. "Melville's Shorter Poems: The Substance and the Significance." Ph.D. dissertation, Indiana University, 1967.

Hand, Harry E. " 'And War Be Done': *Battle-Pieces* and Other Civil War

Poetry of Herman Melville." *Journal of Human Relations* 11 (1963): 326–40.

Hibler, David J. "*Drum-Taps* and *Battle-Pieces:* Melville and Whitman on the Civil War." *Personalist* 50 (1969): 130–47.

Hillway, Tyrus. *Herman Melville.* New Haven, Conn.: College and University Press, 1963.

Hitt, Ralph E. "Melville's Poems of Civil War Controversy." *Studies in the Literary Imagination* 2 (1969): 57–68.

Howard, Leon. *Herman Melville: A Biography.* Berkeley: University of California Press, 1951.

Jarrard, Norman. "Poems by Herman Melville: A Critical Edition of the Published Verse." Ph.D. dissertation, University of Texas, 1960.

Kaplan, Sidney, ed. *Battle-Pieces and Aspects of the War.* Gainesville, Fla.: Scholar's Facsimiles and Reprints, 1960.

Kenny, Vincent S. "Herman Melville's *Clarel.*" Ph.D. dissertation, New York University, 1965.

Knapp, Joseph G., S. J. "Tortured Torturer of Reluctant Rhymes: Melville's *Clarel,* An Interpretation of Post-Civil War America." Ph.D. dissertation, University of Minnesota, 1962.

———. *Tortured Synthesis: The Meaning of Melville's "Clarel."* New York: Philosophical Library, 1972.

Kramer, Aaron. *The Prophetic Tradition in American Poetry, 1835–1900.* Rutherford, N.J.: Fairleigh Dickinson University Press, 1968.

Lindeman, Jack. "Herman Melville's Civil War." *Modern Age* 9 (1965): 387–98.

———. "Herman Melville's Reconstruction." *Modern Age* 10 (1966): 168–72.

Martin, Lawrence H., Jr. "Melville and Christianity: The Late Poems." *Massachusetts Studies in English* 2 (1969): 11–18.

Mason, Ronald. *The Spirit above the Dust: A Study of Herman Melville.* London: John Lehmann, 1951.

Matthiessen, F. O. *American Renaissance: Art and Expression in the Age of Emerson and Whitman.* New York: Oxford University Press, 1941.

———, ed. *Herman Melville: Selected Poems.* Norfolk, Conn.: New Directions, 1944. Introduction reprinted in *The Responsibilities of the Critic: Essays and Reviews.* New York: Oxford University Press, 1952.

Mayoux, Jean-Jacques. *Melville.* New York: Grove Press, 1960. A translation of *Melville par lui-meme.* Paris: Editions du seuil, 1958.

Meldrum, Barbara. "Melville on War." *Research Studies of the State College of Washington* 37 (1969): 130–38.

Miller, James E., Jr. *A Reader's Guide to Herman Melville.* New York: Farrar, Straus and Cudahy, 1962.

Montague, Gene B. "Melville's *Battle-Pieces.*" *University of Texas Studies in English* 35 (1956): 106–15.

Mumford, Lewis. *Herman Melville: A Study of His Life and Vision.* New York: Harcourt, Brace, 1929; revised, 1962.

Packard, Robert Joslin. "A Study of Herman Melville's *Clarel.*" Ph.D. dissertation, Columbia University, 1963.

Parrington, Vernon Louis. *Main Currents in American Thought.* 3 vols. New York: Harcourt, Brace, 1927, 1930.

Plomer, William, ed. *Selected Poems of Herman Melville.* London, 1943.

Pommer, Henry F. *Milton and Melville.* Pittsburgh, Pa.: University of Pittsburgh Press, 1950.

Pops, Martin Leonard. *The Melville Archetype.* Kent, Ohio: Kent State University Press, 1970.

Ryan, Robert C. "*Weeds and Wildings Chiefly: With a Rose or Two,* by Herman Melville; Reading Text and Genetic Text, Edited from the Manuscripts, with Introduction and Notes." Ph.D. dissertation, Northwestern University, 1967.

Sealts, Merton M. "Melville's Burgundy Club Sketches." *Harvard Library Bulletin* 12 (1958): 253–67.

————. *Melville's Reading: A Check-List of Books Owned and Borrowed.* Madison: University of Wisconsin Press, 1966.

Sedgwick, W. E. *Herman Melville: The Tragedy of Mind.* Cambridge, Mass.: Harvard University Press, 1944.

Shaw, Richard O. "The Civil War Poems of Herman Melville." *Lincoln Herald* (Harrogate, Tenn.) 68 (1966): 44–49.

Shulman, Robert. "Melville's 'Timoleon': From Plutarch to the Early Stages of *Billy Budd.*" *Comparative Literature* 19 (1967): 351–61.

Shurr, William H. "The Symbolic Structure of Herman Melville's *Clarel.*" Ph.D. dissertation, University of North Carolina, 1968.

Spiller, Robert E. "Melville: Our First Tragic Poet." *Saturday Review of Literature* 33 (November 25, 1950): 24–25.

Stein, William Bysshe. "Melville and the Creative Eros." *Lock Haven Bulletin* 2 (1960): 13–26.

————. "Melville's Eros." *Texas Studies in Literature and Language* 3 (1961): 297–308.

————. "Melville's Poetry: Its Symbols of Individuation." *Literature and Psychology* 7 (1959): 21–26.

————. "Melville's Poetry: Two Rising Notes." *Emerson Society Quarterly* 27 (1966): 10–13.

————. "The Old Man and the Triple Goddess: Melville's 'The Haglets.'" *Journal of English Literary History* 25 (1958): 43–59.

————. *The Poetry of Melville's Late Years: Time, History, Myth, and Religion.* Albany: State University of New York Press, 1970.

Stone, Geoffrey. *Melville.* New York: Sheed and Ward, 1949.

Sutton, Walter. "Melville's 'Pleasure Party' and the Art of Concealment." *Philological Quarterly* 30 (1951): 316–27.

Thorp, Willard, ed. *Herman Melville: Representative Selections, with Introduction, Bibliography, and Notes.* American Writers Series. New York: American Book Co., 1938.

Tilton, Elanor M. "Melville's 'Rammon': A Text and Commentary." *Harvard Library Bulletin* 13 (1959): 50–91.

Vargish, Thomas. "Gnostic *Mythos* in *Moby-Dick.*" *PMLA* 81 (1966): 272–77.

Vincent, Howard P., ed. *Collected Poems of Herman Melville.* Chicago: Packard and Company, 1947.

Vogel, Dan. "Melville's Shorter Published Poetry: A Critical Study of the Lyrics in *Mardi*, of *Battle-Pieces, John Marr* and *Timoleon.*" Ph.D. dissertation, New York University, 1956.

Waggoner, Hyatt H. *American Poets: From the Puritans to the Present.* Boston: Houghton Mifflin, 1968.

Warren, Robert Penn. "Melville's Poems." *Southern Review* 3, n.s. (1967): 799–855.

———. "Melville the Poet." *Kenyon Review* 8 (1946): 208–23. Reprinted in Warren's *Selected Essays.* New York: Random House, 1958.

———, ed. *Selected Poems of Herman Melville: A Reader's Edition.* New York: Random House, 1970.

Weaver, Raymond. *Herman Melville, Mariner and Mystic.* New York: George H. Doran Co., 1921; reprinted, New York: Pageant Books, 1960, and New York: Cooper Square Publishers, 1961.

Wells, Henry W. *The American Way of Poetry.* New York: Columbia University Press, 1943.

———. "Herman Melville's *Clarel.*" *College English* 4 (1943): 478–82.

Wilson, Edmund. *Patriotic Gore.* New York: Oxford University Press, 1962.

Woodward, C. Vann. *The Burden of Southern History.* Baton Rouge: Louisiana State University Press, 1960; revised, 1968.

Wright, Nathalia. "Form as Function in Melville." *PMLA* 67 (1952): 330–40.

———. *Melville's Use of the Bible.* Durham, N. C.: Duke University Press, 1949.

———. "A Source for Melville's *Clarel*: Dean Stanley's *Sinai and Palestine.*" *Modern Language Notes* 62 (1947): 110–16.

Zolla, Elémire. "La struttura e fonti di *Clarel.*" *Studi Americani* (Roma) 10 (1964): 101–34.

INDEX

*This book has been set in
W. A. Dwiggins' Caledonia, a modified
Scotch face. Eric Gill's Perpetua
is used for display.*

*Composition & printing
by Heritage Printers, Inc.*

*Binding by
The C. J. Krehbiel Co.*

Design by Jonathan Greene